# The Java™ Programming Language

# The Java™ Series

*Lisa Friendly, Series Editor*
*Bill Joy, Technical Advisor*

## The Java™ Programming Language
Ken Arnold and James Gosling

The Java™ Application Programming Interface,
Volume 1
*Core Packages*
James Gosling, Frank Yellin, and the Java Team

The Java™ Application Programming Interface,
Volume 2
*Window Toolkit and Applets*
James Gosling, Frank Yellin, and the Java Team

The Java™ Language Specification
James Gosling, Bill Joy, and Guy Steele

The Java™ Virtual Machine
Tim Lindholm and Frank Yellin

The Java™ Tutorial
Object-Oriented Programming for the Internet
Mary Campione and Kathy Walrath

The Java™ Class Libraries
An Annotated Reference
Patrick Chan and Rosanna Lee

The Java™ FAQ
Frequently Asked Questions
Jonni Kanerva

# The Java™
# Programming Language

Ken Arnold
James Gosling

**Addison-Wesley Publishing Company, Inc.**

Reading, Massachusetts    Menlo Park, California    New York
Don Mills, Ontario    Wokingham, England    Amsterdam    Bonn
Sydney    Singapore    Tokyo    Madrid    San Juan
Seoul    Milan    Mexico City    Taipei

Copyright © 1996 by Sun Microsystems, Inc.
2550 Garcia Avenue, Mountain View, California 94043-1100 U.S.A.

Duke™ designed by Joe Palrang.

All rights reserved.

RESTRICTED RIGHTS LEGEND: Use, duplication, or disclosure by the United States Government is subject to the restrictions set forth in DFARS 252.227-7013 (c)(1)(ii) and FAR 52.227-19.

The release described in this book may be protected by one or more U.S. patents, foreign patents, or pending applications.

Sun Microsystems, Inc. (SUN) hereby grants to you a fully paid, nonexclusive, nontransferable, perpetual, world-wide limited license (without the right to sublicense) under SUN's intellectual property rights that are essential to practice this specification. This license allows and is limited to the creation and distribution of clean-room implementations of this specification that (i) are complete implementations of this specification, (ii) pass all test suites relating to this specification that are available from SUN, (iii) do not derive from SUN source code or binary materials, and (iv) do not include any SUN binary materials without an appropriate and separate license from SUN.

Java and JavaScript are trademarks of Sun Microsystems, Inc. Sun, Sun Microsystems, Sun Microsystems Computer Corporation, the Sun logo, the Sun Microsystems Computer Corporation logo, Java, and HotJava are trademarks or registered trademarks of Sun Microsystems, Inc. UNIX® is a registered trademark in the United States and other countries, exclusively licensed through X/Open Company, Ltd. All other product names mentioned herein are the trademarks of their respective owners.

THIS PUBLICATION IS PROVIDED "AS IS" WITHOUT WARRANTY OF ANY KIND, EITHER EXPRESS OR IMPLIED, INCLUDING, BUT NOT LIMITED TO, THE IMPLIED WARRANTIES OF MERCHANT-ABILITY, FITNESS FOR A PARTICULAR PURPOSE, OR NON-INFRINGEMENT.

THIS PUBLICATION COULD INCLUDE TECHNICAL INACCURACIES OR TYPOGRAPHICAL ERRORS. CHANGES ARE PERIODICALLY ADDED TO THE INFORMATION HEREIN; THESE CHANGES WILL BE INCORPORATED IN NEW EDITIONS OF THE PUBLICATION. SUN MICROSYSTEMS, INC. MAY MAKE IMPROVEMENTS AND/OR CHANGES IN THE PRODUCT(S) AND/OR THE PROGRAM(S) DESCRIBED IN THIS PUBLICATION AT ANY TIME.

The publisher offers discounts on this book when ordered in quantity for special sales. For more information, please contact:
Corporate & Professional Publishing Group
Addison-Wesley Publishing Company
One Jacob Way
Reading, Massachusetts  01867

Text printed on recycled and acid-free paper

ISBN 0-201-63455-4
1 2 3 4 5 6 7 8 9-MA-99989796
First Printing, May 1996

This book is dedicated to the Java team
From whose hard work and vision
A mighty oak has grown


To Susan—*K.A.*

To Judy and Kate—*J.A.G.*

# Contents

# Preface

*Beautiful buildings are more than scientific. They are true organisms,*
*spiritually conceived; works of art, using the best technology by inspiration*
*rather than the idiosyncrasies of mere taste or any averaging by the committee mind.*
—Frank Lloyd Wright

THE Java™ programming language (hereafter called simply "Java") has been warmly received by the world community of software developers and Internet content providers. Users of the Internet and World Wide Web benefit from access to secure platform-independent applications that can come from anywhere on the Internet. Software developers creating applications in Java benefit by developing code only once, with no need to "port" their applications to every software and hardware platform.

For many, Java is known primarily as a tool to create *applets* for the World Wide Web. "Applet" is the term Java uses for a mini-application that runs inside a web page. An applet can perform tasks and interact with the user on their browser page without using resources from the Web server after being downloaded. Some applets may, of course, interact with the server for their own purposes, but that's their business.

Java is indeed valuable for distributed network environments like the Web. However, Java goes well beyond this domain to provide a powerful general-purpose programming language suitable for building a variety of applications that either do not depend on network features, or want them for different reasons. Java's ability to execute code on remote hosts in a secure manner is a critical requirement for many organizations.

Other groups use Java as a general-purpose programming language for projects where machine independence is less important. Java's ease of programming and safety features help produce debugged code quickly. Some common programming errors never occur because of features like garbage collection and type-safe references. Modern network-based and graphical user interface–based applications that must attend to multiple tasks simultaneously are catered to by Java's support for multithreading, while the mechanisms of *exception handling* ease the task of dealing with error conditions. While its built-in tools are powerful, Java the language is itself a *simple* language in which programmers can quickly become proficient.

Java is designed for maximum portability and is specifically designed to have as few implementation dependencies as possible. An int, for example, is a 32-bit signed two's-complement integer in all Java implementations, whatever the CPU architecture on which the Java program executes. Defining everything possible about the language and its runtime environment enables users to run compiled code anywhere and share code with anyone who has a Java environment.

Java shares many language features common to most programming languages in use today. However, unlike C and C++, Java provides automatic storage management and exception handling, integrated with support for threads.

## ABOUT THIS BOOK

This book teaches Java programming to people familiar with basic programming concepts. It explains Java without being formal or complete. This book is not an introduction to object-oriented programming, although some issues are covered to establish a common terminology.

Java should look familiar to C and C++ programmers, because Java was designed with C and C++ constructs where the languages are similar. Other books in this series, and much online documentation, focus on Java applets. For other references, see the Bibliography.

Chapter 1—"A Quick Tour of Java"—gives a quick overview of Java. Programmers unfamiliar with object-oriented programming notions should read the quick tour, while programmers already familiar with object-oriented programming paradigms will find the quick tour a useful introduction to the object-oriented features of Java.

Chapters 2, 3, and 4 cover the object-oriented core features of Java, namely, class declarations that define components of a program, and objects manufactured according to class definitions. Chapter 2—"Classes and Objects"—describes the basis of the Java language. Chapter 3—"Extending Classes"—describes how an existing class can be extended, or *subclassed*, to create a new class with new data and behavior. Chapter 4—"Interfaces"—describes how to declare interface types that are abstract descriptions of behavior that provide maximum flexibility for class designers and implementers.

Chapters 5 and 6 cover standard language constructs common to most languages. Chapter 5—"Tokens, Operators, and Expressions"—describes the tokens of the language from which statements are constructed, how the tokens and operators are used to build expressions, and how expressions are evaluated. Chapter 6—"Control Flow"—describes how control statements direct the order of execution of statements.

Chapter 7—"Exceptions"—describes Java's powerful error-handling capabilities. Chapter 8—"Strings"—describes the built-in language and runtime support for String objects.

Chapter 9—"Threads"—explains Java's implementation of multithreading. Many applications, such as graphical interface–based software, must attend to multiple tasks simultaneously. These tasks must cooperate to behave correctly, and threads meet the needs of cooperative multitasking.

Chapter 10—"Packages"—describes Java's mechanism for grouping collections of Java classes into their own separate packages.

Chapters 11 through 14 cover the main body of the core Java class library packages. Chapter 11—"The I/O Package"—describes the Java input/output system, based on *streams*. Chapter 12—"Standard Utilities"—covers Java *utility classes* such as vectors and hashtables. Chapter 13—"Programming with Types"—describes Java's type-related classes, both individual objects that describe each class and interface, and classes that wrap primitive data types such as integers and floating point values into their own object types. Chapter 14—"System Programming"—leads you through the system classes that provide access to features of the underlying platform.

Appendix A describes Java support for *native methods*—a means to access code written in the "native" programming language of the underlying platform.

Appendix B lists all the runtime exceptions and errors that the Java system itself can throw.

Appendix C has tables of information that you may find useful for quick reference purposes.

Finally, the Bibliography lists works that may be interesting for further reading on object orientation, programming with threads, and other topics.

*EXAMPLES AND DOCUMENTATION*

All the code examples in the text have been compiled and run on the latest version of the language available at the time the book was written, which was the FCS version of Java release 1.0.2. Generally speaking, only Java 1.0.2 features are covered. We have also covered issues beyond writing programs that simply compile—part of learning a language is to learn to use it *well*. For this reason, we have tried to show principles of good programming style and design.

In a few places we refer to online documentation. Java development environments provide a way to automatically generate documentation (usually HTML documents) from a compiled class using the documentation comments. This documentation is normally viewed using a Web browser.

ACKNOWLEDGMENTS

No technical book-writing endeavor is an island unto itself, and ours was more like a continent. Many people contributed technical help, excellent reviews, useful information, and book-writing advice.

Contributing Editor Henry McGilton of Trilithon Software played the role of "Chief Editorial Firefighter" to help make this book possible. Series Editor Lisa Friendly contributed dogged perseverance and support.

A veritable multitude of reviewers took time out of their otherwise busy lives to read, edit, advise, revise, and delete material, all in the name of making this a better book. Kevin Coyle performed one of the most detailed editorial reviews at all levels. Karen Bennet, Mike Burati, Patricia Giencke, Steve Gilliard, Bill Joy, Rosanna Lee, Jon Madison, Brian O'Neill, Sue Palmer, Stephen Perelgut, R. Anders Schneiderman, Susan Sim, Bob Sproull, Guy Steele, Arthur Van Hoff, Jim Waldo, Greg Wilson, and Ann Wollrath provided in-depth review. Geoff Arnold, Tom Cargill, Chris Darke, Pat Finnegan, Mick Jordan, Doug Lea, Randall Murray, Roger Riggs, Jimmy Torres, Arthur van Hoff, and Frank Yellin contributed useful comments and technical information at critical junctures.

Alka Deshpande, Sharon Flank, Nassim Fotouhi, Betsy Halstead, Kee Hinckley, Dr. K. Kalyanasundaram, Patrick Martin, Paul Romagna, Susan Snyder, and Nicole Yankelovich collaborated to make possible the five words of non-ISO-Latin-1 text on page 92. Jim Arnold provided research help on the proper spelling, usage, and etymology of "smoog" and "moorge." Ed Mooney helped with the document preparation. Herb and Joy Kaiser were our Croatian language consultants. Cookie Callahan, Robert E. Pierce, and Rita Tavilla provided the support necessary to keep this project going at many moments when it would otherwise have stalled with a sputtering whimper.

Thanks to Kim Polese for supplying us the capsule summary of why Java is important to computer users as well as programmers.

Support and advice were provided at critical moments by Susan Jones, Bob Sproull, Jim Waldo, and Ann Wollrath. And we thank our families, who besides their loving support, would at times drag us out to play when we should have been working, for which we are deeply grateful.

And thanks to the folks at Peets Coffee and Tea, who kept us buzzed on the best Java on the planet.

Any errors or shortcomings that remain in this book—despite all the best combined efforts of these myriads—are completely the responsibility of the authors.

# CHAPTER 1

# A Quick Tour of Java

*See Europe! Ten Countries in Seventeen Days!*
——Sign in a Travel Agent's Window

THIS chapter is a whirlwind tour of the Java programming language that gets you started writing Java code quickly.[1] We cover the main points of the language quickly, without slowing you down with full-blown detail. Subsequent chapters contain detailed discussions of specific Java features.

## 1.1 Getting Started

Java programs are built from *classes*. From a class definition, you can create any number of *objects* that are known as *instances* of that class. Think of a class as a factory with blueprints and instructions to build gadgets—objects are the gadgets the factory makes.

A class contains two kinds of *members*, called *fields* and *methods*. Fields are data belonging either to the class itself or to objects of the class; they make up the *state* of the object or class. Methods are collections of *statements* that operate on the fields to manipulate the state.

The first sample program in many languages prints "Hello, world". Here is the Java version:

```
class HelloWorld {
    public static void main(String[] args) {
        System.out.println("Hello, world");
    }
}
```

---

[1]. The Java Programming Language is written simply as "Java" throughout.

Use your favorite text editor to type this program source into a file. Then run the Java compiler to compile the source of this program into Java *bytecodes*, the "machine language" for the Java Virtual Machine. Details of editing source and compiling vary from system to system and aren't described here—consult your system manuals for specific information. When you run the program, it displays:

```
Hello, world
```

Now you have a small Java program that does something, but what does it mean?

The program above declares a class called `HelloWorld` with a single method called `main`. Class members appear between curly braces `{` and `}` following the class name. `HelloWorld` has only one method, and no fields.

The `main` method's only *parameter* is an array of `String` objects that are the program's arguments from the command line with which it was invoked. Arrays and strings are covered later, as well as what `args` means for the `main` method.

The `main` method is declared `void` because it doesn't return a value. It is one of a few special method names in Java: the `main` method of a class, if declared as above, is executed when you run the class as an application. When run, `main` can create objects, evaluate expressions, invoke other methods, and do anything else needed to define an application's behavior.

In the example above, `main` contains a single statement that invokes a method on the `System` class's `out` object. Methods are invoked by supplying an object reference and a method name, separated by a dot (.). `HelloWorld` uses the `out` object's `println` method to print a newline-terminated string on the standard output stream.

### Exercise 1.1

Enter, compile, and run `HelloWorld` on your system.   ▲

### Exercise 1.2

Try changing parts of `HelloWorld` and see what errors you get.   ▲

## 1.2   Variables

The next example prints the *Fibonacci sequence*—an infinite sequence whose first few terms are:

```
1
1
2
3
5
```

```
8
13
21
34
```

The Fibonacci sequence starts with the terms 1 and 1, and successive terms are the sum of the previous two terms. A Fibonacci printing program is simple, but it demonstrates how to declare *variables*, write a simple loop, and perform basic arithmetic. Here is the Fibonacci program:

```java
class Fibonacci {
    /** Print out the Fibonacci sequence for values < 50 */
    public static void main(String[] args) {
        int lo = 1;
        int hi = 1;

        System.out.println(lo);
        while (hi < 50) {
            System.out.println(hi);
            hi = lo + hi;       // new hi
            lo = hi - lo;       /* new lo is (sum - old lo)
                                   i.e., the old hi */
        }
    }
}
```

This example declares a `Fibonacci` class that, like `HelloWorld`, has a `main` method. The first two lines of `main` declare two variables, `hi` and `lo`. Every variable must have a *type* that precedes its name. `hi` and `lo` are of type `int`, 32-bit signed integers with values in the range $-2^{32}$ through $2^{32}-1$.

Java has built-in "primitive" data types to support integer, floating-point, boolean, and character values. These primitive types hold data that Java understands directly, as opposed to object types defined by programmers. Java has no "default" types; the type of every variable must be defined explicitly. The primitive data types of Java are:

| | |
|---|---|
| boolean | either true or false |
| char | 16-bit Unicode 1.1 character |
| byte | 8-bit integer (signed) |
| short | 16-bit integer (signed) |
| int | 32-bit integer (signed) |
| long | 64-bit integer (signed) |
| float | 32-bit floating point (IEEE 754-1985) |
| double | 64-bit floating point (IEEE 754-1985) |

In the Fibonacci program, we declared `hi` and `lo` with initial values of 1. The starting values are set by initialization expressions, using the = operator, when the variables are declared. The = operator sets the variable named on the left-hand side to the value of the expression on the right-hand side. In this program `hi` is the last term in the series and `lo` is the previous term.

Variables are *undefined* prior to initialization. Should you try to use variables before assigning a value, the Java compiler will refuse to compile your program until you fix the problem.

The `while` statement in the example provides one way of looping in Java. The expression inside the `while` is evaluated—if true, the body of the loop is executed and the expression tested again. The `while` is repeated until the expression becomes false. If it never becomes false, the program will run forever, unless something intervenes to break out of the loop, like a `break` statement, or an exception happening.

The expression that `while` tests is a boolean expression that has the value `true` or `false`. The boolean expression above tests whether the current high value of the sequence is less than 50. If the high value is less than 50, its value is printed and the next value calculated. If the high value equals or exceeds 50, control passes to the first line of code following the body of the `while` loop. That is the end of the `main` method in this example, so the program is finished.

Notice that the `println` method accepts an integer argument in the Fibonacci example above, whereas it accepted a string argument in the `HelloWorld` example. The `println` method is one of many methods that are *overloaded* such that they can accept arguments of different types.

*Exercise 1.3*

Add a title to the printed list.   ▲

*Exercise 1.4*

Write a program that generates a different sequence, such as a table of squares (multiplication is done using *, such as i * i)   ▲

## 1.3   Comments in Code

The English-like things scattered through the code are *comments*. Java has three styles of comments, all illustrated in the example.

Text following // up to the end of the line is ignored by the compiler, as is text between /* and the next */.

Comments enable you to write descriptive text beside your code, to annotate it for future programmers who may read your code in the future. The "future programmer" may well be *you* months or years later. You save yourself effort by commenting your own code. Also, you often find bugs when you write comments: because explaining what the code is supposed to do forces you to think about it.

The third kind of comment appears at the very top, between /** and */. A comment starting with two asterisks is a *documentation comment* ("doc comment" for short). Documentation comments are intended to describe declarations that follow them. The comment in the above example is for the `main` method. A tool called `javadoc` extracts documentation comments and generates HTML documentation.

## 1.4  Named Constants

*Constants* are values like 12, 17.9, and "Strings Like This". Constants are how you specify values that are not computed and recomputed, but remain, well, constant for the life of a program.

Programmers prefer *named constants* for two reasons. One reason is that the name of the constant is a form of documentation. The name can (and should) describe what the particular value is used for.

Another reason is that you define a named constant in a single place in a program. When the constant needs to be changed or corrected, it can be changed in only one place, easing program maintenance. Named constants in Java are created by declaring a variable as `static` and `final`, and providing its initial value in the declaration:

```
class CircleStuff {
        static final double  π = 3.1416;
}
```

The value of $\pi$ can be changed in just one place when we discover that five significant digits of precision are not enough. We declared $\pi$ as `double`—a double-precision 64-bit floating-point number. Now we could change $\pi$ to a more precise value, like 3.14159265358979323846.

You can group related constants within a class. For example, a card game might use these constants:

```
class Suit {
    final static int CLUBS    = 1;
    final static int DIAMONDS = 2;
```

```
    final static int HEARTS  = 3;
    final static int SPADES  = 4;
};
```

With this declaration, suits in a program would be accessed as `Suit.HEARTS`, `Suit.SPADES`, and so on, thus grouping all the suit names within the single name `Suit`.

### 1.4.1   Unicode Characters

We take a minor diversion to note the π symbol as the name of a constant in the previous example. In most programming languages, identifiers are usually limited to the letters and digits available in the ASCII character set.

Java moves you toward the modern world of internationalized software: you write Java code in *Unicode*—an international character set standard. Unicode characters are 16 bits and provide a character range large enough to write the major languages used in the world, which is why we can use π for the name of the value in the example above. π is a valid letter from the Greek section of Unicode, and therefore valid in Java source. Most existing Java code is written in ASCII, a 7-bit character standard, or ISO-Latin-1, an 8-bit character standard commonly called "Latin-1." But they are translated into Unicode before processing so the Java character set is always Unicode.

*Exercise 1.5*

Change the `HelloWorld` application to use a named string constant as the string to print.   ▲

*Exercise 1.6*

Change the `Fibonacci` application to use a named constant in its loop instead of a literal constant.   ▲

## 1.5   Flow of Control

"Flow of Control" is the term for deciding which statements in a program are executed. The `while` loop in the Fibonacci program above is one way. Other flow of control statements include `if`/`else`, `for`, `switch`, `do`/`while`, and *blocks*—multiple statements grouped within `{` and `}`. We change the Fibonacci sequence program by numbering the elements of the sequence, and marking even numbers with an asterisk:

```
class ImprovedFibonacci {
    /** Print out the first few Fibonacci
     * numbers, marking evens with a '*' */
    static final int MAX_INDEX = 10;

    public static void main(String[] args) {
        int lo = 1;
        int hi = 1;
        String mark;

        System.out.println("1: " + lo);
        for (int i = 2; i < MAX_INDEX; i++) {
            if (hi % 2 == 0)
                mark = " *";
            else
                mark = "";
            System.out.println(i + ": " + hi + mark);
            hi = lo + hi;         // new hi
            /* new lo is (sum - old lo) i.e., the old hi */
            lo = hi - lo;
        }
    }
}
```

Here is the new output:

```
1: 1
2: 1
3: 2 *
4: 3
5: 5
6: 8 *
7: 13
8: 21
9: 34 *
```

To number the elements of the sequence, we used a for loop instead of a while loop. A for loop is shorthand for a while loop, but with an initialization and increment phase added. The for loop above is equivalent to this while loop:

```
{
    int i = 2;
```

```
while (i < MAX_INDEX) {
    // .. do the printing stuff
    i++;
}
}
```

The ++ operator in the code fragment above may be unfamiliar if you're new to C-derived programming languages. The plus-plus operator increments by one the value of any variable it abuts—the contents of variable i in this case. The ++ operator is a *prefix* operator when it comes before its operand, and *postfix* when it comes after. Similarly, minus-minus decrements by one the value of any variable it abuts, and can also be prefix or postfix. The ++ and -- operators come from the C programming language. In the context of the example above, a statement like

```
i++;
```

is equivalent to

```
i = i + 1;
```

Beyond simple assignment, Java supports other assignment operators that apply an arithmetic operation to the value on the left-hand side of the operator. For example, another way to write i++ in the for loop above would be to write

```
i += 1;
```

which adds the value on the right-hand side of the += operator (namely 1) to the variable on the left-hand side (namely i). Many of the binary operators in Java (operators that take two operands) can be joined with = in a similar way.

Inside the for loop we use an if/else to see if the current hi value is even. The if statement tests the expression between the parentheses. If the expression is true, the first statement or block in the body of the if is executed. If the expression is false, the statement or block following the else clause is executed. The else part is optional: if the else is not present, nothing is done when the expression is false. After figuring out which (if any) clause to execute, control passes to the code following the body of the if statement.

The example tests if hi is even, using the % or *remainder* operator. It produces the remainder after dividing the value on the left side by the value on the right. If the left-side value is even, the remainder is 0, and the following statement assigns a string containing the even-number indicator to marker. The else clause is executed for odd numbers, setting marker to an empty string.

The println invocation is more complex, using the + operator to concatenate strings representing i, a separator, a string representing hi, and the marker string. The + operator is a concatenation operator when used with strings, whereas it is an addition operator when used in arithmetic expressions.

***Exercise 1.7***

Change the loop so that i counts backwards instead of forwards.   ▲

## 1.6   Classes and Objects

Java, like any object-oriented programming language, provides a tool to solve programming problems using the notions of classes and objects. Objects in Java have a *type*; that type is the object's class. Each class type has two kinds of members, namely, fields and methods.

- ◆ Fields are data variables associated with a class and its objects. Fields store results of computations performed by the class's methods.

- ◆ Methods contain the executable code of a class. Methods are built from statements. The way in which methods are *invoked*, and the statements contained within those methods, is what ultimately directs program execution.

Here is the declaration of a simple class that might represent a point on a two-dimensional plane:

```
class Point {
    public double x, y;
}
```

This Point class has two fields representing the *x* and *y* coordinates of a point, and has (as yet) no methods. A class declaration like this one is, conceptually, a plan that defines what objects manufactured from that class look like, plus sets of instructions that define the behavior of those objects. The blueprint of an object adds its maximum value when you use the plans and instructions in the blueprint to manufacture goods (objects) from those plans.

Members of a class can have various levels of visibility. The public declaration of x and y in the Point class means that any code with access to a Point object can read or modify those values. Other levels of visibility limit member access to code in the class itself, or to other related classes.

### 1.6.1   Creating Objects

Objects are created using an expression containing the new keyword. Creating an object from a class definition is also known as *instantiation*; thus, objects are often called instances.

In Java, newly created objects are allocated within an area of system memory known as the *heap*. All objects in Java are accessed via *object references*—any variable that appears to hold an object actually contains a reference to that object. Object references are `null` when they do not reference any object.

Most of the time, you can be imprecise in the distinction between actual objects and references to objects. You can say "pass the object to the method" when you really mean "pass an object reference to the method." We are careful about this distinction only where it makes a difference. Most of the time, you can use "object" and "object reference" interchangeably.

Getting back to the `Point` class defined previously, suppose you are building a graphics application in which you need to track lots of points. You represent each point by its own concrete `Point` object. Here is how you might create and initialize `Point` objects:

```
Point  lowerLeft = new Point();
Point  upperRight = new Point();
Point  middlePoint = new Point();

lowerLeft.x = 0.0;
lowerLeft.y = 0.0;

upperRight.x = 1280.0;
upperRight.y = 1024.0;

middlePoint.x = 640.0;
middlePoint.y = 512.0;
```

Each `Point` object is unique and has its own copy of the x and y fields. Changing x in the `lowerLeft`, for example, does not affect the value of x in `upperRight` object. The fields in objects are known as *instance variables*, because there is a unique copy of the field in each object (instance) of the class.

### 1.6.2 Static or Class Fields

Per-object fields are usually what you need. You usually want a field in one object to be distinct from the similarly named field in every other object instantiated from that class.

Sometimes, though, you want fields that are shared among all objects of that class. These shared variables are known as *class variables*—variables specific to the class as opposed to objects of the class.

Why would you want to use class variables? Consider the Sony Walkman factory. Each Walkman has a unique serial number. In object terms, each Walkman object has its own unique serial number field. However, the factory needs to keep a record of the next serial number to be assigned. You don't want to keep that number with every Walkman object—you'd keep only one copy of that number in the factory, or in object terms, as a class variable.

In Java, you obtain class-specific fields by declaring them `static`, and they are therefore sometimes called *static fields*. For example, a `Point` object to represent the origin might be common enough that you should provide it as a `static` field in the `Point` class:

```
public static Point origin = new Point();
```

If this declaration appears inside the declaration of the `Point` class, there will be exactly one piece of data called `Point.origin` that always refers to an object at (0,0). This `static` field is there no matter how many `Point` objects are created, even if none are created. The values of x and y are zero because that is the default for numeric fields that are not explicitly initialized to a different value.

You saw one `static` object in your first program. The `System` class is a standard Java class that has a `static` field named `out` for printing output to the standard output stream.

When you see "field" in this book, it generally means a per-object field, although the term "non-static field" is sometimes used for clarity.

### 1.6.3   The Garbage Collector

After creating an object using `new`, how do you get rid of the object when you no longer want it? The answer is simple—you don't. Unused Java objects are automatically reclaimed by a *garbage collector*. The garbage collector runs in the background and tracks object references. When an object no longer has any reference, it can be removed from the storage allocation heap, although its actual removal may be delayed until a propitious time.

## 1.7   Methods and Parameters

Objects of the `Point` class as defined above are exposed to manipulation by any code that has a reference to a `Point` object, because its fields are declared `public`. The `Point` class is an example of the very simplest kind of class. Indeed, some classes *are* this simple, when they are designed to fit purely internal needs for a package, or when simple data containers are all you need.

The real benefits of object orientation, however, come from hiding the implementation of a class behind operations performed on its internal data. In Java, operations of a class are declared via its methods—instructions that operate on an object's data to obtain results. Methods access internal implementation details that are otherwise hidden from other objects. Hiding data behind methods so that it is inaccessible to other objects is the fundamental basis of data encapsulation.

Methods have zero or more parameters. A method can return a value, or it can be declared `void` to indicate that it does not return any value. A method's statements appear in a block of code between curly braces `{` and `}` that follow the method's name and the declaration of its *signature*. The signature is the name of the method and the number and types of the method's parameters. If we enhance the `Point` class with a simple `clear` method, it might look like this:

```
public void clear() {
    x = 0;
    y = 0;
}
```

The `clear` method has no parameters, hence the empty `(` and `)` after its name; in addition, `clear` is declared `void` because it does not return any value. Inside a method, fields and other methods of the class can be named directly—we can simply say `x` and `y` without an explicit object reference.

### 1.7.1 Invoking a Method

Objects in general do not operate directly on the data of other objects although, as you saw in the `Point` class, a class *can* make its fields publicly accessible. In general, though, well-designed classes hide their data so that it can be changed only by methods of that class. To *invoke* a method, you provide an object reference and the method name, separated by a dot (.). *Parameters* are passed to the method as a comma-separated list of values enclosed in parentheses. Methods that take no parameters still require the parentheses, with nothing between them. The object on which the method is invoked (the object receiving the method invocation) is often known as the *receiving object*, or the *receiver*.

A method may return a single value as a result. To return more than one value from a method, create an object whose sole purpose is to hold return values in a single unit, and return that object.

Here is a method called `distance` that's part of the `Point` class shown in previous examples. The `distance` method accepts another `Point` object as a parameter, computes the Euclidean distance between itself and the other point, and returns a double-precision floating-point result:

```
public double distance(Point that) {
    double xdiff, ydiff;
```

```
        xdiff = x - that.x;
        ydiff = y - that.y;
        return Math.sqrt(xdiff * xdiff + ydiff * ydiff);
    }
```

Based on our `lowerLeft` and `upperRight` objects created in the section on instantiating objects previously, you could invoke `distance` like this:

```
    double d = lowerLeft.distance(upperRight);
```

After this statement executes, the variable d contains the Euclidean distance between `lowerLeft` and `upperRight`.

### 1.7.2   The `this` Reference

Occasionally, the receiving object needs to know its own reference. For example, the receiving object might want to add itself to a list of objects somewhere. An implicit reference named `this` is available to methods, and `this` is a reference to the current (receiving) object. The following definition of `clear` is equivalent to the one just presented:

```
public void clear() {
    this.x = 0;
    this.y = 0;
}
```

You usually use `this` as a parameter to other methods that need an object reference. The `this` reference can also be used to explicitly name the members of the current object. Here's another one of `Point`'s methods, named `move`, that sets the x and y fields to specified values:

```
public void move(double x, double y) {
    this.x = x;
    this.y = y;
}
```

This `move` method uses `this` to clarify which x and y are being referred to. Naming the parameters of `move` "x" and "y" is reasonable, because you pass *x* and *y* coordinates to the method. But then those parameters have the same names as `Point`'s fields, and therefore the parameter names are said to *hide* the field names. If we simply wrote x = x we would assign the value of the x parameter to itself, not to the x field as required. The expression `this.x` refers to the object's x field, not the x parameter of `move`.

### 1.7.3   Static or Class Methods

Just as you can have per-class static fields, you can also have per-class static methods, often known as *class methods*. Class methods are usually intended to do class-like operations specific to the class itself, and usually on static fields, not on specific instances of that class. Class methods are declared using the `static` keyword, and are therefore also known as static methods.

As with the term "field," when you see "method," it generally means a per-object method, although the term "non-static method" is sometimes used for clarity.

Why would you need static methods? Consider the Sony Walkman factory again. The record of the next serial number to be assigned is held in the factory, not in every Walkman. A method to operate on the factory's copy of the next available serial number must be a static method, not a method to operate on specific Walkman objects.

The implementation of `distance` in the previous example uses the static method `Math.sqrt` to calculate a square root. The `Math` class supports many methods useful for general mathematical manipulation. These methods are declared as static methods because they do not act on any particular object, but group a related set of functionality in the class itself.

A static method cannot directly access non-static members. When a static method is invoked, there's no specific object reference for the method to operate on. You could work around this by passing an explicit object reference as a parameter to the static method. In general, however, static methods do class kinds of operations and non-static methods do object kinds of things. Asking a static method to work on object fields is like asking the Walkman factory to change the serial number of a Walkman hanging on the belt of a jogger in Golden Gate Park.

## 1.8   Arrays

Simple variables that hold one value are useful, but are not sufficient for many applications. A program that plays a game of cards would want a number of `Card` objects it can manipulate as a whole. To meet this need, Java provides *arrays*.

An array is a collection of variables all of the same type. The components of an array are accessed by simple integer indices. In a card game, a `Deck` object might look like this:

```
class Deck {
    final int DECK_SIZE = 52;
```

```
        Card[] cards = new Card[DECK_SIZE];

    public void print() {
        for (int i = 0; i < cards.length; i++)
            System.out.println(cards[i]);
    }
}
```

First we declare a constant called DECK_SIZE to define the number of cards in a deck. We declare a cards field as an array of type Card, by following the type name in the declaration with brackets [ and ]. We initialize cards to a new array with DeckSize Card variables, initialized to null. An array's length is fixed when it is created, and can never change.

The print method invocation shows how array components are accessed, by enclosing the index of the desired element within brackets [ and ] following the array name.

You can probably tell from reading the code that array objects have a length field that says how many elements the array contains. The *bounds* of an array are integers between 0 and length-1. An IndexOutOfBoundsException is thrown if you use an index outside the bounds of the array.

The example also introduced a new variable declaration mechanism—declaring the control variable of a for statement in its initialization clause. Declaring variables in the initialization section of a for loop is a concise and convenient way to declare simple loop variables. This construct is allowed only in the initialization of for statements; you cannot declare variables in the test clause of an if or while statement.

The loop variable i is available only within the code of the for statement. A loop variable declared in this manner disappears when the loop terminates, which means you can reuse that variable name in subsequent for statements.

## Exercise 1.8

Modify the Fibonacci application to store the sequence into an array, and print the list of values at the end.   ▲

## Exercise 1.9

Modify the ImprovedFibonacci application to store its sequence in an array. Do this by creating a new class to hold both the value and a boolean value that says whether the value is even, and then having an array of object references to objects of that class.   ▲

## 1.9    String Objects

Java provides a String object type to deal specifically with sequences of character data, and provides language-level support for initializing them. The Java String class provides a variety of methods to operate on String objects.

You've already seen String literals in examples like the HelloWorld program. When you write a statement like

```
System.out.println("Hello, world");
```

the Java compiler actually creates a String object initialized to the value of the specified string literal, and passes that String object as the parameter to the println method.

Unlike arrays, you don't need to specify the length of a String object when you create it. You can create a new String object and initialize it all in one statement, as shown in this example:

```
class StringsDemo {
    static public void main(String args[]) {
        String  myName = "Petronius";

        myName = myName + " Arbiter";
        System.out.println("Name = " + myName);
    }
}
```

Here we create a String object reference called myName and initialize it with a String literal. Following initialization, we use the String concatenation + operator to make a new String object with a new value. Finally, we print the value of myName on the standard output stream. The output when you run the above program is:

```
Name = Petronius Arbiter
```

In addition to the + sign as a concatenation operator, you can use the += operator as a shorthand for placing the variable name on the right-hand side of the assignment. Here's an upgraded version of the above example:

```
class BetterStringsDemo {
    static public void main(String args[]) {
        String myName = "Petronius";
        String occupation = "Reorganization Specialist";
```

```
            myName = myName + " Arbiter";
            myName += " ";
            myName += "(" + occupation + ")";
            System.out.println("Name = " + myName);
    }
}
```

Now, when you run the program you get this output:

```
Name = Petronius Arbiter (Reorganization Specialist)
```

`String` objects have a `length` method that returns the number of characters in the `String`. Characters are indexed from 0 through `length()` - 1.

`String` objects are *read-only,* or *immutable:* the contents of a `String` never change. When you see statements like

```
str = "redwood";
// ... do something with str ..
str = "oak";
```

the second assignment gives a new value to the *object reference* `str`, not to the *contents* of the string. Every time you perform operations that seem to modify a `String` object, such as `+=` as used above, you end up with a new `String` object that is also read-only, while the original `String` object's contents remain unchanged. The `StringBuffer` class provides for mutable strings, and is described in Chapter 8 where `String` is also described in detail.

The `equals` method is the simplest way to compare two `String` objects to see if they have the same contents:

```
if (oneStr.equals(twoStr))
    foundDuplicate(oneStr, twoStr);
```

Other methods for comparing over a subpart of the strings or ignoring case differences are also covered in Chapter 8.

*Exercise 1.10*

Modify the `StringsDemo` application to use different strings.   ▲

*Exercise 1.11*

Modify `ImprovedFibonacci` to store the `String` objects it creates into an array instead of invoking `println` with them directly.   ▲

## 1.10  Extending a Class

One of the major benefits of object orientation is the ability to *extend*, or *subclass*, the behavior of an existing class and continue to use code written for the original class.

When you extend a class to create a new class, the new extended class *inherits* all the fields and methods of the class that was extended. The original class on which the extension is based is known as the *superclass*.

If the subclass does not specifically *override* the behavior of the superclass, the subclass inherits all the behavior of its superclass, because, as we said, the extended class inherits the fields and methods of its superclass.

The Walkman example can itself be extended in this way. Later models incorporated two sets of jacks so two people could listen to the same tape. In the object-oriented world, the two-jack model extends, or is a subclass of, the basic model. The two-jack model inherits the characteristics and behavior of the basic model and adds new behavior of its own.

Customers told Sony they wanted to talk to each other while sharing a tape in the two-jack model. Sony enhanced the two-jack model to include two-way communications so people could chat while listening to music. The two-way communications model is a subclass of the two-jack model, inherits all of *its* behavior, and adds new behavior.

Sony created many other Walkman models. Later models extend the capabilities of the basic model—they subclass the basic model and inherit features and behavior from it.

Let's look at an example of extending a Java class. Here we extend our former Point class to represent a screen pixel. The new Pixel class requires a color in addition to *x* and *y* coordinates:

```
class Pixel extends Point {
    Color color;

    public void clear() {
        super.clear();
        color = null;
    }
};
```

Pixel extends both *data* and *behavior* of its Point superclass. Pixel extends the data by adding an additional field, namely color, to Point. Pixel also extends the behavior of Point by overriding Point's clear method. Here is an illustration of the concept:

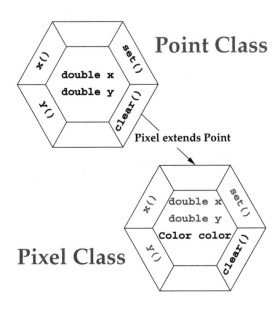

Pixel objects can be used by any code designed to work with Point objects. If a method expects a parameter of type Point, you can hand it a Pixel object and it just works. All the Point code can be used by anyone with a Pixel in hand. This feature is known as *polymorphism*—a single object like Pixel can have many (*poly-*) forms (*-morph*) and can be used as both a Pixel object and a Point object.

Pixel's behavior extends Point's behavior. Extended behavior could be entirely new (adding color in this example) or can be a restriction on old behavior that follows all the original requirements. An example of restricted behavior might be Pixel objects that live inside some kind of Screen object, restricting x and y to the dimensions of the screen. The original Point class made no restriction on coordinates, but a class with restricted range is still within the original unbounded range.

An extended class often *overrides* the behavior of its *superclass* (the class that was extended) by providing new implementations of one or more of the inherited methods. In the example above, we override clear to obtain proper behavior that Pixel requires—the clear that Pixel inherited from Point knows only about Point's fields, but obviously can't know about the new color field declared in the Pixel subclass.

*Exercise 1.12*

Write a set of classes that reflect the class structure of the Sony Walkman product family. Use methods to hide the data, making all the data `private` and the methods `public`. What methods would belong in the base `Walkman` class? Which methods would be added for which extended classes?   ▲

### 1.10.1  The `Object` Class

Classes that do not explicitly extend any other class implicitly extend the `Object` class. All object references are polymorphically of class `Object`, so `Object` is the generic class for references that can refer to objects of any class:

```
Object oref = new Pixel();
oref = "Some String";
```

In this example, `oref` is legally assigned references to `Pixel` and `String` objects, even though those classes have no relationship other than the direct or indirect implicit superclass of `Object`.

The `Object` class also defines several important methods that are discussed in Chapter 3.

### 1.10.2  Invoking Methods from the Superclass

To make `Pixel` do the correct "clear" behavior, we provide a new implementation of `clear` that first invokes its superclass's `clear` using the `super` reference. The `super` reference is a lot like the `this` reference described previously, except that `super` references things from the superclass, where `this` references things from the current object.

The invocation `super.clear()` looks to the superclass to execute `clear` as it would for an object of the superclass type—namely, `Point`. After invoking `super.clear()`, we add new functionality, to set `color` to a reasonable empty value. We choose `null`—a reference to no object.

What would happen had we not invoked `super.clear()` in the example on page 19? `Pixel`'s `clear` method would set the color to its `null` value, but the x and y variables that `Pixel` inherited from `Point` would not be set to any "cleared" values. Not clearing all the values of a `Pixel` object, including its `Point` parts, is probably a bug.

When you invoke `super.`*method*`()`, the object runtime system looks back up the inheritance hierarchy to the first superclass that contains the required *method*`()`. If `Point` didn't have a `clear` method, for example, the object runtime would look at `Point`'s superclass for such a method, and invoke that, and so on.

For all other references you use, invoking a method uses the actual type of the *object*, not the type of the object *reference*. Here is an example:

```
Point point = new Pixel();

point.clear();  // uses Pixel's clear()
```

In this example Pixel's version of clear is invoked, even though the variable that holds the Pixel is declared as a Point reference. But if we write super.clear() inside one of Pixel's methods, Point's clear method is invoked.

## 1.11  Interfaces

Sometimes you need only *define* methods an object must support, but not necessarily supply the *implementation* of those methods. As long as their behavior meets specific criteria, implementation details of the methods are irrelevant. For example, to ask whether a particular value is contained in a set of values, details of how those values are stored are irrelevant. You would want the methods to work equally well with a linked list of values, a hashtable of values, or any other data structure.

Java enables you to define an *interface*, which is a like a class, but with only declarations of its methods. The designer of the interface declares which methods are supported by classes that *implement* the interface, and what those methods should do. Here is a Lookup interface:

```
interface Lookup {
    /** Return the value associated with the name, or
     *  null if there is no such value */
    Object find(String name);
}
```

The Lookup interface defines one method, find, that takes a String and returns the value associated with that name, or null if there is no associated value. No implementation is given for the method—the class that *implements* the interface is responsible for the specific implementation. Code that uses references to Lookup objects (objects that implement the Lookup interface) can invoke the find method and get the expected results, no matter the actual type of the object:

```
void processValues(String[] names, Lookup table) {
    for (int i = 0; i < names.length; i++) {
        Object value = table.find(names[i]);
```

```
        if (value != null)
            processValue(names[i], value);
    }
}
```

A class can implement as many interfaces as it chooses. This example implements Lookup using a simple array (methods to set or remove values are left out for simplicity):

```
class SimpleLookup implements Lookup {
    private String[] Names;
    private Object[] Values;

    public Object find(String name) {
        for (int i = 0; i < Names.length; i++) {
            if (Names[i].equals(name))
                return Values[i];
        }
        return null;    // not found
    }

    // ...
}
```

Interfaces can be extended, too, using the extends keyword. An interface can extend one or more other interfaces, adding new constants and new methods that must be implemented by any class that implements the extended interface.

A class's *supertypes* are the class it extends and the interfaces it implements, including all the supertypes of those classes and interfaces. So the type of an object is not only its class, but any of its supertypes, including interfaces. An object can be used polymorphically with both its superclass and any superinterfaces, including any of their supertypes.

### Exercise 1.13

Write an extended interface of Lookup that has add and remove methods. Implement the extended interface in a new class.   ▲

## 1.12  Exceptions

What do you do when an error occurs in a program? In many languages, error conditions are signaled by unusual return values like −1. Programmers often don't check for exceptional values because they may assume errors "can't happen." On the other hand, adding error-detection and recovery to what should be a straight-forward flow of logic can obscure that logic to the point where the normal flow is incomprehensible. An ostensibly simple task such as reading a file into memory might require about seven lines of code. Error checking and reporting expands this to 40 or more lines. Making normal operation the needle in your code hay-stack is undesirable.

Java uses *checked exceptions* to manage error handling. Exceptions force you to deal with errors. If a checked exception is not handled, this is noticed when the error happens, not later when problems have compounded because of the unchecked error.

A method that detects an unusual error condition *throws* an exception. Excep-tions can be *caught* by code farther back on the calling stack—this prior code can handle the exception as needed and then continue executing. Uncaught exceptions are handled by a default handler in the Java implementation, which may report the exception and terminate the thread of execution.

An exception in Java is an object, with type, methods, and data. Representing exceptions as objects is useful, because an exception object can include data or methods or both to report on or recover from specific kinds of exceptions. Excep-tion objects are generally derived from the Exception class, which provides a string field to describe the error. Java requires all exceptions to be extensions of a class named Throwable.

The general paradigm of exceptions in Java is the *try–catch–finally* sequence: you *try* something; if that something throws an exception, you *catch* the excep-tion; and *finally*, clean up from either the normal code path or the exception code path, whichever actually happened.

Below you see an averageOf method that returns the average of two ele-ments in an array. If either index is outside the bounds of the array, it wants to throw an exception describing the error. First, we define a new exception type IllegalAverageException to describe such an error. Then we declare that the averageOf method throws that exception using a throws clause:

```java
class IllegalAverageException extends Exception {
}

class MyUtilities {
    public double averageOf(double[] vals, int i, int j)
        throws IllegalAverageException
    {
        try {
            return (vals[i] + vals[j]) / 2;
```

```
    } catch(IndexOutOfBoundsException e) {
        throw new IllegalAverageException();
    }
  }
}
```

During the averaging calculation, if both i and j are within the array bounds, the calculation succeeds and the average value is returned. But if either index is out of bounds, an IndexOutOfBoundsException is thrown, and the matching catch clause is executed. The catch clause creates a new IllegalAverageException object and throws it, in effect translating the general array index exception into a specific exception that more precisely describes the real failure. Methods further back on the execution stack have a chance to catch the new exception, and react to it appropriately.

If execution of a method can result in checked exceptions, it must declare the types of these exceptions in a throws clause, as shown for averageOf. Other than exceptions of type RuntimeException and Error, or subclasses of these exception types, which can be thrown anywhere, a method can throw only those exceptions it declares, whether it throws those exceptions directly with throw, or indirectly by invoking a method that throws exceptions.

Declaring exceptions that a method throws means the compiler can ensure that the method throws only those exceptions it declared, and no others. This check prevents errors in cases where your method should handle another method's exceptions, but did not. In addition, the method that invokes your method is assured that your method will not result in unexpected exceptions. This is why the exceptions you must declare in a throws clause are called *checked exceptions*. Exceptions that are extensions of RuntimeException and Error need not be declared and are not checked; they are called *unchecked exceptions*.

**Exercise 1.14**

Add fields to IllegalAverageException to hold the array and indices so that whoever catches the exception will know details about the error.   ▲

## 1.13  Packages

Name conflicts are a major problem when developing reusable code. No matter how carefully you pick names for classes and methods, somebody else is likely to use that name for a different purpose. If you use simple, descriptive names, the problem gets worse—such names are more likely to be used by someone else who was also trying to use simple, descriptive names. Words like "set," "get," "clear," and so on are used a lot and are almost certain to clash with other people's uses.

The standard solution for name collision in many programming languages is to use a "package prefix" at the front of every class, type, global function, and so on. Prefix conventions create *naming contexts* to ensure that names in one package do not conflict with names in other packages. These prefixes are usually a few characters long and are usually an abbreviation of the package product name, such as Xt for "X Toolkit," or WIN32 for the 32-bit Windows API.

When code uses only a few packages, likelihood of prefix conflict is small. However, since prefixes are abbreviations, the probability of a name conflict increases with the number of packages used.

Java has adopted a more formal notion of package that has a set of types and subpackages as members. Packages are named and can be imported. Package names are hierarchical, with components separated by dots. When you use part of a package, either you use its fully qualified name, or you *import* all or part of the package. Hierarchical package names enable longer package names. Hierarchical package names also give you control over name conflicts—if two packages contain classes with the same name, you can use a package-qualified form of the class name for one or both of them.

Here is an example of a method that uses fully qualified names to print the current day and time using Java's utility class Date (documented in Chapter 12):

```java
class Date1 {
    public static void main(String[] args) {
        java.util.Date now = new java.util.Date();
        System.out.println(now);
    }
}
```

And here is a version that uses import to declare the type Date:

```java
import java.util.Date;

class Date2 {
    public static void main(String[] args) {
        Date now = new Date();
        System.out.println(now);
    }
}
```

The name collision problem is not completely solved by the Java package mechanism. Two projects can *still* give their packages the same name. This problem can be solved only by convention. The standard convention is to use the reversed Internet domain name of the organization to prefix the package name. For example, if the Acme Corporation had the Internet domain `acme.com`, it would use package names of the form `COM.acme.package`.

Having dots separate package components may occasionally cause confusion, because the dot is also used to invoke methods and access fields in object references. This may lead to confusion as to what can be imported. Java novices often try to import `System.out` so they don't have to type it in front of every `println`. This does not work because `System` is a class, in which `out` is a staticfield whose type supports the `println` method.

On the other hand, `java.util` is a package, so you can import `java.util.Date` (or `java.util.*` if you want everything from the package). If you are having problems importing something, stop and make sure that you are importing a type.

Java classes are always in a package. A package is named by providing a package declaration at the top of the source file:

```
package com.sun.games;

class Card
{
    // ...
}

// ...
```

If a name is not provided via a `package` declaration, the class is made part of an *unnamed package*. Although this is adequate for an application (or applet) that is not loaded with any other code, classes destined for a library should be written in named packages.

## 1.14  The Java Infrastructure

Java is designed to maximize portability. Many details about Java are specifically defined for all implementations. For example, an `int` is a 32-bit two's-complement signed integer. Many languages leave precise definitions to particular implementations, making only general guarantees such as minimum range, or provide a way to ask the system what the range is on the current platform.

Java makes these definitions specific all the way down to the machine language into which Java code is translated. Java source code is compiled into Java *bytecodes*, designed to be run on a Java *virtual machine*. Bytecodes are a machine language for an abstract machine, but are interpreted by the virtual machine on each system that supports Java.[2]

The virtual machine assigns each application its own *runtime*, which both isolates applications from each other and provides a security model. Each runtime's security manager decides on the capabilities available to the application. The security manager could, for example, forbid the application from reading or writing the local disk, or allow network connections only to particular machines.

These features combined give Java code complete platform independence to provide a security model suitable for executing code downloaded across the network at varying levels of trust. Java source code compiled into Java bytecodes can be run on any machine with a Java virtual machine. The code can be executed with an appropriate level of protection to prevent careless or malicious class writers from harming the system. The level of trust can be adjusted depending on the source of the bytecodes—bytecodes on the local disk or protected network can be trusted more than bytecodes fetched from arbitrary machines elsewhere in the world.

## 1.15  Other Topics Briefly Noted

Java has several other features which we mention briefly here, and which are covered later:

- ◆ *Threads:* Java has built-in thread support for creating multithreaded applications. It uses per-object and per-class monitor-style locks to synchronize concurrent access to object and class data. See Chapter 9 for more details.

- ◆ *I/O:* Java provides a `java.io` package for many different kinds of input and output operations. See Chapter 11 for specifics of the I/O capabilities.

- ◆ *Type Classes:* Java has classes to represent most of the primitive types (such as `Integer`, `Double`, and `Boolean`) and a `Class` class to represent class types. See Chapter 13 for more information about programming with types.

- ◆ *Utility Classes and Interfaces:* Java provides a `java.util` package that has many useful classes, such as `BitSet`, `Vector`, `Stack`, and `Date`. See Chapter 12 for more information about utility classes.

---

[2.] A system can, of course, implement the Java virtual machine in silicon—that is, using a special-purpose chip. This does not affect the portability of the bytecodes—it is just another virtual machine implementation.

CHAPTER $2$

# Classes and Objects

*First things first, but not necessarily in that order.*
—Dr. Who, *Meglos*

**T**HE fundamental unit of programming in Java is the *class*. Classes contain methods—collections of executable code that are the focus of computation. Classes also provide the structure for *objects,* plus the mechanisms to manufacture objects from the class definitions. You *can* compute with only primitive types—integer, floating-point, and so on—but almost any interesting Java program will create and manipulate objects.

Object-oriented programming strictly separates the notion of *what* is to be done from *how* it is done. "What" is described as a set of methods (and sometimes publicly available data) and their associated semantics. This combination—methods, data, and semantics—is often described as a *contract* between the designer of the class and the programmer who uses it, since it says what happens when certain methods are invoked on an object.

A common assumption is that the methods declared in a class are its entire contract. The *semantics* of those operations are also part of the contract, even though they may be described only in documentation. Two methods may have the same name and signature, but they are not equivalent if they have different semantics. For example, not every method called `print` can be assumed to print out a copy of the object. Someone might define a `print` method with the semantics "process interval" or "prioritize nonterminals." The contract of the method, both signature and semantics, defines what it means.

The "how" of an object is defined by its class, which defines the implementation of the methods the object supports. Each object is an *instance* of a class. When a method is invoked on an object, the class is examined to find the code to be run. An object can use other objects to do its job, but we start with simple classes that implement all of their own methods directly.

## 2.1   A Simple Class

The basics of a class are its fields (data) and its methods (code to manipulate the data). Here is a simple class called Body that could be used to store data about celestial bodies such as comets, asteroids, planets, and stars:

```
class Body {
    public long idNum;
    public String nameFor;
    public Body orbits;

    public static long nextID = 0;
}
```

First we declare the name of the class. A class declaration creates a *type name* in Java, so that references to objects of that type can be declared with a simple

```
Body mercury;
```

This declaration states that mercury is a reference to an object of class Body. The declaration does *not* create an object—it declares only a *reference* to a Body object. The reference is initially null, and the object referenced by mercury does not actually exist until you create it explicitly; in this respect, Java is different from languages where objects are created when you declare variables.

This first version of Body is poorly designed. This is intentional: we will demonstrate the value of certain language features as we improve the class in this chapter.

### Exercise 2.1

Write a simple Vehicle class that has fields for (at least) current speed, current direction in degrees, and owner name.   ▲

### Exercise 2.2

Write a LinkedList class that has a field of type Object and a reference to the next LinkedList element in the list.   ▲

## 2.2   Fields

A class's variables are called *fields;* the Body class's nameFor and orbits are examples. Every Body object has its own specific instances of these fields: a long that uniquely identifies the body from all others, a String that is its name, and a reference to another Body around which it orbits.

Giving each separate object a different instance of the fields means that each object has its own unique state. Changing the `orbits` field in one Body object does not affect the `orbits` field in any other Body object.

Sometimes, though, you want only one instance of a field shared by all objects of a class. You obtain such fields by declaring them `static`, so they are called *static fields* or *class variables*. When you declare a `static` field in a class, all objects created from that class share a single copy of that field.

In our case, Body has one `static` field, `nextID`, which contains the next body identifier to use. The `nextID` field is initialized to zero when the class is initialized after it is loaded and linked. You will see below that each newly created Body object will have the current value of `nextID` as its identifier.

In this book when we use the term "field" or "method" we usually mean the non-static kind. When the context makes it ambiguous, we will use the term "non-static field" or "non-static method" to be clear.

### *Exercise 2.3*

Add a static field to your `Vehicle` class for Vehicle Identification Number, and a non-static field to the `Car` class to hold each vehicle's ID number.   ▲

## 2.3   Access Control and Inheritance

All fields and methods of a class are always available to code in the class itself. To control access from other classes, and to control inheritance by subclasses, class members have four possible access control modifiers:

- ◆ *Public:* Members declared `public` are accessible anywhere the class is accessible, and they are inherited by subclasses.

- ◆ *Private:* Members declared `private` are accessible only in the class itself.

- ◆ *Protected:* Members declared `protected` are accessible to and inherited by subclasses, and accessible by code in the same package. Extending objects is covered in Chapter 3.

- ◆ *Package:* Members declared with no access modifier are accessible only to code and inherited only by subclasses in the same package. Packages are discussed in Chapter 10.

We declared the Body class's fields `public` because programmers need access to them to do the work the class is designed for. In a later version of the Body class, you will see that such a design is not usually a good idea.

## 2.4    Creating Objects

In this first version of Body, objects that represent particular celestial bodies are created and initialized like this:

```
Body sun = new Body();
sun.idNum = Body.nextID++;
sun.nameFor = "Sol";
sun.orbits = null; // in solar system, sun is middle

Body earth = new Body();
earth.idNum = Body.nextID++;
earth.nameFor = "Earth";
earth.orbits = sun;
```

First we declare two references (sun and earth) to hold objects of type Body. As mentioned before, these declarations do *not* create objects; they only declare variables that *reference* objects. The references are initially null, and the objects they may reference must be created explicitly.

We create the sun using the new operator. The new construct is by far the most common way to create objects (we cover the other ways later). When you create an object with the new operator, you specify the type of object you want to create and any parameters to its construction. The Java runtime system allocates enough space to store the fields of the object and initializes it in ways you will soon see. When initialization is complete, the runtime system returns a reference to the new object.

If the system cannot find enough free space to create the object, it may have to run the garbage collector to try to reclaim space. If the system still cannot find enough free space, new throws an OutOfMemoryError exception.

Having created a new Body object, we initialize its variables. Each Body object needs a unique identifier, which it gets from the static nextID field of Body. The code must increment nextID so that the next Body object created will get a unique identifier.

This example builds a solar system model. In this model, the Sun is in the center, and sun's orbits field is null because it doesn't orbit anything. When we create and initialize earth, we set its orbits field to sun. A Moon object that orbited the Earth would have its orbits field set to earth. In a model of the galaxy, the sun would orbit around the black hole presumed to be at the middle of the Milky Way.

### *Exercise 2.4*

Write a main method for your Vehicle class that creates a few vehicles and prints out their field values.  ▲

*Exercise 2.5*

Write a `main` method for your `LinkedList` class that creates a few objects of type `Vehicle` and places them into successive nodes in the list.   ▲

## 2.5 Constructors

A newly created object is given an initial state. Fields can be initialized with a value when they are declared, which is sometimes sufficient to ensure a correct initial state.[1] But often you need more than simple data initialization to create the initial state; the creating code may need to supply initial data, or perform operations that cannot be expressed as simple assignment.

For purposes other than simple initialization, classes can have *constructors*. Constructors have the same name as the class they initialize. Like methods, they take zero or more parameters, but constructors are not methods and thus have no return type. Parameters, if any, are provided between the parentheses that follow the type name when the object is created with `new`. Constructors are invoked after the instance variables of a newly created object of the class have been assigned their default initial values, and after their explicit initializers are executed.

This improved version of the `Body` class uses constructors to set up the initial state, partly by initialization and partly in the constructor:

```
class Body {
    public long idNum;
    public String name = "<unnamed>";
    public Body orbits = null;

    private static long nextID = 0;


    Body() {
        idNum = nextID++;
    }
}
```

The constructor for `Body` takes no arguments, but it performs an important function, namely, assigning a proper `idNum` to the newly created object. In the original

---

[1.] Data initialization is covered in detail in "Initial Values" on page 100, but is a simple assignment of an initial value. If no value is assigned to a field it will be a zero, `\u0000`, `false`, or `null`, depending on its type.

code, a simple programmer error—forgetting to assign the idNum, or not incrementing nextID after use—could result in different Body objects with the same idNum, creating bugs in code relying on the part of the contract that says "all idNum values are different."

By moving responsibility for idNum generation inside the Body class, we have prevented errors of this kind. The Body constructor is now the only entity that assigns idNum, and is therefore the only entity needing access to nextID. We can and should make nextID private, so that only the Body class can access it. By doing so, we remove a source of error for programmers using the Body class.

We also are now free to change the way idNums are assigned to Body objects. A future implementation of this class might, for example, look up the name in a database of known astronomical entities and assign a new idNum only if an idNum had not already been assigned. This change would not affect any existing code, because that existing code wouldn't have been involved at all in the mechanism for idNum allocation.

The data initializations for name and orbits set them to reasonable values. Therefore, when the constructor returns from the invocation shown below, all data fields in the new Body object have been set to some reasonable initial state. You can then set state in the object to the values you want:

```
Body sun = new Body();    // idNum is 0
sun.name = "Sol";

Body earth = new Body(); // idNum is 1
earth.name = "Earth";
earth.orbits = sun;
```

The Body constructor is invoked while the new operator creates the object, but *after* name and orbits have been set to their initial values. Initializing orbits to null means that sun.orbits doesn't need to be set in our code.

The case shown here—where you create a body knowing its name and what it orbits—is likely to be fairly common. You can provide another constructor that takes both the name and orbited body:

```
Body(String bodyName, Body orbitsAround) {
    this();
    name = bodyName;
    orbits = orbitsAround;
}
```

As shown here, one constructor can invoke another constructor from the same class using the this() invocation as its first executable statement. This is called an explicit constructor invocation. If the constructor you want to invoke has parameters, they can be passed to the constructor invocation. Here we use it to call the constructor that has no arguments in order to set up the idNum. Now the allocation code is much simpler:

```
Body sun = new Body("Sol", null);
Body earth = new Body("Earth", sun);
```

You could, if you wanted, provide a one-argument constructor for those cases where you're constructing a Body object that doesn't orbit anything, rather than invoking the two-argument Body constructor with a second argument of null.

Some classes always require that the creator supply certain kinds of data. For example, your application might require that all Body objects have a name. To ensure that all statements creating Body objects supply a name, you would define all Body constructors with a name parameter.

Here are some common reasons for providing specialized constructors:

♦ Some classes have no reasonable initial state without parameters.

♦ Providing an initial state is convenient and reasonable when constructing some kinds of objects (the two-argument constructor of Body is an example).

♦ Constructing an object can be a potentially expensive operation, so you want objects to have a correct initial state when they're created. For example, if each object of a class had a table, a constructor to specify the initial size would enable the object to create the table with the right size from the beginning.

♦ A constructor that isn't public restricts who can create objects using it. You could, for example, prevent programmers using your package from extending a class by making all its constructors accessible only inside the package. You can also mark as protected constructors that make sense only for subclasses.

Constructors without arguments are so common that there is a term for them: they are called *no-arg* (for "no arguments") constructors.

If you don't provide any constructors of any kind in a class, the language provides a default no-arg constructor that does nothing. This constructor is provided automatically only if no other constructors exist because there are classes for which a no-arg constructor would be incorrect (like the Attr class you will see in the next chapter).

If you want both a no-arg constructor and one or more constructors with arguments, you can explicitly provide a no-arg constructor. The automatically provided no-arg constructor for a class that has no superclass is equivalent to the following (you will see one for an extended class in Chapter 3):

```
class SimpleClass {
    /** Same as default constructor */
    public SimpleClass() {
    }
}
```

The default constructor is `public` if the class is, and not if the class is not.

### Exercise 2.6

Add two constructors to `Vehicle`—a no-arg constructor and one that takes an initial owner's name. Modify the `main` program so it generates the same output it did before.  ▲

### Exercise 2.7

What constructors should you add to `LinkedList`?  ▲

## 2.6    Methods

A class's *methods* typically contain the code that understands and manipulates an object's state. Some classes have `public` fields for programmers to manipulate directly, but in most cases this isn't a very good idea (see "Designing a Class to Be Extended" on page 72). Many objects have tasks that cannot be represented as a simple value to be read or modified, but require computation.

Methods are *invoked* as operations on objects via references using the `.` operator:

```
reference.method(parameters)
```

Each method takes a specific number of parameters. Java does not include methods that can accept a variable number of parameters. Each parameter has a specified type, either a primitive type or a reference type. Methods also have a return type, which is declared before the method name. For example, here is a method of the Body class to create a `String` that describes a particular Body object:

```
public String toString() {
    String desc = idNum + " (" + name + ")";
    if (orbits != null)
        desc += " orbits " + orbits.toString();
    return desc;
}
```

This method uses + and += to concatenate `String` objects. It first builds a string that describes the identifier and name. If the body orbits another body, we append the string that describes *that* body by invoking its `toString` method. This recursion builds a string of bodies orbiting other bodies until the chain ends with some object that doesn't orbit anything.

The `toString` method is special. If an object has a method named `toString` that takes no parameters and returns a `String`, it is invoked to get a `String` when that object is used in a string concatenation using the + operator. In these expressions:

```
System.out.println("Body " + sun);
System.out.println("Body " + earth);
```

the `toString` methods of `sun` and `earth` are invoked implicitly, and produce the following output:

```
Body 0 (Sol)
Body 1 (Earth) orbits 0 (Sol)
```

Methods can return more than one result in several ways: return references to objects that store the results as fields, take one or more parameters that reference objects in which to store the results, or return an array containing the results.

Suppose, for instance, you want to write a method to return what a particular person can do with a given bank account. Multiple actions are possible (deposit, withdraw, and so on), so multiple permissions must be returned. Here is a `Permissions` object that stores boolean values to say whether a particular action is allowed:

```
class Permissions {
    public boolean canDeposit,
                   canWithdraw,
                   canClose;
}
```

And here is the method that fills in the fields to return multiple values:

```
class Account {
    public Permissions permissionsFor(Person who) {
        Permissions perm = new Permissions();
        perm.canDeposit = canDeposit(who);
        perm.canWithdraw = canWithdraw(who);
        perm.canClose = canClose(who);
        return perm;
    }

    // ... define canDeposit() et al ...
}
    }
```

If a method does not return any value, the place where a return type would go, filled with a void. In methods that return a value, every path through the method must return a value assignable to a variable of the declared return type. The permissionsFor method could not return, say, a String, since you cannot assign a String object to a variable of type Permissions. But you could declare the return type of permissionsFor as Object without changing the return statement, because you can assign a Permissions object reference to a variable of type Object.

### 2.6.1 Parameter Values

All parameters to methods Java are "call by value." That is, values of parameter variables in a method are copies of the values the invoker specified. If you pass a boolean to a method, its parameter is a copy of whatever value was being passed, and the method can change it without affecting values in the code that invoked the method. For example:

```
class PassByValue {
    public static void main(String[] args) {
        double one = 1.0;

        System.out.println("before: one = " + one);
        halveIt(one);
        System.out.println("after:  one = " + one);
    }

    public static void halveIt(double arg) {
        arg /= 2.0;      // divide arg by two
        System.out.println("halved: arg = " + arg);
    }
}
```

The following output illustrates that the value of arg inside halveIt is divided by two without affecting the value of the variable one in main:

```
before: one = 1
halved: arg = 0.5
after:  one = 1
```

When the parameter is an object reference, however, the object *reference* is what is passed "by value," not the object itself. Thus, you can change which object a parameter refers to inside the method without affecting the reference that was passed. But if you change any fields of the object, or invoke methods that change the object's state, the object is changed for every part of the program that holds a reference to it. Here is an example to show this distinction:

```
class PassRef {
    public static void main(String[] args) {
        Body sirius = new Body("Sirius", null);

        System.out.println("before: " + sirius);
        commonName(sirius);
        System.out.println("after:  " + sirius);
    }

    public static void commonName(Body bodyRef) {
        bodyRef.name = "Dog Star";
        bodyRef = null;
    }
}
```

This produces the following output:

```
before: 0 (Sirius)
after:  0 (Dog Star)
```

Notice that the contents of the object have been modified with a name change, while the reference bodyRef still refers to the Body object, even though common-Name changed the value of its bodyRef parameter to null.

The diagram below shows the state of the references just after main invokes commonName. At this point, the two references sirius (in main) and bodyRef (in

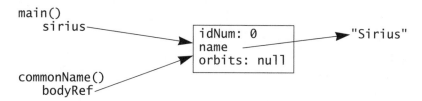

commonName) both refer to the same underlying object. When commonName changes the field bodyRef.name, the name is changed in the underlying object that the two references share. When commonName changes the value of bodyRef to null, only the value of the bodyRef reference is changed, while the value of sirius remains unchanged, since the parameter bodyRef is a pass-by-value copy of sirius. Inside the method commonName, all you are changing is the value in the parameter variable bodyRef, just as all you changed in halveIt was the value in the parameter variable arg. If changing bodyRef affected the value of sirius in main, the "after" line would say "null". However, the variables bodyRef in commonName and sirius in main both refer to the same underlying object, so the change made inside commonName is reflected in the object that sirius refers to.

### 2.6.2   Using Methods to Control Access

The Body class with its various constructors is considerably easier to use than its simple data-only form, and we have ensured that the idNum is set both automatically and correctly. But a programmer could still mess up the object by setting its idNum field after construction, because the idNum field is public and therefore exposed to change. The idNum should be read-only data. Read-only in objects is common, but there is no keyword to apply to a field that allows read-only access outside the class.

To enforce read-only access, you must hide the field. You do this by making the idNum field private and providing a new method so that code outside the class can read its value using that method:

```
class Body {
    private long idNum; // now "private"

    public String name = "<unnamed>";
    public Body orbits = null;
    private static long nextID = 0;

    Body() {
        idNum = nextID++;
    }

    public long id() {
        return idNum;
    }

    //...
}
```

Now programmers who want to use the body's identifier will invoke the id method, which returns the value. There is no longer any way for programmers to modify the identifier—it has effectively become a read-only value outside the class. It can be modified only by the internal methods of the Body class.

Methods that regulate access to internal data are sometimes called *accessor methods*. You could also use accessor methods to protect the name and orbits fields, and you probably should.

Even if an application doesn't require fields to be read-only, making fields private and adding methods to set and fetch them enables you to add actions that may be needed in the future. If programmers can access a class's fields directly, you have no control over what values they will use or what happens when values are changed. For these reasons, you will see very few `public` fields in subsequent examples in this book.

### *Exercise 2.8*

Make the fields in your `Vehicle` class `private`, and add accessor methods for the fields. Which fields should have methods to change them, and which should not? ▲

### *Exercise 2.9*

Make the fields in your `LinkedList` class `private`, and add accessor methods for the fields. Which fields should have methods to change them, and which should not? ▲

### *Exercise 2.10*

Add a `changeSpeed` method that changes the current speed of the vehicle to a passed-in value, and a `stop` method that sets the speed to zero. ▲

### *Exercise 2.11*

Add a method to `LinkedList` to count the number of elements in a list. ▲

## 2.7 this

You have already seen (on page 34) how you can use an explicit constructor invocation to invoke another one of your class's constructors at the beginning of a constructor. You can also use the special object reference `this` inside a non-static method, where it refers to the current object on which the method was invoked. The `this` reference is most commonly used as a way to pass a reference to the current object as a parameter to other methods. Suppose a method requires adding the object to a list of objects awaiting some service. It might look something like this:

```
Service.add(this);
```

An implicit `this` is added to the beginning of any field or method reference inside a method if it is not provided by the programmer. For example, the assignment to `str` in this class:

```
class Name {
    public String str;
```

```
    Name() {
        str = "<unnamed>";
    }
}
```

is equivalent to the following:

```
    this.str = "<unnamed>";
```

Conventionally, you use `this` only when needed, which is when the name of the field you need to access is hidden by a variable or parameter declaration. For example:

```
class Moose {
    String hairdresser;

    Moose(String hairdresser) {
        this.hairdresser = hairdresser;
    }
}
```

The `hairdresser` field is hidden inside the constructor by the parameter of the same name. To ensure we access the `hairdresser` field instead of the `hairdresser` parameter, we prefix it with `this` to specify that the field is the one belonging to "this" object. Deliberately hiding identifiers in this manner is considered good programming practice only in this idiomatic use in constructors and accessor methods.

In addition to `this`, the keyword `super` can be used to access hidden fields and invoke overridden methods of the superclass. The `super` keyword is covered in more detail in "Overriding Methods and Hiding Fields" on page 58.

## 2.8  Overloading Methods

In Java, each method has a *signature*, which is its name together with the number and types of its parameters. Two methods can have the same name if their signatures have different numbers or types of parameters. This feature is called *overloading*, because the simple name of the method has overloaded (more than one) meaning. When a programmer invokes a method, the compiler compares the number and type of parameters to find the method that best matches the available signatures. Here are some `orbitsAround` methods for our Body class:

```
public Body orbitsAround() {
    return orbits;
}
public void orbitsAround(Body around) {
```

```
        orbits = around;
    }
```

These methods are written using a programming style that uses overloading to differentiate between fetching a value (no parameters) and setting the value (a parameter with the new value). The number of parameters is different, so the overload resolution is simple. If orbitsAround is invoked with no parameters, the method that returns the current value is used. If orbitsAround is invoked with one argument that is a Body, the method that sets the value is used. If the invocation matches neither of these signatures, it is invalid, and the code will not compile.

A full discussion of how the language chooses which available overloaded method to invoke for a given invocation can be found in "Member Access" on page 108.

### *Exercise 2.12*

Add two turn methods to Vehicle—one that takes a number of degrees to turn, and one that takes simply either a Vehicle.TURN_LEFT or a Vehicle.TURN_RIGHT constant. ▲

## 2.9 Static Members

A class has two kinds of members: fields and methods. Each member specifies how it may be accessed and how it may be inherited (private, protected, public, or package). Each member can also be made static if so desired.

A *static* member is a member that is only one per class, rather than one in every object created from that class. For static fields (class variables), there is exactly one variable, no matter how many objects (even zero) there are of the class. The nextID field in our Body class above is an example.

The static fields of a class are initialized before any static field in that class is used or any method of that class is run. In the following example, the unset method can assume that the UNSET variable has been set to the value Double.NaN before the unset method wants to use it:

```
class Value {
    public static double UNSET = Double.NaN;

    private double V;

    public void unset() {
        V = UNSET;
    }
```

```
    // ...
}
```

### 2.9.1  Static Initialization Blocks

A class can also have *static initialization blocks* to set up static fields or other necessary states. A static initializer is most useful when simple initialization clauses
on the field declaration aren't up to the task of initialization. For example, creating
a static array and initializing its members often must be done with executable
statements. Here is example code to initialize a small array of primes:

```
class Primes {
    protected static int[] knownPrimes = new int[4];

    static {
        knownPrimes[0] = 2;
        for (int i = 1; i < knownPrimes.length; i++)
                knownPrimes[i] = nextPrime();
    }

}
```

The order of static initialization within a class is left-to-right and top-to-bottom.
Each static variable's initializer or static block of code is run before the next one,
in order from the first line of the source to the bottom. With this guarantee, our
static block in the example is assured that the knownPrimes array is already created before the initialization code block executes.

What if a static initializer in class X invokes a method in Y, but Y's static initializers invoke a method in X to set up *its* static values? This cyclic static initialization cannot be reliably detected during compilation, since the code for Y may
not yet be written when X is compiled. If this happens, X's static initializers will
only have been executed up to the point where Y's method was invoked. When Y,
in turn, invokes the X method, that method runs with the rest of the static initializers yet to be executed. Any static fields in X that haven't had their initializers executed will still have their default values (false, '\u0000', zero, or null
depending on their type).

Initializers for static fields can not invoke methods that declare that they can
result in checked exceptions: initializers are run when the class is loaded, which
can be at an arbitrary time during program execution when nothing is prepared to
handle the exceptions.

A static initialization code block *can* invoke methods that throw exceptions,
but only if it is prepared to catch all of them.

## 2.9.2   Static Methods

A *static method* is invoked on behalf of an entire class, not on a specific object instantiated from that class. Such methods are also known as *class methods*. A static method might perform a general task for all objects of the class—such as returning the next available serial number or something of that nature.

A static method can access only static variables and static methods of the class. There is no `this` reference, because there is no specific object being operated upon.

Outside a class, a static member is usually accessed by using the class name, rather than through an object reference:

```
prime = Primes.nextPrime();
knownCnt = Primes.knownPrimes.length;
```

### *Exercise 2.13*

Add a static method to `Vehicle` that returns the highest identification number used thus far.   ▲

## 2.10   Garbage Collection and `finalize`

Java performs garbage collection for you and eliminates the need to free objects explicitly.

In simple terms, when an object is no longer referenced, the space it occupies can be reclaimed. You do not have to do anything to make this happen—in fact, there is nothing you *can* do. An object is "no longer referenced" when there is no reference to the object in any static data, nor in any variable of any currently executing method, nor can you find a reference to the object by starting with static data and method variables and then following each field or array element, and so on. You create objects using `new`, but there is no corresponding `delete`. When you are finished with an object, you simply stop referring to it (change its reference to refer to another object or to `null`, or return from a method so its local variables no longer exist and hence refer to nothing). When an object has no references to it anywhere, except in other objects which are also unreferenced, it can be collected. We use the phrase "can be" because space is reclaimed only if more is needed or if the garbage collector wants to avoid running out of memory. A program may exit without running out of space or even coming close, and so never need to perform garbage collection.

Garbage collection means never having to worry about "dangling references." In systems where you directly control when objects are deleted, you can delete an object to which some other object still has a reference. That other reference is now "dangling," meaning it references space that the system considers free. Space that is thought to be "free" might be allocated to a new object, and the dangling reference would then reference something completely different from what the object thinks it references. This would cause all manner of havoc when it uses the values in that space as if they were part of something they are not. Java solves the dangling reference problem for you, because an object that's still referenced somewhere will never be garbage-collected.

Garbage is collected without your intervention, but collecting garbage still takes work. Creating and collecting large numbers of objects can interfere with time-critical applications. You should design systems to be judicious in the number of objects they create.

Garbage collection is not a guarantee that memory will always be available for new objects. You could create objects indefinitely, place them in lists, and continue doing so until there is no more space, and no unreferenced objects to reclaim. You could create a memory leak, for example, by allowing a list of objects to refer to objects you no longer need, and eventually run out of space. Garbage collection solves many, but not all, memory allocation problems.

### 2.10.1  finalize

You won't normally notice when an orphaned object's space is reclaimed—"it just works." But a class can implement a finalize method that is executed before the space is reclaimed and when the virtual machine exits. Such a finalize method gives you a chance to use the state contained in the object to reclaim other non-Java resources. It is declared like this:

```
protected void finalize() throws Throwable {
    super.finalize();
    // ...
}
```

Using finalize methods is important when dealing with non-Java resources that are too valuable to wait until garbage collection. For example, open files (usually a limited resource) cannot wait until the finalize phase to be reclaimed. There is no guarantee that the object holding the open file will be garbage-collected before all the open file resources are used up.

Still, objects that allocate external resources should provide a finalize method that cleans them up so the class doesn't create a resource leak. You will also need to provide a mechanism for programmers to explicitly reclaim those resources. For example, a class that opens a file to do its work should have some form of close method to close the file, enabling programmers using that class to manage the "number of open files" resource explicitly.

Sometimes `close` may not be invoked even though a client is finished with an object. Some programmers may not yet have run into problems that require them to do so. You can delay the consequences of this "open file" leak by adding a `finalize` method that invokes `close`, thereby ensuring that, whatever the quality of the other programmer's code, it never leaks open files. Here is how that might look:

```
public class ProcessFile {
    private Stream File;

    public ProcessFile(String path) {
        File = new Stream(path);
    }

    // ...

    public void close() {
        if (File != null) {
            File.close();
            File = null;
        }
    }

    protected void finalize() throws Throwable {
        super.finalize();
        close();
    }
}
```

Note that `close` is carefully written to be correct if it is invoked more than once. Otherwise if someone did invoke `close`, finalizing the object would cause another close on the file, which might not be allowed.

Note also that in the example above, the `finalize` method invokes `super.finalize`. Train your fingers so that you always do so in any `finalize` method you write. If you don't invoke `super.finalize`, you will correctly finalize your own class, but superclasses that used to be correctly finalized will no longer work. Remembering to invoke `super.finalize` is one of those good habits you should adopt even when your class doesn't extend any other. Besides being good training, invoking `super.finalize` in such a case means that you can always add a superclass to a class like `ProcessFile` without remembering to examine its `finalize` method for correctness.

The body of a `finalize` method can use `try/catch` to handle exceptions in methods it invokes, but any uncaught exceptions raised while executing a `finalize` method are ignored. Exceptions are covered in detail in Chapter 7.

The garbage collector may reclaim objects in any order, or never. Memory resources are reclaimed when the garbage collector thinks the time is appropriate. Not being bound to an ordering guarantee lets the garbage collector operate in whatever manner is most efficient, which helps minimize the overhead of garbage collection. You can directly invoke the garbage collector to try and force earlier collection—see "Memory Management" on page 260.

When an application exits, the `finalize` methods of all existing objects are run. This happens no matter how the exit occurs. However, various system errors can prevent all `finalize` methods from being invoked. For example, should the program exit because it runs out of memory, the garbage collector may not be able to get any memory it needs to find all objects and invoke `finalize`. In general, though, you can expect that all `finalize` methods will be executed for each object.

### 2.10.2  Resurrecting Objects During `finalize`

A `finalize` method can "resurrect" an object by making it referenced again, possibly by adding it to a static list of objects. This is *not* recommended behavior, but there is nothing Java can do to stop you.

However, Java invokes `finalize` exactly once on any object, even if that object is garbage-collected more than once because a previous `finalize` resurrected it. If resurrecting objects is important to your design, the object would be resurrected only once, which is highly unlikely to be the behavior you actually wanted.

If you really think you need to resurrect objects, you should review your design carefully, because you may uncover a flaw. If your design review convinces you that you still need to resurrect objects, the correct answer is to clone the object or create a new object, not to resurrect it. The `finalize` method can insert a reference to a new object that will continue the state of the dying object, rather than a reference to the dying object itself. Being new, the cloned object's `finalize` method will be invoked in the future (if needed), enabling it to insert yet another copy of itself in yet another list, ensuring the survival, if not of itself, at least of its progeny.

## 2.11  `main`

Details of invoking a Java application vary from system to system, but whatever the details, you must always provide the name of a Java class that drives the application. When you run a Java program, the system locates and runs the `main` method for that class. The `main` method must be `public`, `static`, and `void` (it returns nothing), and it must accept a single argument of type `String[]`. Here is an example that prints its parameters:

```
class Echo {
    public static void main(String[] args) {
        for (int i = 0; i < args.length; i++)
            System.out.print(args[i] + " ");
        System.out.println();
    }
}
```

The arguments in the string array are the "program arguments." These are usually typed by users when they run the program. For example, on a command-line system such as UNIX or a DOS shell, you might invoke the `Echo` application like this:

```
java Echo in here
```

In this command, `java` is the Java bytecode interpreter, `Echo` is the name of the class, and the rest of the parameters are the program arguments. The `java` command finds the compiled bytecodes for the class `Echo`, loads them into a runtime in a virtual machine, and invokes `Echo.main` with the program arguments contained in strings in the `String` array. The result is the following output:

```
in here
```

The name of the class is not included in the strings passed to `main`. You already know the name because it is the name of the enclosing class.

An application can have any number of `main` methods, since each class can have one. Only one `main` is used for any given program. The `main` that's actually used is specified when the program is run, as `Echo` was above. Being able to have multiple `main` methods has one salutary effect—each class can have a `main` that tests its own code, providing an excellent hook for unit-testing a class. This is something we recommend as a coding technique.[2]

### *Exercise 2.14*

Change `Vehicle.main` to create cars with owners whose names are specified on the command line, and then print them out.   ▲

---

[2.] Many of the example classes in this book have `main` methods. Space does not allow us to show the `main` method for every example, but it is how we usually write our own classes for nontrivial applications and libraries.

## 2.12  The `toString` Method

If an object supports a public `toString` method that takes no parameters and returns a `String` object, that method is invoked whenever an expression has an object of that type where a `String` is expected for a + or += operator. Here, for instance, is code that would print out an array of celestial bodies:

```
static void displayBodies(Body[] bodies) {
    for (int i = 0; i < bodies.length; i++)
        System.out.println(i + ": " + bodies[i]);
}
```

If you examine the `println` invocation, you will see two implicit string conversions: the first for the index `i` and the second for the Body objects, with a separating string in between. All primitive types are implicitly converted to `String` objects when used in expressions, but not at other times.

There is no universal `String`-to-object mechanism in Java. You can, of course, provide your own class decoding function. This will typically either be some kind of `fromString` method that replaces an existing object's state, or a constructor that takes a `String` parameter that sets up the object's initial state.

### Exercise 2.15

Add a `toString` method to `Vehicle`.  ▲

### Exercise 2.16

Add a `toString` method to `LinkedList`.  ▲

## 2.13  `native` Methods

If you need to write a Java program that will use some existing code that isn't written in Java, or if you need to directly manipulate some hardware, then you can write *native methods*. A native method enables you to implement a method that can be invoked from Java, but is written in a "native" language, usually C or C++.

If you use a native method, all portability and safety of the code is lost. You cannot, for instance, use a native method in almost any code you expect to download and run from across a network connection (an applet, for example)—the downloading system may or may not be of the same architecture, and even if it is, it might not trust your system well enough to run arbitrary compiled C code.

For details on writing native methods, see Appendix A.

# CHAPTER 3

# Extending Classes

*You will understand this when I tell you that I can trace*
*my ancestry back to a protoplasmal primordial atomic globule.*
—Gilbert and Sullivan, *The Mikado*

**T**HE quick tour described briefly how a class can be *extended*, or *subclassed*, and how an extended class can be used wherever the original class was legal. The term for this capability is *polymorphism*, meaning that an object of a given class can have multiple forms, either as its own class or as any superclass it extends. The extended class is called a *subclass* or *extended class* of the class it extends; the class that is extended is called its *superclass*.

The collection of methods and fields that are accessible from outside a class, together with how those members are expected to behave, is often referred to as the class's *contract*. The contract is what the class designer has promised the class will do. Whenever you extend a class to add new functionality, you create a new class with an expanded contract. You do not, however, change the part of the contract you *inherit* from the class you extended. Changing the way that the superclass's contract is *implemented* is reasonable, but you should never change the implementation in a way that violates the superclass's contract.

## 3.1 An Extended Class

Every class you have seen so far is an extended class, whether or not it is declared with an `extends` clause. A class such as `Body` that does not explicitly extend another class implicitly extends Java's `Object` class. In other words, `Object` is at the root of the total class hierarchy. The `Object` class declares methods that are implemented by all objects. Variables of type `Object` can refer to any object, whether it is a class instance or an array.

For example, if you make a list class whose elements can be any type of object, you can declare it to have field of type `Object`. The list still would not be able to hold primitive types (`int`, `boolean`, etc.), but you can make objects of these types if you need to, using the "wrapping" classes (`Integer`, `Boolean`, etc.) described in Chapter 13. The `Object` class itself is described in more detail on page 63.

To demonstrate subclassing, we start with a basic attribute class designed to store name–value pairs. Attribute names are human-readable strings (such as "color" or "location." Attributes can have any type of value, so the value is stored in a variable of type `Object`:

```
class Attr {
    private String name;
    private Object value = null;

    public Attr(String nameOf) {
        name = nameOf;
    }

    public Attr(String nameOf, Object valueOf) {
        name = nameOf;
        value = valueOf;
    }

    public String nameOf() {
        return name;
    }

    public Object valueOf() {
        return value;
    }

    public Object valueOf(Object newValue) {
        Object oldVal = value;
        value = newValue;
        return oldVal;
    }
}
```

An attribute must have a name, so the `Attr` constructors require name parameters. The name must be read-only, because it may well be used, for example, as a key into a hashtable or sorted list. In such a case, if the name field were modified from outside the class, the attribute object would become "lost" because it would be filed under the old name, not the modified one. The value, however, can be changed at any time.

The next class extends the notion of attribute to store color attributes, which might be strings that name or describe colors. Color descriptions might be color names like "red" or "ecru" that must be looked up in a table, or numeric values that can be decoded to produce a standard, more efficient color representation we call ScreenColor (assumed to be defined elsewhere). Decoding a description into a ScreenColor object is expensive enough that you would like to do it only once. So we extend the Attr class to create a ColorAttr class to support a method to retrieve a decoded ScreenColor object, implemented so the decoding is done only once:

```java
class ColorAttr extends Attr {
    private ScreenColor myColor; // the decoded color

    public ColorAttr(String name, Object value) {
        super(name, value);
        decodeColor();
    }

    public ColorAttr(String name) {
        this(name, "transparent");
    }

    public ColorAttr(String name, ScreenColor value) {
        super(name, value.toString());
        myColor = value;
    }

    public Object valueOf(Object newValue) {
        // do the superclass's valueOf() work first
        Object retval = super.valueOf(newValue);
        decodeColor();
        return retval;
    }

    /** Set value to ScreenColor, not description */
    public ScreenColor valueOf(ScreenColor newValue) {
        // do the superclass's valueOf() work first
        super.valueOf(newValue.toString());
```

```
        myColor = newValue;
        return newValue;
    }

    /** Return decoded ScreenColor object */
    public ScreenColor color() {
        return myColor;
    }

    /** set ScreenColor from description in valueOf() */
    protected void decodeColor() {
        if (valueOf() == null)
            myColor = null;
        else
            myColor = new ScreenColor(valueOf());
    }
}
```

First we create a new `ColorAttr` class that extends the `Attr` class. The `ColorAttr` class does everything the `Attr` class does, but adds new behavior. The `Attr` class is the superclass of `ColorAttr`, and `ColorAttr` is a subclass of `Attr`. The *class hierarchy* for these classes looks like this, going top-down from super-class to subclass:

The extended `ColorAttr` class does three primary things:

- ◆ It provides three constructors: two to mirror its superclass, and one to directly provide a `ScreenColor` object.
- ◆ It both overloads and overrides the `valueOf` method of its base class so it can set the color object when the value is changed.
- ◆ It provides a new `color` method to return a value that is the color description decoded into a `ScreenColor` object.

### *Exercise 3.1*

Starting with the `Vehicle` class from Chapter 2, create an extended class called `PassengerVehicle` to add a capability for counting the number of seats available in the car and the number currently occupied. Provide a new `main` method in `PassengerVehicle` to create a few of these objects and print them out. ▲

## 3.2 What protected Really Means

We noted briefly that making a class member `protected` means it can be accessed by classes that extend that class, but that is loose language. More precisely, a protected member can be accessed from a class through object references that are of at least the same type as the class. An example will make this easier to understand. Assume the following class hierarchy:

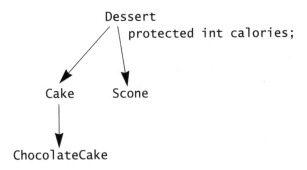

The `Calories` field in the `Dessert` class is protected. Each class that extends `Dessert` inherits its `Calories` field. However, code in the `Cake` class can access the `Calories` field *only* through a reference to a type that is a `Cake`, or a subclass of `Cake`, including, for example, references of type `ChocolateCake`. Code in the `Cake` class could not access the `Calories` field through a reference of type `Scone`. This restriction ensures that the `protected` fields of a class are not accessed outside the part of the class hierarchy of the class using it. If your `Cake` code had a reference of the more generic `Dessert` type, you couldn't use it to access `Calories`, but you could cast it to a `Cake` reference and use the result—assuming, of course, that the object being referenced really was (at least) a `Cake`.

A `protected` method is treated just the same—you can invoke it only using a reference to a type that is at least the type of the class code using the reference.

Protected static fields and methods can be accessed in any extended class. If `Calories` were a static field, any method (static or not) in `Cake`, `ChocolateCake`, and `Scone` could access it through references of any `Dessert` type.

Members declared `protected` are also available to any code within the package. If the `Dessert` classes shown above are all in the same package, they can access each others' `Calories` fields.

## 3.3    Constructors in Extended Classes

When you extend a class, the new class must choose one of its superclass's constructors to invoke. The part of the object controlled by the superclass must be constructed properly, in addition to ensuring a correct initial state for any added fields.

In a constructor in the subclass, you can directly invoke one of the super-class's constructors using another kind of explicit constructor invocation, the super() construct. This is shown in the first ColorAttr constructor above. If you do not invoke a superclass constructor as the new constructor's first executable statement, the superclass's no-arg constructor is automatically invoked before any statements of the new constructor are executed. If the superclass doesn't have a no-arg constructor, you must explicitly invoke your superclass's constructor with some parameters to invoke a constructor. If you use super(), it must be the first statement of the new constructor.

The first constructor of ColorAttr shows how to invoke a superclass con-structor. It passes the name and value up to its superclass's two-argument con-structor. Then, it invokes its own decodeColor method to make myColor hold a reference to the correct color object.

You can defer the choice of which superclass constructor to use by invoking one of the class's own constructors using this() instead of super(). The second constructor of ColorAttr does precisely this. We chose to ensure that every color attribute has a color, and so if a color value is not supplied, we provide a default of "transparent."

The third constructor of ColorAttr enables the programmer creating a ColorAttr object to specify the ScreenColor object itself. The first two con-structors have to convert their parameters to ScreenColor objects using the decodeColor method, which presumably has some overhead. When the program-mer already has a ScreenColor object to provide as a value, we want to avoid the overhead of that conversion. This is an example of providing a constructor that adds efficiency, not capability.

In this example ColorAttr has constructors with exactly the same signatures as its superclass's constructors, but this is by no means required. Sometimes part or all of an extended class's benefit is to provide useful parameters to its superclass's constructors, based on few or no parameters of its own. It is common to have an extended class that has no constructor signatures in common with its superclass.

The language provides a default no-arg constructor for you. The default con-structor for an extended class starts by invoking the superclass's no-arg construc-tor. However, if the superclass does not have a no-arg constructor, the new extended class must provide at least one constructor. The default constructor for an extended class is equivalent to

```
public class ExtendedClass extends SimpleClass {
    public ExtendedClass() {
        super();
    }
}
```

Remember that a constructor is as public as its class. Because `ExtendedClass` is `public`, the default constructor is too.

### 3.3.1   Constructor Order Dependencies

When an object is created, all its fields are set to default initial values for their respective types (zero for all numeric types, \u0000 for `char`, `false` for `boolean`, and `null` for object references). Then the constructor is invoked. Each constructor has three phases:

1. Invoke a superclass's constructor
2. Initialize the fields using their initialization statements
3. Execute the body of the constructor

Here is an example we can trace:

```
class X {
    protected int xMask = 0x00ff;
    protected int fullMask;

    public X() {
        fullMask = xMask;
    }

    public int mask(int orig) {
        return (orig & fullMask);
    }
}

class Y extends X {
    protected int yMask = 0xff00;

    public Y() {
        fullMask |= yMask;
    }
}
```

If you create an object of type Y and follow the construction step by step, here are the values of the fields after each step:

| Step | What Happens | xMask | yMask | fullMask |
|------|--------------|-------|-------|----------|
| 0 | Fields set to default values | 0 | 0 | 0 |
| 1 | Y constructor invoked | 0 | 0 | 0 |
| 2 | X constructor invoked | 0 | 0 | 0 |
| 3 | X field initialization | 0x00ff | 0 | 0 |
| 4 | X constructor executed | 0x00ff | 0 | 0x00ff |
| 5 | Y field initialization | 0x00ff | 0xff00 | 0x00ff |
| 6 | Y constructor executed | 0x00ff | 0xff00 | 0xffff |

This ordering creates important issues when invoking methods during construction. When you invoke a method, you always get the implementation of that method for the actual type of the object. If the method uses fields of the actual type, they may not have been initialized yet. From step 4 above, if the constructor X invokes mask, it would mask against 0x00ff, not 0xffff, even though a later invocation of mask—after the object was completely constructed—uses 0xffff.

Also, imagine if class Y overrides mask with an implementation that explicitly uses the yMask field in its calculations. When the constructor X uses the mask method, it actually invokes Y's mask method, and at that point yMask is zero, not the expected 0xff00.

Methods you invoke during the construction phase of an object must be designed with these factors in mind. You should also document carefully any non-final methods your constructor invokes, to alert anyone wanting to override the constructors of their potential limitations.

### Exercise 3.2

Type in the classes X and Y as shown above, and add print statements to trace the values of the masks. Add a main method and run it to see the results. Add an override of mask to Y and run the test again.   ▲

### Exercise 3.3

If setting up these masks properly was critical during construction, how could you work around these problems?   ▲

## 3.4    Overriding Methods and Hiding Fields

In our new ColorAttr class we have both *overridden* and *overloaded* the valueOf method that sets the attribute's value:

- ◆ *Overloading* a method is what we have already discussed: providing more than one method with the same name, but with different signatures to distinguish them.

- ◆ *Overriding* a method means replacing the superclass's implementation of a method with one of your own. The signatures must be identical. Note that only non-static methods may be overridden.

In the `ColorAttr` class, we overrode `Attr.valueOf(Object)` by providing a new `ColorAttr.valueOf(Object)` method that uses the `super` keyword to invoke the superclass's implementation, and then invokes `decodeColor`. The `super` reference can be used in method invocations to access methods from the superclass that are otherwise overridden in this class. We discuss `super` in detail later.

When overriding methods, the signature must be the same, as well as the return type. The overriding method's `throws` clause can be different from the `throws` clause of the superclass's method, as long as the `throws` clause doesn't declare any types not covered in the original method definition. The `throws` clause of an overriding method can have fewer types listed than the method in the superclass. The overriding method can even have no `throws` clause, which means that it results in no checked exceptions.

Overridden methods have their own access specifiers. An extended class can change the access of a superclass's methods, but only if it provides more access. A method declared `protected` in the superclass can be redeclared `protected` (the usual thing to do), or `public`, but cannot be declared `private`. Making a method less accessible than it was in a superclass would actually be a meaningless restriction, since the increased restriction could be foiled by simply casting a reference to a supertype with more public access and using *that* reference to access the method.

Fields cannot be overridden; they can only be *hidden*. If you declare a field in your class with the same name as one in your superclass, that other field still exists, but can no longer be directly accessed by its simple name. You must use `super` or another reference of your superclass's type to access it.

When you invoke a method on an object, the *actual type* of the *object* governs which implementation is used. When you access a field, the *declared type* of the *reference* is used. The following example will help to explain:

```
class SuperShow {
    public String str = "SuperStr";

    public void show() {
        System.out.println("Super.show: " + str);
    }
}
```

```
class ExtendShow extends SuperShow {
    public String str = "ExtendStr";

    public void show() {
        System.out.println("Extend.show: " + str);
    }

    public static void main(String[] args) {
        ExtendShow ext = new ExtendShow();
        SuperShow sup = ext;
        sup.show();
        ext.show();
        System.out.println("sup.str = " + sup.str);
        System.out.println("ext.str = " + ext.str);
    }
}
```

There is only one object, but we have two references to it—one reference as its actual type and the other as its superclass. Here is the output of the example when run:

```
Extend.show: ExtendStr
Extend.show: ExtendStr
sup.str = SuperStr
ext.str = ExtendStr
```

For the show method, the behavior is as you expect: the actual type of the object, not the type of the reference, governs which version of the method is called. When we have an ExtendShow object, invoking show always calls ExtendShow's show, even if we access it via a reference declared with the type SuperShow.

For the str field, the declared type of the *reference*, not the actual type of the *object*, decides which class's field is accessed. In fact, each ExtendShow object has *two* String variables, both called str, one of which is inherited and hidden by ExtendShow's own, different field called str:

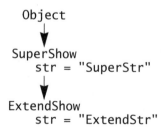

You've already seen that method overriding enables you to extend existing code by reusing it with objects of expanded, specialized functionality not foreseen by the inventor of the original code. But where fields are concerned, one is hard pressed to think of cases where hiding them is a useful feature.

If an existing method had a parameter of type SuperShow, and accessed str with that object's reference, it would always get SuperShow.str, even if the method was actually handed an object of type ExtendShow. If the classes were designed to use a method instead of a field to access the string, the overridden method would be invoked in such a case, and the ExtendShow.str could be returned. This is often another reason to prefer defining classes with private data accessed only by methods.

Hiding fields is allowed in Java because implementors of existing super-classes must be free to add new public or protected fields without breaking subclasses. If Java forbade the same field name in both a superclass and a sub-class, adding a new field to an existing superclass could potentially break any sub-classes already using those names.

If adding new fields to existing superclasses would break some unknown number of subclasses, you'd be effectively immobilized, unable to ever add public or protected fields to a superclass. Purists might well argue that classes should have only private data, but Java supports both styles.

### 3.4.1 The super Keyword

The super keyword is available in all non-static methods of an extended class. In field access and method invocation, super acts as a reference to the current object as an instance of its superclass. Using super is the only case where the type of the *reference* governs selection of the method implementation to be used. An invocation of super.*method* always uses the superclass's implementation of *method,* not any overridden implementation of that method farther down the class hierarchy.

The special method invocation using the super keyword is different in this way from all other references, which choose the method based on the actual type of the object, not the type of the reference. When you invoke a method via super, you get the implementation of the method based on the superclass's type. Here is an example that shows super in action:

```
class That {
    /** return the class name */
    protected String nm() {
        return "That";
    }
}
```

```
class More extends That {
    protected String nm() {
        return "More";
    }

    protected void printNM() {
        That sref = super;

        System.out.println("this.nm()  = " + this.nm());
        System.out.println("sref.nm()  = " + sref.nm());
        System.out.println("super.nm() = " + super.nm());
    }
}
```

And here is the output of printNM:

```
this.nm()  = More
sref.nm()  = More
super.nm() = That
```

You can also use super to access protected members of the superclass.


## 3.5    Marking Methods and Classes final

Marking a method final means that no extended class can override the method to change its behavior. In other words, this is the *final* version of that method.

Entire classes can also be marked final:

```
final class NoExtending {
    // ...
}
```

A class marked final cannot be subclassed by any other class, and all the methods of a final class are themselves implicitly final.

There are two major ramifications to marking a method as final. The first is security: anyone who uses the class can be sure that the behavior will not change, no matter what actual type of object is given to them.

Final classes and methods improve security. If a class is final, you can't declare a class that extends it, and therefore can't violate its contract. If a method is final, you can rely upon its implementation (unless it invokes non-final methods, of course). You could use final, for example, on a validatePassword method to ensure that it does what it is advertised to do, instead of being overridden to always return `true`. Or you can mark as `final` the class that contains the method so that it can never be extended to confuse the implementation of `validatePassword`.

In many cases, the security of marking a class `final` can be achieved by leaving the class extensible and marking each method in the class as `final`. In this way, you can rely on the behavior of those methods, while still allowing extensions that can add functionality without overriding methods. Of course, fields that the `final` methods rely upon should be `private`, or an extended class could change behavior by changing those fields.

Marking a method or class `final` is a serious restriction on the use of the class. If you make a method `final`, you should really intend that its behavior be completely fixed. You restrict the flexibility of your class for other programmers who might want to use your class as a basis to add functionality to their code. Marking an entire class `final` prevents anyone else from extending your class, limiting its usefulness to others. If you make anything `final`, be sure that you want to create these restrictions.

The second ramification is that `final` simplifies optimizations. When a non-`final` method is invoked, the Java runtime system determines the actual type of the object, binds the method call to the correct implementation of the method for that type, and then invokes that implementation.

But if the `nameOf` method was `final` in the `Attr` class, for example, and you have a reference to an object of type `Attr` or any extended type, it is possible to skip the steps to invoke the method. In the simplest case, such as `nameOf`, an invocation can be replaced with the actual body of the method. This mechanism is known as "inlining." The inlined method makes the following two statements perform equivalently:

```
System.out.println("id = " + rose.name);
System.out.println("id = " + rose.nameOf());
```

Although the two statements are equally efficient, a `nameOf` method allows the `name` field to be read-only, and gives you the benefits of abstraction, allowing you to change the implementation.

For the kinds of optimization discussed here, `private` and `static` methods are equivalent to `final` methods because they cannot be overridden.

Some type checks become faster with `final` classes. In fact, many type checks become compile-time checks, and errors can be caught earlier. If the Java compiler has a reference of a `final` class, it knows that the object referred to is exactly that type. The entire class hierarchy for that class is known, so the compiler can check whether any use is valid or invalid. With a non-`final` reference, some checks can happen only at run time.

### Exercise 3.4

Which methods (if any) of `Vehicle` and `PassengerVehicle` might reasonably be made `final`?  ▲

## 3.6    The `Object` Class

All classes extend the `Object` class, directly or indirectly, and therefore inherit `Object`'s methods. These methods fall into two categories: general utility methods and methods that support threads. Thread support is covered in Chapter 9. This section describes `Object`'s utility methods and how they affect classes. The utility methods are:

`public boolean` **`equals(Object obj)`**
    Compares the receiving object and the object referenced by `obj` for equality, returning `true` if they have the same value, and `false` if they don't. If you want to determine if two references refer to the same object, you can compare them using `==` and `!=`. The `equals` method is concerned with value equality. The default implementation of `equals` in `Object` assumes that an object is only equal to itself.

`public int` **`hashCode()`**
    Returns a hash code for this object. Each object has a hash code for use in hashtables. The default implementation returns a value that is usually unique for different objects. It is used when storing objects in `Hashtable` objects, described in "`Hashtable`" on page 230.

`protected Object` **`clone()`** `throws CloneNotSupportedException`
    Returns a clone of this object. A clone is a new object that is a copy of the object on which `clone` was invoked. Cloning is discussed in greater detail later, in Section 3.8.

`public final Class` **`getClass()`**
    Returns the particular object of type `Class` that represents the class of this object. Java has runtime representation for classes—an object of class `Class`—which the method `getClass` returns. The `Class` class is described on page 244.

`protected void` **`finalize()`** `throws Throwable`
    Finalize the object during garbage collection. This method was discussed in detail in "`finalize`" on page 46.

Both the `hashCode` and `equals` methods should be overridden if you want to provide a notion of equality different from the default implementation provided in the `Object` class. The default is that any two different objects are not `equal` and their hash codes are usually distinct.

If your class has a notion of equality in which two different objects can be `equal`, those two objects should return the same value from `hashCode`. This is because the `Hashtable` mechanism relies on `equals` returning `true` when it finds a key of the same value in the table. For example, the `String` class overrides `equals` to return `true` if the two `String` objects have the same contents. It also overrides `hashCode` to return a hash based on the contents of the `String`, so that two strings with the same contents have the same `hashCode`.

### Exercise 3.5

Override `equals` and `hashCode` for `Vehicle`.  ▲

## 3.7 Abstract Classes and Methods

An extremely useful feature of object-oriented programming is the concept of the *abstract class*. Using abstract classes, you can declare classes that define only part of an implementation, leaving extended classes to provide specific implementation of some or all of the methods.

Abstraction is helpful when some of the behavior is true for most or all objects of a given type, but some behavior makes sense only for particular types of objects, and not a general superclass. In Java, such a class is declared `abstract`, and each method not implemented in the class is specifically marked `abstract`.

(If all you need is to define a set of methods that someone will support, but provide no implementation, you probably want to use interfaces instead, described in Chapter 4.)

For example, suppose you want to create a benchmarking harness to provide an infrastructure for writing benchmarked code. The class implementation could understand how to drive and measure a benchmark, but it couldn't know in advance what benchmark would be run. Most `abstract` classes fit a pattern where a particular area of expertise that a class is good at requires someone else to provide a missing piece. In this benchmarking example, the missing piece is code that needs to be benchmarked. Here is how such a class might look:

```
abstract class Benchmark {
    abstract void benchmark();

    public long repeat(int count) {
        long start = System.currentTimeMillis();
        for (int i = 0; i < count; i++)
            benchmark();
        return (System.currentTimeMillis() - start);
    }
}
```

The class is declared `abstract` because a class with any `abstract` methods is declared `abstract`. This redundancy helps the reader quickly see that the class is `abstract` without scanning to see if any method in the class declared `abstract`.

The `repeat` method provides the benchmarking expertise. It knows how to time a run of `count` invocations of the benchmark. If the timing needs become more complex (possibly measuring the time of each run and computing statistics about the variations), this method can be enhanced without affecting any extended class's implementation of its specialized benchmark code.

The `abstract` method `benchmark` must be implemented by each subclass that is not `abstract` itself. This is why it has no implementation in this class, only a declaration. Here is an example of a simple `Benchmark` extension:

```
class MethodBenchmark extends Benchmark {
    void benchmark() {
    }

    public static void main(String[] args) {
        int count = Integer.parseInt(args[0]);
        long time = new MethodBenchmark().repeat(count);
        System.out.println(count + " methods in " +
                            time + " milliseconds");
    }
}
```

This class times how long it takes to simply invoke a method by using `benchmark`. You can now time method invocations by running the application `MethodBenchmark` with the number of times to repeat the test. The count is taken from the program arguments and decoded using the `Integer` class's `parseInt` method on the argument string, as described in "String Conversions" on page 150.

You cannot create an object of an `abstract` class, since there would be no implementation for some methods that might well be invoked.

Any class can override methods from its superclass to declare them `abstract`, turning a concrete method into an `abstract` one at that point in the type tree. This is useful, for example, when a class's default implementation is invalid for a part of the class hierarchy.

*Exercise 3.6*

Write a new extended class that benchmarks something else, such as how long it takes to run a loop from 0 to some passed-in parameter.   ▲

### Exercise 3.7

Change `Vehicle` so that it has an `EngergySource` object reference, which is associated with the `Vehicle` in its constructor. `EnergySource` must be an `abstract` class, because a `GasTank` object will have a different notion of how full it is than a `Battery` object would have. Put an `abstract` empty method in `EnergySource`, and implement it in `GasTank` and `Battery` classes. Add a `start` method to `Vehicle` that ensures that the energy source isn't `empty`.  ▲

## 3.8 Cloning Objects

The `Object.clone` method helps you write *clone* methods for your own classes. A clone method returns a new object whose initial state is a copy of the current state of the object on which `clone` was invoked. Subsequent changes to the new clone object should not affect the state of the original object.

There are three major considerations in writing a `clone` method:

◆ The `Cloneable` interface, which you must implement to provide a working `clone` method.[1]

◆ The `Object.clone` method, which performs a simple clone by copying all fields of the original object to the new object. This works for many classes, but may need to be supplemented by an overridden method (see below).

◆ The `CloneNotSupportedException`, which can be used to signal that a class's `clone` method shouldn't have been invoked.

A given class can have one of four different attitudes towards `clone`:

◆ Support `clone`. Such a class implements `Cloneable`, and usually declares its `clone` method to throw no exceptions.

◆ Conditionally support `clone`. Such a class might be a collection class that can be cloned in principle, but cannot successfully be cloned unless its contents can be cloned. This kind of class will implement `Cloneable`, but let its `clone` method pass through any `CloneNotSupportedException` it may receive from other objects it tries to clone as part of its cloning. Or a class

---

[1.] `Cloneable` should have been spelled `Clonable`, and the current, incorrect spelling may be deprecated in a future release.

may want the ability to be cloned itself, but not require that all subclasses also have the ability to be cloned.

◆ Allow subclasses to support `clone`, but don't publicly support it. Such a class doesn't implement `Cloneable`, but provides a `clone` implementation that clones its fields correctly if the default implementation isn't correct.

◆ Forbid `clone`. Such a class does not implement `Cloneable` and provides a `clone` method that always throws `CloneNotSupportedException`.

`Object.clone` first checks to see if the object on which `clone` was invoked implements the `Cloneable` interface, and throws a `CloneNotSupportedException` if it does not. Otherwise, it creates a new object of exactly the same type as the original object on which `clone` is invoked, and initializes the fields of the new, cloned object to have the same value as the fields of the original object. When `Object.clone` is finished, it returns a reference to the new object.

The simplest way to make a class that can be cloned is to declare that it implements the `Cloneable` interface:

```
public class MyClass extends AnotherClass
    implements Cloneable
{
    // ...
}
```

The `clone` method in the `Cloneable` interface is declared `public`, so the `MyClass.clone` method inherited from `Object` will also be `public`. Now, any other code can make a clone of a `MyClass` object. In this simple case, all fields of `MyClass` will be assigned by `Object.clone` into the new object that is returned.

`Cloneable.clone` has the `throws CloneNotSupportedException` declaration, so a class can declare that it can be cloned, but a subclass can decide that it can't be cloned. Such a subclass would implement the `Cloneable` interface because it extends a class that does so, but the subclass could not, in fact, be cloned. The extended class would make this known by overriding `clone` to always throw `CloneNotSupportedException`, and documenting that it does so. Be careful—this means that you cannot determine if a class can be cloned by a runtime check to see if the class implements `Cloneable`. Some classes that can't be cloned will be forced to signal this condition by throwing an exception.

Most classes can be cloned in principle. Even if you do not support the `Cloneable` interface yourself, you must ensure that your `clone` method is correct. In many classes, the default implementation of `clone` will be wrong, because it duplicates a reference to an object that shouldn't be shared. In such cases `clone` should be overridden to behave correctly. The default implementation assigns each field from the source to the same field in the destination object.

If, for instance, your objects have a reference to an array, a clone of one of your objects will refer to the same array. If the array holds read-only data, such a shared reference is probably fine. But if it is a list of objects that should be distinct from each other, you probably don't want the clone's manipulation of its own list to affect the list of the original source object, or vice versa.

Here is an example of the problem. Suppose you have a simple integer stack class:

```java
public class IntegerStack implements Cloneable {
    private int[] buffer;
    private int top;

    public IntegerStack(int maxContents) {
        buffer = new int[maxContents];
        top = -1;
    }

    public void push(int val) {
        buffer[++top] = val;
    }

    public int pop() {
        return buffer[top--];
    }
}
```

Now let's look at some code that creates an `IntegerStack` object, puts some data onto the stack, and then clones it:

```java
IntegerStack first = new IntegerStack(2);
first.push(2);
first.push(9);
IntegerStack second = (IntegerStack)first.clone();
```

With the default `clone` method, the data in memory will look something like this:

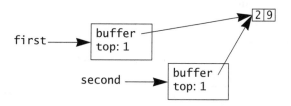

Now consider what happens when future code invokes first.pop(), followed by first.push(17). The top element in the stack first will change from 9 to 17, which is expected. The programmer will probably be surprised, however, to see that the top element of second will *also* change to 17, since there is only one array that is shared by the two stacks.

The solution is to override clone to make a copy of the array:

```java
public Object clone() {
    try {
        IntegerStack nObj = (IntegerStack)super.clone();
        nObj.buffer = (int[])buffer.clone();
        return nObj;
    } catch (CloneNotSupportedException e) {
        // Cannot happen -- we support
        // clone() and so do arrays
        throw new InternalError(e.toString());
    }
}
```

First the clone method invokes super.clone, which is very important, because the superclass may be working around its own problems of shared objects. If you do not invoke the superclass's method, you solve your own shared object problem, but may create another. Further, super.clone will eventually reach Object.clone, which creates an object of the correct type. If IntegerStack.clone used new to create an IntegerStack object, it would be incorrect for any object that extended IntegerStack. The extended class's invocation of super.clone would give it an IntegerStack object, not an object of the correct, extended type.

The return value of super.clone is then cast to an IntegerStack reference. Casting is described in "Type Conversions" on page 104, and changes a reference of one type (in this case, Object as the return value of clone) to a reference of another type (in this case, IntegerStack). A cast succeeds only if the referenced object is actually of the type to which the reference is being cast.

Object.clone initializes each field in the new clone object by assigning it the value from the same field of the object being cloned. You then need only write special code to deal with fields for which copying by value is incorrect. IntegerStack.clone doesn't copy the top field, since it is already correct from the copy-by-value default.

With the specialized clone method in place, the example code now creates memory that looks like this:

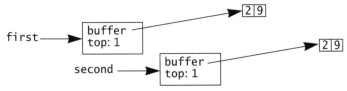

Sometimes making `clone` work correctly is not worth the trouble, and some classes should not support `clone`. In such cases, you should declare a `clone` method that throws `CloneNotSupportedException` so that objects with bad state will never be created by your `clone` method.

You can declare that all subclasses of a class must support `clone` properly if you override the `clone` method with a signature that drops the declaration of `CloneNotSupportedException`. Now, subclasses implementing the `clone` method cannot throw `CloneNotSupportedException`, because methods in the subclass cannot add an exception to a method. In the same way, if your class makes its `clone` method `public`, all extended classes must have `public` `clone` methods, too, since a subclass cannot make a method less visible than it was in its superclass.

### Exercise 3.8

Make `Vehicle` and `PassengerVehicle` into `Cloneable` types. Which of the four described attitudes should each class take towards cloning? Is the simple copying done by `Object.clone` correct for the clone methods of these classes?   ▲

### Exercise 3.9

Write a `Garage` class whose objects can hold up to some number of `Vehicle` objects in an array. Make `Garage` a `Cloneable` type, and write a proper `clone` method for it. Write a `Garage.main` method to test it.   ▲

### Exercise 3.10

Make your `LinkedList` class `Cloneable`, with `clone` returning a new list that refers to the same values as the original list, not clones of the values. In other words, changes to one list should not affect the other list, but changes to the objects referenced by the list would be visible in both lists.   ▲

## 3.9   Extending Classes: How and When

Writing extended classes is a large part of the benefit of object-oriented programming. When you extend a class to add new functionality, you create what is commonly termed an *IsA* relationship—the extension creates a new kind of object that "is a" type of the original class. The *IsA* relationship is quite different from a *HasA* relationship, in which one object uses another object to store its state or do its work—it "has a" reference to that other object.

Let's look at an example. Consider a `Point` class that represents a point in two-dimensional space by an $(x, y)$ pair. You might extend `Point` to create, say, a `Pixel` class to represent a colored point on a screen. A `Pixel` IsA `Point`: anything that is true of a simple `Point` would also be true of a `Pixel`. The `Pixel` class might add mechanisms to represent the color of the pixel, or a reference to an object that represents the screen on which the pixel is drawn. As a point in a two-dimensional space (the plane of a display) with an extension to the contract (it has color and a screen), a `Pixel` IsA `Point`.

On the other hand, a circle is not a point. Although a circle can be described by a point and a radius, it has properties that no point would have. For instance, if you had a method to place the center of a rectangle at a particular point, would it really make sense to pass in a circle? A circle HasA center that IsA point, but a circle Is*Not*A point with a radius, and therefore should not be a subclass of `Point`.

There are times when the correct choice is not obvious, and for which different choices will be correct depending on the application. In the end, applications must run and make sense.

Getting IsA versus HasA relationships correct is both subtle and potentially critical. For instance, one obvious and common way to design an employee database using object-oriented tools is to use an `Employee` class having the data all persons share (such as name and employee number) and extend it to classes for particular kinds of employee, like `Manager`, `Engineer`, and `FileClerk`.

This design fails in real-world situations, in which one person operates simultaneously in more than one role. For example, an engineer might be an acting manager in a group, and must now appear in two guises. As another example, a teaching assistant is often both a student and a staff member at a university.

A more flexible design would create a `Role` class, and extend it to create classes for roles such as `Manager`. Then you would change the design of the `Employee` class to have a set of `Role` objects. Now a person could be associated with an ever-changing set of roles in the organization. We have changed from saying that a manager IsAn employee to saying manager IsA role, and an employee can HaveA manager's role as well as others.

If the wrong initial choice is made, changing deployed systems later on will be hard, because changes could require major alterations in code. For example, methods in the first employee database design above would no doubt rely on the fact that a `Manager` object could be used as an `Employee`. If we changed to our second design, this would no longer be true, and all the original code would break.

## 3.10  Designing a Class to Be Extended

Now we can justify the complexity of our `Attr` class defined on page 51. Why weren't `name` and `value` simply public variables? That would avoid three methods entirely, since the fields could be accessed and modified directly.

The answer is that the `Attr` class is designed to be extended. If we store our data in public members, it will have two bad effects:

◆ The `name` field could be modified at any time by the programmer—a bad move because the `Attr` object represents the (mutable) value of a particular (immutable) name. For example, changing the name after inserting the attribute into a list sorted by name would result in an out-of-order list.

◆ There would be no way to add functionality. By providing accessor methods, you can override them to enhance functionality, as we did in `ColorAttr` to pre-decode a new value into an actual `ScreenColor` object. If `value` were a `public` field, the programmer could change it at any time, and we would have to provide a different way to get the `ScreenColor` object that remembered the last value and compared it to the current to see if it needed to do some new decoding. The resulting code would be more complex and usually less efficient.

A non-`final` class has two interfaces. The *public* interface is for programmers *using* your class. The *protected* interface is for programmers *extending* your class. Both interfaces are real contracts, and both should be designed carefully.

For example, suppose you want to provide a benchmarking harness for comparing varieties of sorting algorithms. Some things can be said of all sorting algorithm benchmarks: they all have data on which they must operate; that data must support an ordering mechanism; and the number of comparisons and swaps they require to do their work is an important factor in the benchmark.

You can write an `abstract` class that helps you with these features, but you cannot write a generic `sort` method—the actual operations of the sort are determined by each derived class. Here is a `SortDouble` class that sorts arrays of double, tracking the number of swaps and compares required in a `SortMetrics` class we will define later:

```
abstract class SortDouble {
    private double[] values;
    private SortMetrics curMetrics = new SortMetrics();

    /** Invoked to do the full sort */
    public final SortMetrics sort(double[] data) {
        values = data;
        curMetrics.init();
        doSort();
        return metrics();
    }
```

```
public final SortMetrics metrics() {
    return (SortMetrics)curMetrics.clone();
}

protected final int dataLength() {
    return values.length;
}

/** For derived classes to probe elements */
protected final double probe(int i) {
    curMetrics.probeCnt++;
    return values[i];
}

/** For derived classes to compare elements */
protected final int compare(int i, int j) {
    curMetrics.compareCnt++;
    double d1 = values[i];
    double d2 = values[j];
    if (d1 == d2)
        return 0;
    else
        return (d1 < d2 ? -1 : 1);
}

/** For derived classes to swap elements */
protected final void swap(int i, int j) {
    curMetrics.swapCnt++;
    double tmp = values[i];
    values[i] = values[j];
    values[j] = tmp;
}

/** Derived classes implement this -- used by sort() */
protected abstract void doSort();
}
```

This class defines fields to hold the array being sorted (values) and a reference to a metrics object (curMetrics) to track the measured operations. To ensure that these counts are correct, SortDouble provides routines to be used by extended sorting classes when they need to examine data, or perform comparisons and swaps.

When you design a class, you can decide whether to trust its extended classes. The SortDouble class is designed *not* to trust them, and that is generally the best way to design classes for others to extend. A guarded design not only prevents malicious use, it also prevents bugs.

SortDouble carefully restricts access to each member to the appropriate level. It uses final on all its non-abstract methods. These are all part of the contract of the SortDouble class, which includes protecting the measurement of the sort algorithm from tampering. Making the methods final also allows the compiler to make them as efficient as possible, as well as ensuring that no derived class overrides these methods to change behavior.

SortMetrics objects describe the cost of a particular sorting run. The class has three public fields. Its only task is to communicate data, so there is no need to hide that data behind accessor methods. SortDouble.metrics returns a *copy* of the data so that it doesn't give out a reference to its internal data. This prevents both the code that creates SortDouble objects and the code in the extended classes from changing the data. Here is the SortMetrics class:

```
final class SortMetrics implements Cloneable {
    public long probeCnt,        // simple data probes
                compareCnt,      // comparing two elements
                swapCnt;         // swapping two elements

    public void init() {
        probeCnt = swapCnt = compareCnt = 0;
    }

    public String toString() {
        return probeCnt + " probes " +
                compareCnt + " compares " +
                swapCnt + " swaps";
    }

    /** this class supports clone() */
    public Object clone() {
        try {
            return super.clone(); // default mechanism works
        } catch (CloneNotSupportedException e) {
            // can't happen: this and Object both clone
```

```
                  throw new InternalError(e.toString());
            }
        }
    }
```

Here is a class that extends SortDouble. The BubbleSortDouble class implements doSort with a bubble sort, a very slow but simple sort algorithm whose primary advantage is that it is easy to code and easy to understand:

```
class BubbleSortDouble extends SortDouble {
    protected void doSort() {
        for (int i = 0; i < dataLength(); i++) {
            for (int j = i + 1; j < dataLength(); j++) {
                if (compare(i, j) > 0)
                    swap(i, j);
            }
        }
    }
    static double[] testData = {
                    0.3, 1.3e-2, 7.9, 3.17,
                };


    static public void main(String[] args) {
        BubbleSortDouble bsort = new BubbleSortDouble();
        SortMetrics metrics = bsort.sort(testData);
        System.out.println("Bubble Sort: " + metrics);
        for (int i = 0; i < testData.length; i++)
            System.out.println("\t" + testData[i]);
    }
}
```

The main method shows how code that drives a test works: it creates an object of a class extended from SortDouble, provides it with the data to be sorted, and invokes sort. The sort method initializes the metrics, then invokes the abstract method doSort. Each extended class implements doSort to do its sorting, invoking dataLength, compare, and swap when it needs to. When doSort returns, the counts reflect the number of each operation performed.

BubbleSortDouble contains a main method that serves as test code, and here is its output:

```
Bubble Sort: 0 probes 6 compares 2 swaps
        0.013
        0.3
        3.17
        7.9
```

Now let us return to the issue of designing a class to be extended, with these classes as examples. We carefully designed the protected interface of SortClass to allow extended classes more intimate access to the data in the object, but only to things we *want* them to manipulate. The access for each part of the class design has been carefully chosen:

◆ *Public:* The public part of the class is designed for use by the timing code—that is, the code that tests how expensive the sorting algorithm is. An example of testing code is in BubbleSort.main. This code provides the data to be sorted, and gets the results of the test. For the test code, the metrics are read-only. The public sort method we provide for the test code ensures that the metrics are initialized before they are used.

Making the actual doSort method protected, the test code forces to invoke it indirectly via the main sort method; thus, we guarantee that the metrics are always initialized and avoid another possible error.

We used methods and access protection to hide whatever should not be exposed to the user of the public part of the class. To the test code, the only available functionality of the class is to drive a test of a particular sorting algorithm and provide the results.

◆ *Protected:* The protected part of the class is designed for use by the sorting code to produce a properly metered sort. The protected contract lets the sorting algorithm examine and modify the data to produce a sorted list by whatever means the sort desires. It also gives the sorting algorithm a context where it will be properly driven so it can be measured. This home is the doSort method.

The extended class is not considered trustworthy, which is why it can access the data only indirectly, through methods that have access to the data. For instance, to hide a comparison by avoiding compare, the sort would have to use probe to find out what is in the array. Since calls to probe are also metered, this does not, in the end, hide anything.

In addition, `metrics` returns a *copy* of the actual metrics, so a sorting implementation cannot modify the values.

♦ *Private:* The class keeps private to itself data that should be hidden from the outside, namely the data being sorted and the metrics. Outside code cannot access these fields, directly or indirectly.

As we said above, `SortDouble` is designed not to trust its extended classes, to prevent intentional cheating and accidental misuse. For example, if `SortDouble.values` (the array being sorted) were `protected` instead of `private`, we could eliminate the `probe` method, because sort algorithms normally count only comparisons and swaps. But if we had, the programmer writing an extended class could avoid using `swap` to swap data. The results would be invalid in ways that might be hard to notice. Counting probes and declaring the array `private` precludes some bugs, as well as intentionally devious programming.

If a class is not *designed* to be extended, it can and often will be misused by extensions. If a class is expected to be extended, its `protected` interface should be carefully designed (although the end result may be to have protected members, if extended classes need to special access). Otherwise it should probably be declared `final`, forcing someone to design a protected interface when the time comes to lift the `final` restricton

### Exercise 3.11

Find at least one security hole in `SortDouble` that would let a sorting algorithm cheat on its metrics without getting caught. Fix the security hole. Assume that the sorting algorithm author doesn't get to write `main`.  ▲

### Exercise 3.12

Write a generic `SortHarness` class that can sort any object type. How would you provide a way to represent ordering for the objects in a generic way, since you cannot use < to compare them?  ▲

CHAPTER 4

# Interfaces

*"Conducting" is when you draw "designs" in the nowhere—with your stick,
or with your hands— which are interpreted as "instructional messages"
by guys wearing bow ties who wish they were fishing.*
—Frank Zappa

**T**HE fundamental units of *design* in Java are the `public` methods that can be invoked on objects. *Interfaces* are a way to declare a type consisting only of abstract methods and constants, enabling any implementation to be written for those methods. An interface is an expression of pure design, where a class is a mix of design and implementation.

A class can implement the methods of an interface in any way that the designer of the class chooses. An interface thus has many more possible implementations than a class.

## 4.1    An Example Interface

The previous chapter introduced the `Attr` class and showed how to extend it to make specialized types of attribute objects. Now all you need is the ability to associate attributes with objects. There are two ways to do this: one is *composition;* the other is *inheritance*. An object could, if you chose, contain a set of attributes and allow programmers access to that set. Or you could say that being able to store attributes on an object is a part of its type, and so should be part of the class hierarchy. Both are legitimate positions. We believe that representing the ability to hold attributes in the class hierarchy is most useful. We will create an `Attributed` type to be used for objects that can be attributed by attaching `Attr` objects to them.

However, Java has *single inheritance* of *implementation*, which means you can extend only from a single class. If you create an `Attributed` class for programmers to inherit from, then either `Attributed` has to be at the base of all classes, or programmers have to decide whether to inherit from `Attributed` or from some other useful class.

Every time you create a useful feature like `Attributed`, you would end up wanting to add its capabilities to the root `Object` class, which would grow quickly to unmanageable proportions.

Java has multiple interface inheritance, so instead of adding the capabilities of `Attributed` to `Object`, we make `Attributed` into an interface. To make an attributed version of our celestial body class, for example, its declaration might look like this:

```
class AttributedBody extends Body
    implements Attributed
```

Of course to do this, we need an `Attributed` interface:

```
interface Attributed {
    void add(Attr newAttr);
    Attr find(String attrName);
    Attr remove(String attrName);
    java.util.Enumeration attrs();
}
```

This interface declares four methods: one for adding a new attribute to an `Attributed` object; one for finding whether an attribute of a given name has been added to that object; one for removing an attribute from an object; and one for returning a list of the attributes currently attached to the object. This last is returned using the `Enumeration` interface defined for Java's collection classes. `java.util.Enumeration` is covered in detail in Chapter 12.

All methods in an interface are implicitly `abstract`, and because an interface can not provide an implementation of its declared methods, an interface doesn't need to declare its methods `abstract`. Each class that implements the interface must implement all of its methods, or, if the class implements only some of the methods in an interface, that class is (and must be declared) `abstract`.

Methods in an interface are always public. Interface methods may not be `static`, because `static` methods are class-specific, never `abstract`, and an interface can have only `abstract` methods.

Fields in an interface, on the other hand, are always `static` and `final`. They are a way to define constants used when invoking methods. An interface that had differing levels of verbosity in its contract might have the following:

```
interface Verbose {
    int SILENT  = 0;
    int TERSE   = 1;
```

```
        int NORMAL  = 2;
        int VERBOSE = 3;

        void setVerbosity(int level);
        int getVerbosity();
    }
```

The constants SILENT, TERSE, NORMAL, and VERBOSE can be passed to the verbosity method, giving names to constant values that represent specific meanings. These values must be constant, so all fields in an interface are implicitly static and final.

## 4.2  Single Inheritance versus Multiple Inheritance

In Java, a new class can extend exactly one superclass—a model known as *single inheritance.* Extending a class means that the new class inherits not only its superclass's contract, but also its superclass's implementation. Some object-oriented languages employ *multiple inheritance,* where a new class can have two or more superclasses.

Multiple inheritance is useful when a new class wants to add new behavior and keep most or all of the old behavior. But when there is more than one superclass, problems arise when a superclass's behavior is inherited in two ways. Assume, for a moment, the following type tree:

This is commonly called "diamond inheritance," and there is nothing wrong with it. Many legitimate designs show this structure. The problems exist in the inheritance of implementation, when W's implementation stores some state. If class W had, for example, a public field named goggin, and you had a reference to an object of type Z called zref, what would zref.goggin refer to? It might refer to X's copy of goggin, or it might refer to Y's copy, or X and Y might properly share a single copy of goggin since Z is really only a W once, even though it is both an X and a Y.

Java uses the single-inheritance model of object-oriented programming to avoid such issues.

Single inheritance precludes some useful and correct designs. The problems of multiple inheritance arise from multiple inheritance of implementation, so Java provides a way to inherit a contract without inheriting implementation. The way is to declare an `interface` type, instead of a `class` type.

Interfaces in the class hierarchy, therefore, add multiple inheritance to Java.

In a given class, the classes that are extended and the interfaces that are implemented are collectively called the *supertypes,* and from the viewpoint of the supertypes, the new class is a *subtype.* The full type of the new class includes all of its supertypes, so a reference to an object of its type can be used polymorphically, that is, anywhere a reference to an object of any of its supertypes (class or interface) is required. Interface definitions create type names just as class definitions do; you can use the name of an interface as a type name of a variable, and any object that implements that interface can be assigned to that variable.

## 4.3    Extending Interfaces

Interfaces may be extended, too, with the `extends` keyword. Interfaces, unlike classes, can extend more than one interface:

```
interface Shimmer extends FloorWax, DessertTopping {
    double amazingPrice();
}
```

The `Shimmer` type extends both `FloorWax` and a `DessertTopping`, which means that all the methods and constants defined by `FloorWax` and `DessertTopping` are part of its contract, along with its added `amazingPrice` method.

If you want a class to implement an interface and extend another class, you need multiple inheritance. In other words, you will have a new class that can be used in the places allowed both by its superclass and its superinterface types. Consider the following declaration:

```
interface W { }
interface X extends W { }
class Y implements W { }
class Z extends Y implements X { }
```

This creates something that looks like our diamond inheritance, but there is no question about whether it uses X's fields or Y's fields—X has no fields, because it is an interface, so only Y's fields are available. The diamond looks like this, with interfaces circled:

We could construct the diamond with W, X, and Y all being interfaces, and Z a class. Here is how this would look:

```
interface W { }
interface X extends W { }
interface Y extends W { }
class Z implements X, Y { }
```

Now Z is the only actual class in the hierarchy.

Interfaces, unlike classes, do not have a single root interface akin to the Object class. Even so, you can pass an expression of any interface type to a method that has a parameter of type Object, because that object must be of *some* class, and all classes are subclasses of Object. For example, extending the example above, the following assignment to obj is legal:

```
protected void twiddle(W wRef) {
    Object obj = wRef;
    // ...
}
```

### 4.3.1 Name Conflicts

The last two examples demonstrated that a class or interface can be a subtype of more than one interface. This raises the question of what happens when a method of the same name appears in more than one interface. If methods in interfaces X and Y have the same name but different numbers or types of parameters, the answer is simple: the Z interface will have two overloaded methods with the same name but different signatures. If the two methods have exactly the same signature, the answer is also simple: Z will have one method with that signature. If they differ only in return type, you cannot implement both interfaces.

If the two methods differ only in the types of exceptions they throw, your class must satisfy two method declarations with the same signature (name and parameters) but that throw different exceptions. But methods in a class cannot differ only in the exceptions they throw, so there must be only one implementation that satisfies both throws clauses. This example illustrates the situation:

```
interface X {
    void setup() throws SomeException;
}

interface Y {
    void setup();
}
```

```
class Z implements X, Y {
    public void setup() {
        // ...
    }
}
```

In this case class Z can provide a single implementation that satisfies both X.setup and Y.setup. A method can throw fewer exceptions than its superclass declares, so Z.setup doesn't have to declare that it throws the SomeException type that X.setup says it is allowed to. Of course, this only makes sense if one implementation can also serve the declared contracts for both of the methods—if the two methods *mean* different things, you probably cannot write a single implementation that does what is expected for both meanings.

If two methods disagree in their list of exceptions in such a way that you cannot find an implementation signature that satisfies both interface signatures for the method, an interface cannot extend the two interfaces, nor can a class implement the two interfaces.

Interface *constants* are simpler. If two interfaces have constants of the same name, you can always join them in an inheritance tree, but you must use the qualified name for those constants. For instance, the interfaces PokerDeck and TarotDeck might both have DECK_SIZE constants of different values, and a MultiDeck interface or class could implement both interfaces. But inside MultiDeck and its subtypes, you must use the explicit names PokerDeck.DECK_SIZE and TarotDeck.DECK_SIZE, because a simple DECK_SIZE would be ambiguous.

## 4.4    Implementing Interfaces

Interfaces describe contracts in a pure, abstract form, but an interface is interesting only if a class implements it.

Some interfaces are purely abstract—they do not have any useful general implementation but must be implemented afresh for each new class. Most interfaces, however, may have several useful implementations. In the case of our Attributed interface, we can imagine several possible implementations that use various strategies to store a set of attributes.

One strategy might be simple and fast when only a few attributes are in a set; another might be optimized for attribute sets that are queried more often than they are changed; yet another might be optimized for sets that change frequently. If there were a package of various implementations for the Attributed interface, a class might choose to implement the Attributed interface through any one of them, or through its own implementation.

As an example, here is a simple implementation of `Attributed` that uses the utility `java.util.Hashtable` class. Later, this implementation is used to implement the `Attributed` interface for a specific set of objects to which you would want to add attributes. First, here is the `AttributedImpl` class:

```
import java.util.*;

class AttributedImpl implements Attributed
{
    protected Hashtable attrTable = new Hashtable();

    public void add(Attr newAttr) {
        attrTable.put(newAttr.nameOf(), newAttr);
    }

    public Attr find(String name) {
        return (Attr)attrTable.get(name);
    }

    public Attr remove(String name) {
        return (Attr)attrTable.remove(name);
    }

    public Enumeration attrs() {
        return attrTable.elements();
    }
}
```

The declaration that `AttributedImpl` implements `Attributed`, and implements all of the methods of `Attributed`, is made using a `Hashtable`, described on page 230.

The initializer for `attrTable` creates a `Hashtable` object to hold attributes. This `Hashtable` does most of the actual work. The `Hashtable` class uses the object's `hashCode` method to hash any object it is given as a key. No explicit hash method is needed, since `String` already provides a suitable `hashCode` implementation.

When a new attribute is added, the `Attr` object is stored in the hashtable under its name, and then you can easily use the hashtable to find and remove attributes by name.

The `attrs` method returns an `Enumeration` that lists all the attributes in the set. The `Enumeration` class is an abstract superclass defined in `java.util` for collection classes like `Hashtable` to use when returning lists (see "Enumeration" on page 221). The same type is used here because it is a standard way for Java classes to represent a list. In effect, the `Attributed` interface defines a collection type, so the normal mechanism for returning the contents of a collection is used, namely, the `Enumeration` class. Using `Enumeration` has benefit: implementing `Attributed` is easier using a standard collection class like `Hashtable` that uses `Enumeration`, so you can use its return value directly.

## 4.5    Using an Implementation

You can use an implementing class like `AttributedImpl` by simply extending the class. This is the simplest tool when it is available, since all the methods and their implementations are inherited. But if you need to support more than one interface, or need to extend a different class, you will need to use a different approach. The most common approach is to create an object of an implementing class and *forward* all the methods from the interface to that object, returning any values.

Each method in the class that is inherited from the interface provides a method to invoke the implementation from another object and return the result. Here is an implementation of the `Attributed` interface, which uses an `AttributedImpl` object to build an attributed version of our celestial body class (defined on page 40):

```
import java.util.Enumeration;

class AttributedBody extends Body
    implements Attributed
{
    AttributedImpl attrImpl = new AttributedImpl();

    AttributedBody() {
        super();
    }

    AttributedBody(String name, Body orbits) {
        super(name, orbits);
    }

    // Forward all Attributed calls to the attrImpl object

    public void add(Attr newAttr)
```

```
        { attrImpl.add(newAttr); }
    public Attr find(String name)
        { return attrImpl.find(name); }
    public Attr remove(String name)
        { return attrImpl.remove(name); }
    public Enumeration attrs()
        { return attrImpl.attrs(); }
}
```

The declaration that `AttributedBody` extends Body and implements `Attributed` defines the contract of `AttributedBody`. The implementation of all Body's methods is inherited from the Body class itself. Each method of `Attributed` is implemented by forwarding the call to the `AttributedImpl` object's equivalent method, returning its value (if any). This also means that you have to add a field of type `AttributedImpl` to use in the stubs, and initialize the field to refer to an `AttributedImpl` object.

Forwarding is both straightforward and a lot less work than implementing `Attributed` from scratch. It also enables you to quickly change which implementation you use, should a better implementation of `Attributed` become available at some future date.

## 4.6    When to Use Interfaces

There are two important differences between interfaces and abstract classes:

◆ Interfaces provide a form of multiple inheritance, because you can implement multiple interfaces. A class can extend only one other class, even if that class has only `abstract` methods.

◆ An `abstract` class can have a partial implementation, `protected` parts, `static` methods, and so on, while interfaces are limited to `public` methods with no implementation and constants.

These differences usually direct the choice of which tool is best to use in a particular implementation. If multiple inheritance is important, or even useful, interfaces are used. However, an abstract class enables you to provide some or all of the implementation so that it can be inherited easily, rather than by explicit forwarding. Forwarding is tedious to implement and error-prone, so using an abstract class should not be dismissed lightly.

However, any major class you expect to be extended, whether abstract or not, should be an implementation of an interface. Although this requires a little more work on your part, it enables a whole category of use that is otherwise precluded. For example, had we simply created an `Attributed` *class* instead of an `Attributed` interface with an `AttributedImpl` implementation class, then people who wanted to create new classes that extended other existing classes could never be `Attributed`, since you can only extend one class—AttributedBody could never be created. Because `Attributed` is an interface, programmers have a choice: they can extend `AttributedImpl` directly and avoid the forwarding, or if they cannot extend, they can at least use forwarding to implement the interface. And if the general implementation provided is incorrect, they can write their own implementation. You can even provide multiple possible implementations of the interface to prospective users. Whatever implementation strategy the programmer prefers, the objects they create are `Attributed`.

### Exercise 4.1

Rewrite your solution to Exercise 3.7 on page 67 using an interface if you didn't write it that way in the first place.  ▲

### Exercise 4.2

Rewrite your solution to Exercise 3.12 on page 78 using an interface if you didn't write it that way in the first place.  ▲

### Exercise 4.3

Should the `LinkedList` class from previous exercises be an interface? Rewrite it that way, with an implementation class before you decide.  ▲

### Exercise 4.4

Design a collection class hierarchy using only interfaces.  ▲

### Exercise 4.5

Think about whether the following types should be represented as interfaces, abstract classes, or concrete classes: (a) `TreeNode` to represent nodes in an N-ary tree; (b) `TreeWalker` to walk the tree in a user-controlled order (such as depth-first or breadth-first); (c) `Drawable` for objects that can be drawn by a graphics system; (d) `Application` for programs that could be run from a graphical desktop.  ▲

### Exercise 4.6

What changes in your assumptions about each of the problems in Exercise 4.5 would make you change your answers?  ▲

# CHAPTER 5

# Tokens, Operators, and Expressions

*There's nothing remarkable about it.*
*All one has to do is hit the right keys at the right time*
*and the instrument plays itself.*
—Johann Sebastian Bach

THIS chapter discusses the fundamental building blocks of Java, namely, its types, operators, and expressions. You have already seen a lot of Java code, and have gained familiarity with its components. This chapter describes the basic elements in detail.

## 5.1 Character Set

Most programmers are familiar with source code that is prepared using one of two major families of character representations: ASCII and its variants (including Latin-1) and EBCDIC. Both of these character sets contain characters used in English and other Western European languages.

Java, on the other hand, is written in *Unicode*, a 16-bit character set. The first 256 characters of Unicode are the Latin-1 character set, and most of the first 128 characters of Latin-1 are equivalent to the 7-bit ASCII character set. Current Java environments read standard ASCII or ISO Latin-1 files, converting them to Unicode on the fly.[1]

Few text editors support Unicode characters at this time, so Java recognizes the *escape sequence* \u*dddd* to encode Unicode characters, where each *d* is a

---

[1.] Java uses Unicode 1.1.5 with bug fixes. See the Bibliography for reference information.

hexadecimal digit represented using the ASCII characters 0-9, and a-f or A-F to represent decimal values 10–15. This sequence can appear anywhere in code, not only in character and string constants, but in identifiers as well. More than one u may appear at the beginning; thus, the character 𑀁 can be written as either \u0b87 or \uu0b87.[2]

## 5.2   Comments

There are three kinds of comments in Java:

| | |
|---|---|
| `// comment` | Characters from // to the end of the line are ignored. |
| `/* comment */` | Characters between /* and the next */ are ignored, including line terminators \r, \n, or \r\n. |
| `/** comment */` | Characters between /** and the next */ are ignored, including line terminators as defined above. These documentation comments must come immediately before a class declaration, class member, or constructor, and are included in automatically generated documentation. |

When we say "characters," we mean *any* Unicode characters. A Java comment can include any Unicode character, such as Yin-Yang (\u262f), interrobang (\u203d), Won (\u20a9), scruple (\u2108), or a snowman (\u2603).

Java comments do not nest. This code—tempting though it looks—does not compile:

```
/*Comment this out for now: not implemented

    /* Do some really neat stuff */
    universe.neatStuff();

*/
```

---

[2.]  This "multiple u" allowance seems strange, but there is a good reason for it. When translating a Unicode file into an ASCII file, you have to translate Unicode characters that are outside the ASCII range into an escape sequence. Thus, you would translate 𑀁 into \u0b87. Then, when translating back, you would make the reverse substitution. But what if the original Unicode source had not contained 𑀁, but had used \u0b87 instead? Then the above reverse translation would not result in the original source (to the parser, it would be equivalent, but it might not be to the reader of the code). The solution is to have the translator add an extra u when it encounters an already-existing \u*dddd*, and the reverse translator remove a u and, if there aren't any left, replace the escape sequence with its equivalent Unicode character.

The first /* starts a comment; the very next */ ends it, leaving the code that follows to be parsed, and the invalid stand-alone */ as a syntax error. The best way to remove blocks of code from programs is either to put a // at the beginning of each line, or use if (false) like this:

```
if (false) {
    // call this method when it works
    dwim();
}
```

Of course, this code assumes that the dwim method is defined somewhere.

## 5.3   Tokens

The *tokens* of a language are its basic words. A parser breaks source code into tokens and then tries to figure out what statements, identifiers, and such make up the code. In Java, white space (spaces, tabs, newlines, and form feeds) is not significant except to separate tokens, or as the contents of character or string literals. You can take any valid Java code and replace any amount of intertoken white space (that is, white space outside strings and characters) with a different amount of white space (but not none) without changing the meaning of the program.

White space is *required* to separate tokens that would otherwise constitute a single token. For instance, in the statement

```
return 0;
```

you cannot eliminate the space between return and the 0, since that would create the invalid statement

```
return0;
```

consisting of just the single identifier return0. Use extra white space appropriately to make your code human-readable, even though the parser ignores it. Note that the parser treats comments as white space.

The tokenizer for Java is a "greedy tokenizer." It grabs as many characters as it can to build up the next token, not caring if this creates an invalid sequence of tokens. So, because ++ is longer than +, the expression

```
j = i+++++i;     // INVALID
```

is interpreted as the invalid expression

```
j = i++ ++ +i;   // INVALID
```

instead of the valid

```
j = i++ + ++i;
```

## 5.4   Identifiers

Java *identifiers*, used for names of declared entities (such as variables and constants) and labels, must start with a letter—including an underscore character (_), or a dollar sign ($)—followed by letters or digits or both. This sounds familiar to many programmers, but because Java source code is written in Unicode, the definition of "letter" and "digit" is much wider than in most existing programming languages. Java "letters" can include glyphs from Armenian, Korean, Gurmukhi, Georgian, Devanagari, and almost any script written in the world today. Thus, not only is kitty a valid identifier, but mačka, кошка, پیشی, புனைக்குட்டி, and 猫 are, too.[3] The terms "letter" and "digit" are pretty broad in Unicode, but if something is considered a letter or digit in a language, it probably is in Java, too. For a complete definition, see the tables "Unicode Digits" on page 300 and "Unicode Letters and Digits" on page 301.

Any differences in characters within an identifier makes that identifier unique. Case is significant: A, a, á, À, Å, and so on, are different identifiers. Characters that look the same, or nearly the same, can be confused for each other. For example, the Latin capital letter n "N" and the Greek capital ν "N" look alike, but are different Unicode characters (\u004e and \u039d, respectively). The only way to avoid this confusion is to write each identifier in only one language—and thus in one known set of characters—so that programmers trying to type the identifier will know whether you meant E or E.[4]

Java identifiers can be any length.

### 5.4.1   Java Reserved Words

Java language keywords cannot be used as identifiers. Here is a list of Java's keywords (those marked with a [†] are reserved but currently unused):

---

[3.]   These are the words "cat" or "kitty" in English, Serbo-Croatian, Russian, Farsi, Tamil, and Japanese, respectively. If these characters spell other words in other languages, we sincerely hope the words are not offensive, and apologize if they are, since such offense is completely unintentional.

[4.]   One of these is a Cyrillic letter, one is ASCII. Determine which is which and win a prize.

| | | | |
|---|---|---|---|
| abstract | double | int | super |
| boolean | else | interface | switch |
| break | extends | long | synchronized |
| byte | final | native | this |
| case | finally | new | throw |
| catch | float | package | throws |
| char | for | private | transient[†] |
| class | goto[†] | protected | try |
| const[†] | if | public | void |
| continue | implements | return | volatile |
| default | import | short | while |
| do | instanceof | static | |

Although they appear to be keywords, `null`, `true`, and `false` are formally literals, just like the number 12, so they do not appear in the above table. However, you cannot use `null`, `true`, or `false` as identifiers, just as you cannot use 12 as an identifier, although they can be used as part of identifiers. While `null`, `true`, and `false` are not formally keywords, the same restrictions apply.

## 5.5 Primitive Types

Some reserved words are type names. The primitive data types of Java are:

| | |
|---|---|
| boolean | either `true` or `false` |
| char | 16-bit Unicode 1.1.5 character |
| byte | 8-bit signed two's-complement integer |
| short | 16-bit signed two's-complement integer |
| int | 32-bit signed two's-complement integer |
| long | 64-bit signed two's-complement integer |
| float | 32-bit IEEE 754-1985 floating-point number |
| double | 64-bit IEEE 754-1985 floating-point number |

Each primitive Java language type except `short` and `byte` has a corresponding class declared in the `java.lang` package. Values of type `short` and `byte` are always promoted to `int` before being evaluated—they are only stored, never operated upon (see "Expression Type" on page 104). The language classes that wrap the primitive types—`Boolean`, `Character`, `Integer`, `Long`, `Float`, and `Double`—also define useful constants and methods. For example, some of these types declare constants `MIN_VALUE` and `MAX_VALUE` in their corresponding language classes.

The language classes `Float` and `Double` each also have `NEGATIVE_INFINITY`, `POSITIVE_INFINITY`, and `NaN` constants, as well as an `isNan` method that tests if a floating point value is "Not a Number"—that is, if it is the result of a floating-point expression that has no valid result, such as dividing by zero. The `NaN` value can be used to indicate an invalid floating-point value, similar to the use of `null` for object references that do not refer to anything. The representative language classes are covered in more detail in Chapter 13.

## 5.6 Literals

Each type in Java has *literals*, which are how constant values of that type are written. The next few subsections describe how literal (unnamed) constants for each type are specified.

### 5.6.1 Object References

The only literal object reference is `null`. It can be used anywhere a reference is expected. `null` conventionally represents an invalid or uncreated object. `null` is not of any type, even `Object`.

### 5.6.2 Boolean

The boolean literals are `true` and `false`.

### 5.6.3 Integers

Integer constants are strings of octal, decimal, or hexadecimal digits. The start of the constant declares the base of the number: a leading `0` (zero) denotes an octal number (base 8); a leading `0x` or `0X` denotes a hexadecimal number (base 16); any other set of digits is assumed to be a decimal number (base 10). The following numbers all have the same value:

```
29 035 0x1D 0X1d
```

Integer constants are `long` if they end in L or l, like 29L; L is preferred over l because l can too easily be confused with 1 (the digit one). Otherwise, integer constants are assumed to be of type `int`. If a literal of type `int` is immediately assigned to a `short` or `byte`, and its value is within the valid range for that type, the integer literal is treated as if it were a `short` or `byte`, respectively.

### 5.6.4    Floating Point

Floating-point numbers are expressed as decimal numbers with an optional decimal point, optionally followed by an exponent. At least one digit must be present. The number may be followed by f or F to denote a single-precision constant, or d or D to denote a double-precision constant. These literals all denote the same floating-point number:

```
18. 1.8e1 .18E2
```

Floating-point constants are of type `double` unless they are specified with a trailing f or F, which makes them `float` constants, like `18.0f`. A trailing d or D specifies a `double` constant. Zero can be positive `0.0` or negative `−0.0`. Positive and negative zero compare equal, but produce different results when used in some calculations. For example, `1d/0d` is $+\infty$, whereas `1d/-0d` is $-\infty$.

A `double` constant cannot be assigned directly to a `float` variable, even if the value of the `double` is within the valid `float` range. A `float` constant must be used for assignment to `float` variables and fields, or the `double` must be cast to a `float`.

### 5.6.5    Characters

Character literals appear between single quotes like `'Q'`. Certain special characters can be represented by an *escape sequence*. These are:

| | |
|---|---|
| \n | newline (\u000A) |
| \t | tab (\u0009) |
| \b | backspace (\u0008) |
| \r | return (\u000D) |
| \f | form feed (\u000C) |
| \\ | backslash itself (\u005C) |
| \' | single quote (\u0027) |
| \" | double quote (\u0022) |
| \\*ddd* | a `char` by octal value, where each *d* is one of 0-7 |

Octal character constants can have three or fewer digits, and cannot exceed \377 (\u00ff). Hexadecimal characters must always have four digits.

### 5.6.6    Strings

String literals appear between double quotes: `"along"`. All of the special escape sequences that are valid for character constants can be included in string literals.

A string literal references an object of type `String`. To learn more about strings, see Chapter 8.

Newlines are not allowed in the middle of strings. If you want to embed a newline character in the string, use the escape sequence `\n`.

Characters in strings can be specified using the octal digit mechanism, but all three octal digits should be used to prevent accidents when an octal value is specified next to a valid octal digit in the string. For example, the string `"\0116"` is equivalent to `"\t6"`, whereas the string `"\116"` is equivalent to `"N"`.

## 5.7    Declarations of Variables

A *declaration* states the type, access, and other attributes of an identifier. A declaration is broken into three parts: *modifiers*, followed by a *type*, followed by a list of *identifiers*.

Modifiers are optional in a variable declaration. The `static` modifier declares that a variable retains its value after a method returns; the `final` modifier declares that the value of the field is assigned only once, when it is initialized. Only fields may be declared `final`.

The type part of a declaration says what kinds of values and behavior are supported by the declared entities.

There is no difference between variables declared in one declaration, or in multiple declarations of the same type. For example:

```
float[] x, y;
```

is the same as

```
float[] x;
float[] y;
```

Declarations can appear at any point in the source code. They need not be at the beginning of a class, method, or block of code. In general, identifiers are available any time after their declaration inside the block in which they are declared (see "Statements and Blocks" on page 121), with the proviso that non-static fields are not available to static methods.

Fields that are declared `final` must be initialized in their declaration.

A declaration of a class member can be preceded by any of several modifiers. Modifiers are allowed in any order, but we recommend a standard order for consistency. Here is the order we use throughout the book: first are any access modifiers (`public`, `private`, or `protected`), followed by `static`, then `synchronized`, and then `final`. Using a consistent order improves readability of code.

### 5.7.1 The Meanings of Names

When an identifier is created, it lives in a particular *namespace*. Identifiers in the same namespace must have names that are unique. When you use an identifier to name a variable, class, or method, the meaning of the name is determined by searching as follows:

1. Local variables declared in a code block, `for` loop, or the parameters to an exception handler. A code block is one or more statements enclosed within braces. Variables can be declared in a `for` loop's initialization statement.

2. If the code is in a method or constructor, the parameters to the method or constructor.

3. A member of the enclosing class or interface type. These are the fields and methods of the type, including any inherited members.

4. Explicitly named imported types.

5. Other types declared in the same package.

6. Implicitly named imported types.

7. Packages available on the host system.

Each new nested block or `for` statement may declare new names. To avoid confusion, you cannot use this nesting to redeclare an identifier that is in an outer code block, in a `for` statement, or used for a parameter. Once there is a local identifier or parameter called, say, über, you cannot create a new, different identifier with the name über in a nested block.

These namespaces are further subdivided by the type of identifier involved. A variable can have the same name as a package, type, method, field, or statement label. The degenerate case of this is something like the following:

```
class Reuse {
    Reuse Reuse(Reuse Reuse) {
      Reuse:
        for (;;) {
            if (Reuse.Reuse(Reuse) == Reuse)
                break Reuse;
        }
        return Reuse;
    }
}
```

The order of lookup means that identifiers declared inside a method can hide identifiers outside it. Hiding is generally bad style, because a human reading the code must check all levels of the hierarchy to determine which variable is being used.

The nesting of scope gives variables a meaning in a region of the code corresponding to their intended use. For example, a variable declared in the initializer clause of a for statement is unavailable outside the scope of the for. This is often appropriate so that code outside the for loop cannot discover where the iteration ended.

Nesting is needed to make local code robust. If hiding outer variables were not allowed, adding a new field to a class or interface could break existing code that used variables of the same name. Scoping is meant as protection for the system as a whole, rather than support for reusing identifier names.

## 5.8    Array Variables

Java *arrays* provide ordered collections of elements. Components of an array can be primitive types or references to objects, including references to other arrays. The declaration

```
int[] ia = new int[3];
```

declares an array named ia that initially refers to an array of three int values.

Array dimensions are omitted in the declaration of any array variable. The number of components in an array is determined when it is *created* using new, not when it is declared. An array object's length is fixed at its creation, and cannot be changed. Note that it is the length of the array *object* that is fixed. In the example above, a new array of a different size could be assigned to the array reference ia at any time.

The first element of the array ia has index 0 (zero), and the last has index *length*–1. In our example above, the last element of the array is ia[2]. Every subscript use is checked to ensure that it is within the proper range. An out-of-range array access throws an IndexOutOfBoundsException.

The length of an array is available via the length field. In our example, the following code would loop over the array, printing out each value:

```
for (int i = 0; i < ia.length; i++)
    System.out.println(i + ": " + ia[i]);
```

Arrays are implicit extensions of Object. Given a class X, a class Y that extends X, and arrays of each, the class hierarchy looks something like this:

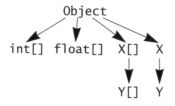

This allows polymorphism for arrays. You can assign an array to a variable of type Object, and cast it back. An array of objects of type Y is usable wherever an array of objects of its base type X is required.

Like any other object, arrays are created and are subject to normal garbage collection mechanisms.

The major limitation on the object-ness of arrays is that they cannot be extended to add new methods. The following construct is not valid:

```
class ScaleVector extends double[] { // INVALID
    // ...
}
```

When you declare an array of an object type, you are really declaring an array of *variables* of that type. Consider the following code:

```
Attr[] attrs = new Attr[12];

for (int i = 0; i < attrs.length; i++)
    attrs[i] = new Attr(names[i], values[i]);
```

After the initial new of the array, attrs has a reference to an array of 12 variables that are initialized to null. The Attr objects are created only when the loop is executed.

If you prefer, Java allows the array brackets to come after the variable instead of the type, as in:

```
int ia[] = new int[3];
```

This is equivalent to the original definition of ia above. However, the first style is generally preferable, because it places the type declaration entirely in one place.

### 5.8.1  Arrays of Arrays

Java arrays supports arrays of arrays. The code to declare and print a two-dimensional matrix, for example, might look like this:

```
float[][] mat = new float[4][4];
setupMatrix(mat);
for (int y = 0; y < mat.length; y++) {
    for (int x = 0; x < mat[y].length; x++)
        System.out.print(mat[x][y] + " ");
    System.out.println();
}
```

The first (leftmost) dimension of an array must be specified when the array is created. Other dimensions may be left unspecified, to be filled in later. Specifying more than the first dimension is a shorthand for a nested set of new statements. Our new creation above could have been written more explicitly as:

```
float[][] mat = new float[4][];
for (int y = 0; y < mat.length; y++)
    mat[y] = new float[4];
```

One advantage of arrays-of-arrays is that each nested array can have a different size. You can emulate a 4×4 array, but you can also create an array of four int arrays, each of which has a different length necessary to hold its own data.

### Exercise 5.1

Write a program that calculates Pascal's triangle to a depth of 12, storing each row of the triangle in an array of the appropriate length, and putting each of the row arrays into an array of 12 int arrays. Design your solution so that the results are printed by a method that prints the array of arrays using the lengths of each array, not a constant 12. Now change the code to use a constant other than 12 without modifying your printing method. ▲

## 5.9 Initial Values

A variable can be initialized in its declaration. The initial value for the variable can be given by following the variable name with an = and an expression:

```
final double    π = 3.14159;
float           radius = 1.0f;  // start with unit circle
```

Java assigns a default initial value to fields of a class if one isn't specified. The default value depends on the type of the field:

| Field Type | Initial Value |
| --- | --- |
| boolean | false |
| char | '\u0000' |
| integer (byte, short, int, long) | 0 |
| floating point | +0.0f or +0.0d |
| object reference | null |

Java does not assign any default initial value to local variables in a method, constructor, or static initializer. Failure to provide an initial value for a local variable is usually a bug, and you must initialize local variables before using their values.

A variable's scope determines when it is initialized. Local variables are initialized each time their declaration is executed. Object fields and members of arrays are initialized when the object or array is created with new—see "Constructor Order Dependencies" on page 57 for precise details. Class `static` variables are initialized before any code for that class is run.

Field initializers cannot throw checked exceptions, nor invoke methods that can, since there is no way to catch them. This rule can be worked around for non-static fields by placing the assignment inside a constructor, since the constructor can handle the exception. For static fields, the work-around is to set the initial value inside a static initializer that handles the exception.

### 5.9.1   Array Initializers

Arrays can be initialized by providing values inside braces following their declaration. The following array declaration creates and initializes an array object:

```
String[] dangers = { "Lions", "Tigers", "Bears" };
```

The following code gives the same result:

```
String[] dangers = new String[3];

dangers[0] = "Lions";
dangers[1] = "Tigers";
dangers[2] = "Bears" ;
```

Arrays of arrays can be initialized by nesting array initializers. Here is a declaration that initializes a four-by-four matrix:

```
double[][]  identityMatrix = {
            { 1.0, 0.0, 0.0, 0.0 },
            { 0.0, 1.0, 0.0, 0.0 },
            { 0.0, 0.0, 1.0, 0.0 },
            { 0.0, 0.0, 0.0, 1.0 },
        };
```

## 5.10  Operator Precedence and Associativity

Operator precedence is the "stickiness" of operators relative to each other. Operators have different precedences. For example, relational operators have a higher precedence than boolean operators, so you can say

```
if (i >= min && i <= max)
    process(i);
```

without any confusion. Since * (multiply) has a higher precedence than - (minus), the expression

```
5 * 3 - 3
```

has the value 12, not zero. Precedence can be overridden using parentheses; if zero were the desired value, for example, the following would do the trick:

```
5 * (3 - 3)
```

When two operators with the same precedence appear next to each other, the associativity of the operator determines which is evaluated first. Since + (add) is left-associative, the expression

```
a + b + c
```

is equivalent to

```
(a + b) + c
```

The following table lists all the operators in order of precedence from highest to lowest. All the operators are binary, except those shown as unary with *expr*, the creation and cast operators (which are also unary), and the conditional operator (which is ternary). Operators with the same precedence appear on the same line of the table:

| | |
|---|---|
| postfix operators | [] . (*params*) *expr*++ *expr*-- |
| unary operators | ++*expr* --*expr* +*expr* -*expr* ~ ! |
| creation or cast | new (*type*)*expr* |
| multiplicative | * / % |
| additive | + - |
| shift | << >> >>> |
| relational | < > >= <= instanceof |
| equality | == != |
| bitwise AND | & |
| bitwise exclusive XOR | ^ |

| | |
|---|---|
| bitwise inclusive OR | \| |
| logical AND | && |
| logical OR | \|\| |
| conditional | ?: |
| assignment | = += -= *= /= %= >>= <<= >>>= &= ^= \|= |

All binary operators other than assignment operators are *left-associative*. Assignment is *right-associative*—in other words, a=b=c is equivalent to a=(b=c). 

Precedence can be overridden using parentheses. The expression x+y*z multiplies y by z first and then adds x, whereas (x+y)*z adds x and y first and multiplies the result by z.

Parentheses are often needed in expressions where assignment is embedded in a boolean expression, or in which bitwise operations are used. For an example of the former, examine the following code:

```
while ((v = stream.next()) != null)
    processValue(v);
```

Assignment operators have lower precedence than equality operators; without the parentheses, it would be equivalent to

```
while (v = (stream.next() != null)) // INVALID
    processValue(v);
```

and probably not what you want. It is also likely to be invalid code, since it would be valid only in the unusual case where v is `boolean`.

The precedence of the bitwise operators &, ^, and | is problematic. Binary bitwise operators in complex expressions should be parenthesized for readability and to ensure correct precedence.

Our use of parentheses is sparse—we use them only when code seems otherwise unclear. Operator precedence is part of the language and should be generally understood. Others inject parentheses liberally. Try not to use parentheses everywhere—code becomes completely illegible, looking like LISP with none of LISP's saving graces.

## 5.11 Order of Evaluation

Java guarantees that operands to operators will be evaluated left-to-right. For example, given x+y+z, the compiler evaluates x, evaluates y, adds the values together, evaluates z, and adds that to the previous result. The compiler does not evaluate, say, y before x, or z before either y or x.

Order of evaluation matters if x, y, or z have side effects of any kind. If they are, for instance, invocations of methods that affect the state of the object or print something, you would notice if they were evaluated in any other order. The language guarantees that this will not happen.

Except for the operators &&, ||, and ?: (see below), every operand of an operator will be evaluated before the operation is performed. This is true even for operations that raise exceptions. For example, an integer division by zero results in an ArithmeticException, but it will only do so after both operands have been fully evaluated.

## 5.12 Expression Type

All expressions have a type. The type of an expression is determined by the types of its component parts, and the semantics of operators. If an arithmetic or bitwise operator is applied to an integer value, the result is of type int unless one or both sides are long, in which case the result is long. All integer operations are performed in either int or long precision, so the smaller byte and short integer types are always promoted to int before evaluation.

If either operand of an arithmetic operator is floating-point, the operation is performed in floating-point arithmetic. Such operations are done in float unless at least one operand is a double, in which case double is used for the calculation and result.

A + operator is a String concatenation when either operand to + is of type String, or if the left-hand side of a += is a String.

When used in an expression, a char value is converted to an int by setting the top 16 bits to zero. For example, the Unicode character \uffff would be treated as equivalent to the integer 0x0000ffff. This is different from how a short with the value 0xffff would be treated—sign extension makes it equivalent to -1, and its int equivalent would be 0xffffffff.

## 5.13 Type Conversions

Java is a *strongly typed* language, which means that it checks for type compatibility at compile time in almost all cases. Java prevents incompatible assignments by forbidding anything questionable, and provides casts for use when the compatibility of a type can be determined only at run time. We discuss these conversions in terms of assignment, but what we say also applies to conversions within expressions and when assigning values to method parameters.

### 5.13.1  Implicit Conversion

Some kinds of conversions happen automatically, without any work on your part. There are two kinds of *implicit* conversions.

The first kind of implicit conversion applies to primitive values. Any numeric value can be assigned to any numeric variable whose type supports a larger range of values. A char can be used wherever an int is valid. A floating-point value can be assigned to any floating-point variable of equal or greater precision.

Java also allows implicit conversion of integer types to floating-point, but not vice versa, since there is no loss of range going from integer to floating-point, because the range of any floating-point type is larger than the range of any integer.

Preserving magnitude is not the same as preserving the precision of a value. You can lose precision in some implicit conversions. Consider, for instance, assigning a long to a float. The float is a 32-bit data type, and the long is a 64-bit type. A float stores fewer significant digits than a long, even though it stores numbers of a larger range. You can lose data in an assignment of a long to a float. Consider the following:

```
long orig = 0x7effffffffffffffL;
float fval = orig;
long lose = (long)fval;

System.out.println("orig = " + orig);
System.out.println("fval = " + fval);
System.out.println("lose = " + lose);
```

The first two statements create a long value and assign it to a float value. To show that this loses precision, we explicitly cast fval to a long, and assign it to another variable (explicit casts are covered below). If you examine the output, you can see that the float value lost some precision, since the long variable orig that was assigned to the float variable fval has a different value than the one generated by the explicit cast back into the long variable lose:

```
orig = 9151314442816847871
fval = 9.15131e+18
lose = 9151314442816847872
```

The second type of implicit conversion is reference conversion. An object that is an instance of a class includes an instance of each of its supertypes. You can use an object reference of one type wherever a reference of any supertype is required.

The null object reference is assignable to any object reference type, including array references.

### 5.13.2 Explicit Casts and `instanceof`

When one type cannot be assigned to another with implicit conversion, it can often be explicitly *cast* to the other type. A cast requests a new value of a new type that is the best available representation of the old value in the old type. Some casts are not allowed—a `boolean` cannot be cast to an `int`, for example—but explicit casting can be used to assign a `double` to a `long`, as in this code:

```
double d = 7.99;
long l = (long)d;
```

When a floating-point value is cast to an integer, the fractional part is lost by rounding towards zero; for instance, `(int)-72.3` is `-72`. Methods are available in the `Math` class that round floating point values to integers in other ways—see "Math" on page 269 for details.

A `double` can also be explicitly cast to a `float`, or an integer type can be explicitly cast to a smaller integer type. When casting from a `double` to a `float`, you can lose precision, or you could get a zero, or an infinity where you had a finite larger value before.

Integer types are converted by chopping off the upper bits. If the value in the larger integer fits in the smaller type to which it is cast, no harm is done. But if the larger integer has a value outside the range of the smaller, dropping the upper bits changes the value, including possibly changing sign. The following code:

```
short s = -134;
byte b = (byte)s;

System.out.println("s = " + s + ", b = " + b);
```

produces the following output because the upper bits of s are lost when storing the value in b:

```
s = -134, b = 122
```

A `char` can be cast to any integer type, and vice versa. In casting the integer to a `char`, only the bottom 16 bits of data are used, and the rest are discarded. When a `char` is cast to an integer type, the additional top 16 bits are filled with zeros. Once those bits are assigned, though, they are treated as they would be in any other instance. Here is some code that casts the highest Unicode character to both an `int` (implicitly) and a `short` (explicitly). The `int` is a positive value, equal to `0x0000ffff`, because the upper bits of the character were set to zero. But the same bits in the `short` are a negative value, because the top bit of the `short` is the sign bit:

```
class CharCast {
    public static void main(String[] args) {
        int i = '\uffff';
        short s = (short)'\uffff';

        System.out.println("i = " + i);
        System.out.println("s = " + s);
    }
}
```

And here is the program's output:

```
i = 65535
s = -1
```

Explicit casts can also be used with object types. While an object of an extended type can be used where a supertype is needed, the converse is not generally true. Suppose you had the following class hierarchy:

A reference of type `Coffee` does not necessarily refer to an object of type `Mocha`; the object might be of type `Latte`. So you cannot, for example, pass the `Coffee` reference where an object of type `Mocha` is expected. Such casting is called *narrowing*, or *casting down* the class hierarchy. It is also called *unsafe casting*, because it is not always valid. Going from a more-extended to a less-extended type is called *widening*, or *casting up* the class hierarchy; it is also sometimes called *safe casting*, because it is always valid.

But sometimes you know that the `Coffee` object is actually an instance of `Mocha`. In such a case, you can cast down the type tree using an explicit cast, like this:

```
Mocha fancy = (Mocha)joe;
```

If this is valid—that is, `joe` really refers to a `Mocha` object—`fancy` will refer to the same object `joe` does, but `fancy` can be used to access the functionality that `Mocha` adds. If the cast is not valid, a `ClassCastException` is thrown. If the cast isn't even potentially correct (for instance, if `Mocha` were not an extended class of the declared type for `joe`), this code would not compile. This prevents an error where the code assumes a class hierarchy that isn't correct.

Sometimes a method does not require an object of a more extended type, but if it *has* an extended object, the method wants to use the extended functionality. You could simply do the cast and handle the exception, but using exception handling in this way may be slow and is considered poor style. To determine if an object is of a given type, use `instanceof`, which returns `true` if the cast would be valid:

```java
public void quaff(Coffee joe) {
    // ...
    if (joe instanceof Mocha) {
        Mocha fancy = (Mocha)joe;
        // ... use Mocha's functionality
    }
}
```

The `null` reference is not an instance of any object type at all, so

```java
null instanceof Type
```

is always `false`, for any *Type*.

### 5.13.3 String Conversions

The `String` class is special: it is used implicitly in the + string concatenation operator, and literal strings refer to `String` objects. You've already seen examples of output code: wherever a `String` object is needed when concatenating strings, Java tries to convert the non-`String` side (if any) into a `String`. Such conversions are defined for all primitive types, and for any object by invoking its `toString` method (see "The toString Method" on page 50).

When a null reference is converted to a `String`, the result is the string `"null"`. If no `toString` method is defined for a class, it inherits the one from `Object`, which returns a string representation of the object type.

## 5.14 Member Access

Members of objects are accessed using the `.` operator, as in `obj.method()`. You can also use `.` to access static members, using either a class name or an object reference. If you use an object reference for a static member, the declared type of the reference, not the actual type of the object, is used to determine which class's static members to use. Elements of arrays are accessed using brackets, as in `array[i]`.

If you use either `.` or `[]` on a reference with the value `null`, a `NullPointerException` is thrown, unless you are using `.` to invoke a static method. If an array index is out of bounds, `IndexOutOfBoundException` is thrown. This is checked every time an array is indexed.[5]

For an invocation of a method to be correct, arguments of the proper number and type must be provided so that exactly one matching method can be found in the class. If a method is not overloaded, this is simple, because only one parameter count is associated with the method name. Matching is also simple if there is only one method declared with name and number of arguments provided.

If two or more overloads of a method have the same number of parameters, choosing the correct method overload is more complex. Java uses a "most specific" algorithm to do the match:

1. Find all the methods that could possibly apply to the invocation, namely all the overloaded methods that have the correct name, and whose parameters are of types that can be assigned the values of all the arguments. If one method matches exactly for all arguments, you invoke that method.

2. If any method in the set has parameter types that are all assignable to any other method in the set, the other method is removed from the set because it is less specific. Repeat until no eliminations can be made.

3. If you are left with one method, that method is the most specific and will be the one invoked. If you have more than one method left, then the call is ambiguous, there being no most specific method, and the invoking code is invalid.

For instance, suppose you had an expanded version of the dessert types shown in Section 3.2:

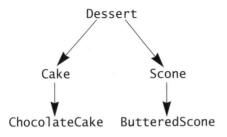

---

At least the runtime behaves as if this were true, but the compiler can often avoid the test when it knows, for example, that a loop index is always within range.

Further suppose you had several overloaded methods that took particular combinations of Dessert parameters:

```
void moorge(Dessert d, Scone s)       { /* first form  */ }
void moorge(Cake c, Dessert d)        { /* second form */ }
void moorge(ChocolateCake cc, Scone s) { /* third form  */ }
```

Now consider the following invocations of moorge:

```
moorge(dessertRef, sconeRef);
moorge(chocolateCakeRef, dessertRef);
moorge(chocolateCakeRef, butteredSconeRef);
moorge(cakeRef, sconeRef);       // INVALID
```

The first invocation uses the first form of moorge, because the parameter and argument types match exactly. The second invocation uses the second form, because it is the only form for which the provided arguments can be assigned to the parameter types. In both these cases, the method to invoke is clear after step 1 in the algorithm described above.

The third invocation requires more thought. The list of potential overloads includes all three forms, because a ChocolateCakeRef is assignable to any of the first parameter types, a ButteredScone reference is assignable to either of the second parameter types, and none of the signatures matches exactly. So after step 1 you have a set of three candidate methods.

Step 2 requires you to eliminate less specific methods from the set. In this case, the first form is removed from the set because the third form is more specific—a ChocolateCake reference can be assigned to the first form's Dessert parameter and a Scone reference can be assigned to the first form's Scone parameter, so the first form is less specific. The second form is removed from the set in a similar manner. After this, the set of possible methods has been reduced to one—the third form of moorge—and that method form will be invoked.

The final invocation is invalid. After step 1, the set of possible matches includes the first and second form. Since neither form's parameters are assignable to the other, neither can be removed from the set in step 2. Therefore, you have an ambiguous call that cannot be resolved by the compiler, and therefore an invalid invocation of moorge.

These rules apply to the primitive types, too. An int, for example, can be assigned to a float, and resolving an overloaded invocation will take that into account just the way it considered that a ButteredScone reference was assignable to a Scone reference.

Methods may not differ only in return type and/or the list of exceptions they throw because there are too many ambiguities to determine which overloaded method is wanted. If, for example, there were two doppelgänger methods that differed only because one returned an `int` and the other a `short`, both would make equal sense in the following statement:

```
double d = doppelgänger();
```

A similar problem exists with exceptions, since you can catch any, all, or none of the exceptions a method might throw in the code where you invoke the over-loaded method. There would be no way to determine which of two methods to use when they differed only in thrown exceptions.

## 5.15  Arithmetic Operators

Java supports several binary arithmetic operators that operate on any numerical type:

| | |
|---|---|
| + | addition |
| – | subtraction |
| * | multiplication |
| / | division |
| % | remainder |

Java also supports unary - for negation. The sign of a number can be inverted with code like this:

```
val = -val;
```

There is also a unary +, as in +3. Unary plus is included for symmetry—without it, you could not write constants like +2.0.

### 5.15.1  Integer Arithmetic

Integer arithmetic is modular two's-complement arithmetic—that is, if a value exceeds the range of its type (`int` or `long`), it is reduced modulo the range. So integer arithmetic never overflows or underflows, but just wraps.

Integer division truncates towards zero (that is, 7/2 is 3, and -7/2 is -3). For integer types, division and remainder obey the rule

```
(x/y)*y + x%y == x
```

So 7%2 is 1, and -7%2 is -1. Dividing by zero or remainder by zero is invalid for integer arithmetic and throws `ArithmeticException`.

Character arithmetic is integer arithmetic after the `char` is implicitly con-verted to `int`.

### 5.15.2  Floating-Point Arithmetic

Java uses the IEEE 754-1985 standard on floating-point, both for representation and arithmetic, with default modes. Under this standard, arithmetic can overflow to infinity (become too large for the `double` or `float`) or underflow to zero (become too small for the `double` or `float`). There is also a representation—NaN, for "Not a Number"—for the results of invalid expressions, such as dividing by zero.

Arithmetic with finite operands performs as expected, within the limits of precision of `double` or `float`. Signs of floating-point arithmetic results are also as expected. Multiplying two numbers with the same sign results in a positive value; multiplying two numbers with opposite signs results in a negative value.

Adding two infinities results in the same infinity if their signs are the same, and NaN if their signs differ. Subtracting infinities of the same sign produces NaN; subtracting infinities of opposite signs produces an infinity of the same sign as the left operand. For example, $(\infty - (-\infty))$ is $\infty$. Arithmetic operations involving any value that is NaN have a result that is also NaN. Overflows result in a value that is an infinity of the proper sign. Underflows result in a zero of the proper sign. IEEE floating-point has a negative zero, which compares equal to +0.0, but `1f/0f` results in positive infinity, while `1f/-0f` results in negative infinity.

If the result of an underflow is `-0.0`, and `-0.0 == 0.0`, how do you test for a negative zero? The zero must be used in an expression where sign matters, and the result tested. For instance, if $x$ is zero, the expression $1/x$ will yield negative infinity if $x$ was negative zero, or positive infinity if $x$ was positive zero.

The rules for operations on infinities match normal mathematical expectations. Adding or subtracting any number to or from either infinity results in that infinity. For example, $(-\infty + x)$ is $-\infty$ for any finite number $x$.

To obtain an infinity, you can produce it by arithmetic, or use type-specific names for infinity from type objects `Float` and `Double`: `POSITIVE_INFINITY` and `NEGATIVE_INFINITY`. For example, `Double.NEGATIVE_INFINITY` is the `double` value of minus infinity.

Multiplying infinity by zero yields NaN. Multiplying infinity by a nonzero finite number produces an infinity of the appropriate sign.

Floating-point division and remainder can produce infinities or NaN, but never raises an exception. This table shows the results of the various combinations:

| x | y | x/y | x%y |
|---|---|-----|-----|
| Finite | ±0.0 | ±∞ | NaN |
| Finite | ±∞ | ±0.0 | x |
| ±0.0 | ±0.0 | NaN | NaN |
| ±∞ | Finite | ±∞ | NaN |
| ±∞ | ±∞ | NaN | NaN |

Otherwise, floating-point remainder (%) acts analogously to integer remainder as described above. See the `Math.IEEERemainder` method in Section 14.8 on page 269 for different remainder calculation.

### 5.15.3 Java Floating-Point Arithmetic and IEEE-754

Java floating-point arithmetic is a subset of the IEEE-754-1985 standard. Those with a need for complete understanding of these issues should consult *The Java Language Specification*. Here is a summary of the key differences:

◆ *Nonstop Arithmetic:* The Java system will not throw exceptions, trap, or otherwise signal the IEEE exceptional conditions of invalid operation, division by zero, overflow, underflow, or inexact. Java arithmetic has no signaling NaN value.

◆ *Rounding:* Java arithmetic is *round toward nearest*—it rounds inexact results to the nearest representable value, with ties going to the value with a 0 least-significant bit. This is the IEEE default mode. But Java arithmetic rounds towards zero when converting a floating value to an integer. Java does not provide user-selectable rounding modes for floating-point computations: up, down, or towards zero.

◆ *Relational Set:* Java arithmetic has no relational predicates that include the unordered condition, except for `!=`. However, all cases but one can be constructed by the programmer, using existing relations and logical inversion. The exception is "ordered but unequal," which can be obtained if needed by $x < y \,||\, x > y$.

◆ *Extended Formats:* Java arithmetic does not support any extended formats, except that `double` will serve as single-extended. Other extended formats are not a requirement of the standard.

### 5.15.4 String Concatenation

You can use + to concatenate two strings together. Here is an example:

```
String boo = "boo";
String cry = boo + "hoo";
cry += "!";
System.out.println(cry);
```

And here is its output:

```
boohoo!
```

You can also use + to concatenate a `String` with a string representation of any primitive type or of an object. For example, the following brackets a string with the guillemet characters used for quotations in many European languages:

```
public static String guillemete(String quote) {
    return '«' + quote + '»';
}
```

This implicit conversion of primitive types and objects to strings happens only when using + or += in expressions involving strings—it does not happen anywhere else. A method, for instance, that takes a `String` parameter must be passed a `String`. You cannot pass it an object or `float` and have it converted implicitly.

## 5.16  Increment and Decrement Operators

The ++ and -- operators are the increment and decrement operators, respectively. The expression i++ is equivalent to i = i + 1, except that i is evaluated only once. For example, the statement

```
arr[where()]++;
```

invokes `where` only once, and uses the result as an index into the array only once. On the other hand, in the statement

```
arr[where()] = arr[where()] + 1;
```

the `where` method is called twice: once to determine the index on the right-hand side, and once to determine the index on the left-hand side. If `where` returns a different value each time it is invoked, the results will be quite different from those of the ++ expression above.

The increment and decrement operators can be either *prefix* or *postfix* operators—they can appear either before or after what they operate on. If the operator comes before (prefix), the operation is applied *before* the value of the expression is returned. If it comes after (postfix), the operation is applied *after* the original value is used. For example:

```
class IncOrder {
    public static void main(String[] args) {
        int i = 16;
        System.out.println(++i + " " + i++ + " " + i);
    }
}
```

The output is

```
17  17  18
```

The first value printed is i preincremented to 17; the second value is i after that increment, but before it is postincremented to 18; then finally i is printed out after its postincrement from the middle term.

The increment and decrement operators ++ and -- can also be applied to char variables to get to the next or previous Unicode character.

## 5.17  Relational and Conditional Operators

Java supports a standard set of relational and equality operators:

| | |
|---|---|
| > | greater than |
| >= | greater than or equal to |
| < | less than |
| <= | less than or equal to |
| == | equal to |
| != | not equal to |

All these operators yield boolean values. The unary operator ! inverts a boolean, hence !true is the same as false. Boolean values are normally tested directly—if x and y are booleans, it is considered cleaner to write

```
if (x || !y) {
    // ...
}
```

rather than

```
if (x == true || y == false) {
    // ...
}
```

Results of boolean expressions can be joined with && and Symbol(s):||, which means "conditional AND" and "conditional OR," respectively. These operators avoid evaluating their second operand if possible. For example:

```
if (w && x) {        // outer "if"
    if (y || z) {  // inner "if"
        // ...          inner "if" body
    }
}
```

The inner if is executed only if both w *and* x are true. If w is false, Java does not evaluate x. The body of the inner if is executed if either y or z is true. If y is true, Java does not evaluate z.

Much Java code relies upon this rule for program correctness or efficiency. For example, the evaluation shortcuts make the following code safe:

```
if (ix >= 0 && ix < array.length && array[ix] != 0) {
    // ...
}
```

The range checks are done first—only if ix is within bounds will it be used to access an array element.

Only the equality operators == and != are allowed to operate on boolean values, because the question of whether true is greater than or less than false is meaningless.

This can be used to create a "logical XOR" test. The following code executes sameSign only if both x and y have the same sign (or zero) and otherwise executes differentSign:

```
if (x < 0 == y < 0)
    sameSign();
else
    differentSign();
```

Floating-point values follow normal ordering (-1.0 is less than 0.0 is less than positive infinity), except that NaN is an anomaly. All relational and equality operators that test a number against NaN return false, except !=, which always returns true. This is true even if both values are NaN. For example,

```
Double.NaN == Double.NaN
```

is always false. To test whether a value is NaN, use the type-specific NaN testers: the static methods Float.isNaN(float) and Double.isNan(Double).

Two object references can always be tested for equality. ref1==ref2 is true if the two references both refer to the same object, or if both are null, even if the two references are of different declared types. Otherwise, it is false.

Using equality operators on String objects does not work as expected. Given String objects str1 and str2, str1==str2 tests whether str1 and str2 refer to the same String object. It does *not* test whether they have the same contents. Content equality is tested using String.equals, described in Chapter 8.

## 5.18  Bitwise Operators

Binary bitwise operators are as shown in this table:

    &        bitwise AND
    |        bitwise inclusive OR
    ∧       bitwise exclusive or (XOR)

There is also a unary bitwise complement operator ~, which toggles each bit in its operand. An `int` with value `0x00003333` has a complemented value of `0xffffcccc`. The other bit-related operators shift bits within an integer value. They are:

    <<      Shift bits left, filling with zero bits on the right-hand side
    >>      Shift bits right, filling with the highest (sign) bit on the left-hand side
    >>>   Shift bits right, filling with zero bits on the left-hand side

The left-hand side of a shift expression is what is shifted, and the right-hand side is how much to shift. For example, `var >>> 2` will shift the bits in `var` two places to the right, dropping the top two bits off the end, and filling the top two bits with zero.

Shift operators have a slightly different type rule than most other binary integer operations. For shift operators, the resulting type is the type of the left-hand operand—that is, the value that is shifted. If the left-hand side of the shift is an `int`, the result of the shift is an `int`, even if the shift count is provided as a `long`.

If the shift count is larger than the number of bits in the word, or if it is negative, the actual count will be different from the provided count. The actual count used in a shift is the count you provide, masked by the size of the type minus one. For a 32-bit `int`, for instance, the mask used is `0x1f` (31), so both `(n << 35)` and `(n << -29)` are equivalent to `(n << 3)`.

Bitwise operators can also be used on `boolean` values. `&` and `|` return the same value as their logical counterparts `&&` and `||`, with one important difference: the bitwise operators always evaluate both operands, while the logical operators evaluate both operands only if necessary.

The bitwise ∧ is `true` if the booleans are not the same—one or the other is `true`, but not both. Using ∧ is another way to create "logical XOR":

```
if ((x < 0) ^ (y < 0))
    differentSign();
else
    sameSign();
```

Bitwise operators can be used only on integer types and booleans, not on floating-point or reference values. Shift operators can be used only on integer types. In the rare circumstance where you actually need to manipulate bits in floating-point values, you can use the conversion methods on the type classes `Float` and `Double`, discussed in "Float and Double" on page 257.

## 5.19  The Conditional Operator ?:

The *conditional operator* provides a single expression that yields one of two values based on a boolean expression. The following:

```
value = (userSetIt ? usersValue : defaultValue);
```

is equivalent to

```
if (userSetIt)
    value = usersValue;
else
    value = defaultValue;
```

The primary difference between the if statement and the ?: operator is that the latter has a value. The conditional operator results in a more compact expression, but programmers disagree on whether it is more clear. We use whichever seems clearer at the time. When to use parentheses around a conditional operator expression is a matter of personal style where practice varies widely. They are not required by the language.

The result expressions (the second and third ones) must have assignment-compatible types. The type of one result expression must be assignable to the type of the other without an explicit cast, no matter which is assignable to the other. The type of the result of the conditional operator is the more general of the two types. For example, in

```
double scale = (halveIt ? 1 : 0.5);
```

the two sides are int (1) and double (0.5). An int is assignable to a double, so the 1 is cast to 1.0 and the result of the conditional operator is double. This rule holds for reference types also—if one type is assignable to the other, the least-extended type is the type of the operation. If neither type is assignable to the other, the operation is invalid.

This operator is also called "the question/colon operator" because of its form, and "the ternary operator" because it is the only ternary (three-operand) operator in the Java language.

## 5.20  Assignment Operators

The simple = is the most basic form of assignment operator. Java supports many other assignment forms. Any arithmetic or binary bitwise operator can be concatenated with = to form another assignment operator. For example,

```
arr[where()] += 12;
```

is the same as

```
arr[where()] = arr[where()] + 12;
```

except that the expression on the left-hand side of the assignment is evaluated only once. In the example, `arr[where()]` is evaluated only once in the first expression.

Given the variable `var` of type `Type`, the value `expr`, and the binary operator *op*,

```
var op= expr
```

is equivalent to

```
var = (Type)((var) op (expr))
```

except that `var` is evaluated only once. This means that *op=* is valid only if *op* is valid for the types involved. You cannot, for example, use `<<=` on a `double` variable because you cannot use `<<` on a `double` variable.

Note the parentheses used above. The expression

```
a *= b + 1
```

is the same as

```
a = a * (b + 1)
```

and not

```
a = a * b + 1
```

Although a `+= 1` is the same as `++a`, `++` is considered idiomatic and is preferred.


## 5.21  Package Names

Package names consist of a sequence of identifiers separated by dots (`.`). Unicode-capable editors will be rare for some time, so using only ASCII characters in package names makes sense if the package is expected to be widely distributed.


### *Exercise 5.2*

Using what you've learned in this chapter, but without writing Java code, figure out which of the following expressions are invalid, and what the type and values are of the valid expressions:

```
3 << 2L - 1
(3L << 2) - 1
```

```
10 < 12 == 6 > 17
10 << 12 == 6 >> 17
13.5e-1 % Float.POSITIVE_INFINITY
Float.POSITIVE_INFINITY + Double.NEGATIVE_INFINITY
Double.POSITIVE_INFINITY - Float.NEGATIVE_INFINITY
0.0 / -0.0 == -0.0 / 0.0
Integer.MAX_VALUE + Integer.MIN_VALUE;
Long.MAX_VALUE + 5;
(short)5 * (byte)10
(i < 15 ? 1.72e3f : 0)
i++ + i++ + --i      // i = 3 at start  ▲
```

CHAPTER **6**

# Control Flow

*"Would you tell me, please, which way I ought to go from here?"*
*"That depends a good deal on where you want to get to."*
—Lewis Carroll, *Alice in Wonderland*

**A** program consisting only of a list of consecutive statements is immediately useful because the statements are executed in the order in which they're written. But the ability to control the order in which statements are executed—that is, to test conditions and execute different statements based on the results of the tests—adds enormous value to our programming toolkit. This chapter covers almost all the *control flow statements* that direct the order of execution. Exceptions are covered separately in Chapter 7.

## 6.1 Statements and Blocks

The two basic statements are *expression statements* and *declaration statements*, of which you've seen a plethora. Expression statements, such as i++ or method invocations, are expressions that have a semicolon at the end. The semicolon terminates the statement.[1] Not all expressions can become statements, since it would be almost always meaningless to have, for example, a <= test stand alone as a statement. Only the following types of expressions can be made into statements by adding a terminating semicolon:

◆ Assignment expressions—those that contain = or one of the *op=* operators

◆ Prefix or postfix forms of ++ and --

---

[1]. The distinction between *terminator* and *separator* is important. The comma between identifiers in declarations is a *separator,* because it comes between elements in the list. The semicolon is a *terminator* because it comes after every statement. If the semicolon were a statement separator, the last semicolon in a code block would be unnecessary, and (depending upon the choice of the language designer) possibly invalid.

◆ Method calls (whether they return a value or not)

◆ Object creation expressions—those that use new to create an object

Declaration statements (formally called local variable declaration statements) declare a variable and initialize it to a value. These may appear anywhere inside a block, not just at the beginning. Local variables exist only as long as the block containing their declaration is executing. Local variables must be initialized before use, either by initialization when declared, or by assignment. If any local variable is used before it is initialized, the code will not compile.

Besides the expression statements listed above, several other kinds of statements such as if and for affect flow of control through the program. This chapter covers each type of statement in detail.

Braces ({ and }) group zero or more statements into a *block*. A block can be used where any single statement is allowed because a block *is* a statement, albeit compound.

## 6.2 `if-else`

The most basic form of conditional control flow is the if statement, which chooses whether to execute following statements. Its syntax is

```
if (boolean-expression)
        statement1
else
        statement2
```

First, the boolean expression is evaluated. If its value is true, then *statement1* is executed; otherwise, if there is an else part, *statement2* is executed. The else clause is optional.

A series of tests can be built up by joining another if to the else clause of a previous if. Here is a method that maps a string—expected to be one of a particular set of words—into an action to perform with a value:

```
public void setProperty(String keyword, double value)
    throws UnknownProperty
{
    if (keyword.equals("charm"))
        charm(value);
    else if (keyword.equals("strange"))
        strange(value);
```

```
    else
        throw new UnknownProperty(keyword);
}
```

What happens if there is more than one preceding `if` without an `else`? For example:

```
public double sumPositive(double[] values) {
    double sum = 0.0;

    if (values.length > 1)
        for (int i = 0; i < values.length; i++)
            if (values[i] > 0)
                sum += values[i];
    else    // oops!
        sum = values[0];
    return sum;
}
```

The `else` clause *looks* as if it is bound to the array length check, but that is a mirage of indentation, and Java ignores indentation. Instead, an `else` clause is bound to the most recent `if` that does not have one. Thus, the previous block of code is equivalent to

```
public double sumPositive(double[] values) {
    double sum = 0.0;

    if (values.length > 1)
        for (int i = 0; i < values.length; i++)
            if (values[i] > 0)
                sum += values[i];
            else    // oops!
                sum = values[0];
    return sum;
}
```

This is probably not what was intended. To bind the `else` clause to the first `if`, you can use braces to create blocks:

```
public double sumPositive(double[] values) {
    double sum = 0.0;

    if (values.length > 1) {
```

```
        for (int i = 0; i < values.length; i++)
            if (values[i] > 0)
                sum += values[i];
    } else {           // oops!
        sum = values[0];
    }
    return sum;
}
```

## Exercise 6.1

Using if/else, write a method that takes a string parameter and returns a string
with all the special characters in the original string replaced by their Java equivalents. For example, a string with a " in the middle of it should create a return value
with that " replaced by \".   ▲

## 6.3   switch

A switch statement evaluates an integer expression whose value is used to find an
appropriate case label among those listed inside the following block. If a matching case label is found, control is transferred to the first statement following it. If
not, control is transferred to the first statement following a default label. If there
is no default label, the entire switch statement is skipped.

This example dumps the state of an object, with greater verbosity adding new
output, and then printing out the output of the next lower-level of verbosity:

```
public static final int TERSE = 0,
                        NORMAL = 1,
                        BLATHERING = 2;

// ...

public int Verbosity = TERSE;

public void dumpState()
    throws UnexpectedStateException
{
    switch (Verbosity) {
      case BLATHERING:
        System.out.println(stateDetails);
        // FALLTHROUGH
      case NORMAL:
```

```
          System.out.println(basicState);
          // FALLTHROUGH

      case TERSE:
          System.out.println(summaryState);
          break;

      default:
          throw new UnexpectedStateException(Verbosity);
      }
  }
```

The class defines symbolic constants to represent the verbosity states. When the time arrives to dump the object's state, it is done at the requested verbosity level.

The "FALLTHROUGH" comments indicate that control *falls through* the following case label to the code below. Thus, if verbosity is BLATHERING, all three output parts are printed; if verbosity is NORMAL, two parts are printed; and if verbosity is TERSE, only one part is printed.

A case or default label does *not* force a break out of the switch. Nor does it imply an end to execution of statements. This is why we have a break statement after the TERSE output is finished. Without the break, execution would continue through into the code for the default label and throw the exception every time.

Falling through to the next case can be useful in some circumstances. But in most cases a break should come after the code that a case label selects. Good coding style suggests you always use some form of FALLTHROUGH comment to document an intentional fall-through.

Fall-through is most often used to have multiple case labels for the same code. This example uses fall-through to translate a hexadecimal digit into an int:

```
public int hexValue(char ch) throws NonHexDigitException {
    switch (ch) {
      case '0': case '1': case '2': case '3': case '4':
      case '5': case '6': case '7': case '8': case '9':
        return (ch - '0');

      case 'a': case 'b': case 'c':
      case 'd': case 'e': case 'f':
        return (ch - 'a') + 10;

      case 'A': case 'B': case 'C':
      case 'D': case 'E': case 'F':
        return (ch - 'A') + 10;
```

```
        default:
            throw new NonHexDigitException(ch);
    }
}
```

There are no `break` statements because the `return` statements exit the code blocks before they can fall through.

You should terminate the last group of statements in a switch with a `break`, `return`, or `throw`, as you would a group of statements in an earlier case. Doing so reduces the likelihood that a new `case` added at the end will be accidentally fallen into from what *used* to be the last part of the switch.

All `case` labels must be constant expressions, that is, the expressions must contain only literals and `static final` fields initialized with constant expressions. In any single `switch` statement, each `case` value must be unique, and there can be at most one `default` label.

### Exercise 6.2

Rewrite your method from Exercise 6.1 to use a `switch`.    ▲

## 6.4    `while` and `do-while`

The `while` loop looks like this:

```
while (boolean-expression)
        statement
```

The boolean expression is evaluated, and if it is `true`, the statement (which can, of course, be a block) is executed repeatedly until the boolean expression evaluates to `false`.

A `while` loop executes zero or more times, since the boolean expression might be `false` the first time it is evaluated.

Sometimes you really want to execute a loop body at least once, which is why Java has a do-`while` construct as well:

```
do
        statement
while (boolean-expression);
```

Here, the boolean expression is evaluated *after* the statement is executed. While it is `true`, the statement is executed repeatedly. The statement in a do-`while` loop is almost always a block.

## 6.5   for

The `for` statement is used to loop over a range of values from beginning to end. It looks like this:

```
for (init-expr; boolean-expr; incr-expr)
        statement
```

This is equivalent to

```
{
    init-expr;
    while (boolean-expr) {
        statement
        incr-expr;
    }
}
```

with the proviso that *incr-expr* is always executed if a `continue` is encountered (see "continue" on page 130).

Typically, the `for` loop is used to iterate a variable over a range of values until some logical end to that range is reached.

The initialization and iteration statements of a `for` loop can be a comma-separated list of expressions. The expressions separated by the commas are, like all operators, evaluated left-to-right. For example, to march two indices through an array in opposite directions, the following code would be appropriate:

```
for (i = 0, j = arr.length - 1; j >= 0; i++, j--) {
    // ...
}
```

You can define what an iteration range is. A `for` loop is often used, for example, to iterate through the elements of a linked list or to follow a mathematical sequence of values. This makes the `for` construct more powerful than equivalent constructs in many other languages, which restrict `for`-style constructs to incrementing a variable over a range of values.

Here is an example of such a loop, designed to calculate the smallest power of 10 that is larger than the value:

```
public static int tenPower(int value) {
    int exp, v;
    for (exp = 0, v = value - 1; v > 0; exp++, v /= 10)
        continue;
    return exp;
}
```

In this case, two variables move synchronously through the value range: the exponent (exp) and the value of $10^{exp}$ (v). Both the test value and exponent are looped over. In such cases, a comma-separated list of expressions is the correct technique to use to ensure that they are always in lockstep.

The body of this loop is simply a `continue` statement, which starts the next iteration of the loop. The body of the loop has nothing to do—all the work of the loop is in the test and iteration clauses of the `for` statement itself. The `continue` style shown here is one way to show an empty loop body; another is to put a simple semicolon on a line by itself, or to have an empty block with braces. Simply putting a semicolon at the end of the `for` line is dangerous—if the semicolon is accidentally deleted or forgotten, the statement that follows the `for` can silently become the body of the `for`.

All of the expressions in the `for` construct are optional. If *init-expr* or *incr-expr* is left out, its part in the loop is simply omitted. If *boolean-expr* is left out, it is assumed to be `true`. Thus, the idiomatic way to write an infinite loop is as a "for ever" loop:

```
for (;;)
        statement
```

Presumably the loop is terminated by some other means, such as a `break` statement described below, or by throwing an exception.

Conventionally, the `for` loop is used only when looping through a range of related values. Violating this convention by using initialization or increment expressions that are unrelated to the boolean loop test is bad style.

### Exercise 6.3

Write a method that takes two `char` parameters and prints out the characters including and between those two values.   ▲

## 6.6   Labels

Statements can be labeled. Labels are typically used on blocks and loops. A label precedes a statement like this:

```
label: statement
```

Labeled blocks are useful with `break` and `continue`.

## 6.7   break

A `break` statement can be used to exit from *any* block, not just a `switch`. A `break` is most often used to break out of a loop, but can be used to immediately exit any block. Here is an example where we are looking for the first empty slot in an array of references to Contained objects:

```
class Container {
    private Contained[] Objs;

    // ...

    public void addIn(Contained obj)
        throws NoEmptySlotException
    {
        int i;
        for (i = 0; i < Objs.length; i++)
            if (Objs[i] == null)
                break;
        if (i >= Objs.length)
            throw new NoEmptySlotException();
        Objs[i] = obj;      // put it inside me
        obj.inside(this); // let it know it's inside me
    }
}
```

An unlabeled break terminates the innermost switch, for, while, or do. To terminate an outer statement, label the outer statement and use its label name in the break statement:

```
private float[][] Matrix;

public boolean workOnFlag(float flag) {
    int y, x;
    boolean found = false;

  search:
    for (y = 0; y < Matrix.length; y++) {
        for (x = 0; x < Matrix[y].length; x++) {
            if (Matrix[y][x] == flag) {
                found = true;
                break search;
            }
        }
    }
    if (!found)
        return false;
```

```
    // do some stuff with flagged value at Matrix[y][x]
    return true;
}
```

Whether to always use labels is a matter of individual preference. However, always using labels is a good defensive measure against a later maintainer of the code enclosing your code with a switch statement or a loop.

Note that a labeled `break` is not a `goto`. The `goto` statement enables indiscriminate jumping around in code, obfuscating the flow of control. A `break` or `continue` that references a label, on the other hand, exits from or repeats only that specific labeled block, and the flow of control is obvious by inspection.

## 6.8    continue

A `continue` statement skips to the end of a loop's body and evaluates the boolean expression that controls the loop. A `continue` is often used to skip over an element of a loop range that can be ignored or treated with trivial code. For example, a token stream that included a simple "skip" token might be handled like this:

```
while (!stream.eof()) {
    token = stream.next();
    if (token.equals("skip"))
        continue;
    // ... process token ...
}
```

A `continue` statement has meaning only inside loops—`while`, `do-while`, and `for`. A `continue` statement can specify a label of an enclosing loop, which applies the `continue` to the named loop instead of the innermost loop. A labeled `continue` will break out of any inner loops on its way to the next iteration of the named loop. No label is required on the `continue` in the example above since there is only one enclosing loop.

## 6.9    return

A `return` statement terminates execution of a method and returns to the invoker. If the method returns no value, a simple return statement will do:

```
return;
```

If the method has a return type, the `return` must include an expression of a type that could be assigned to the return type. For example, if a method returns `double`, a `return` could have an expression that was a `double`, `float`, or integer:

```
protected double nonNegative(double val) {
    if (val < 0)
        return 0;   // an int constant
    else
        return val; // a double
}
```

A `return` can also be used to exit constructors and static initializer code. Neither construct has a return value, so `return` is used without specifying a return value. Constructors are invoked as part of the new process which in the end *does* return a reference to an object, but each constructor plays only a part of that role; no constructor "returns" the final reference.

## 6.10   What, No goto?

Java has no `goto` construct to transfer control to an arbitrary statement in a method, although `goto` is common in languages to which Java is related. The primary uses for `goto` in these other languages are:

♦ Controlling outer loops from within nested loops. Java provides labeled `break` and `continue` statements to meet this need.

♦ Skipping the rest of a block of code that is not in a loop when an answer or error is found. Use a labeled `break`.

♦ Executing cleanup code before a method or block of code exits. Use either a labelled break or, more cleanly, the `finally` construct of the `try` statement covered in the next chapter.

Labeled `break` and `continue` have the advantage that they transfer control to a strictly limited place. A `finally` block is even stricter as to where it transfers control, and it works in all circumstances, including exceptions. With these constructs we are able to write clean Java code without a `goto`.

# CHAPTER 7

# Exceptions

*A slipping gear could let your M203 grenade launcher fire when you least expect it.*
*That would make you quite unpopular in what's left of your unit.*
—The U.S. Army's *PS* magazine, August 1993

**D**URING execution, applications can run into many kinds of errors of varying degrees of severity. When methods are invoked on an object, the object can discover internal state problems (inconsistent values of variables), detect errors with objects or data it manipulates (such as a file or network address), determine that it is violating its basic contract (such as reading data from an already closed stream), and so on.

Many programmers do not test for all possible error conditions, and for good reason: code becomes unintelligible if each method invocation checks for all possible errors before the next is executed. This trade-off creates a tension between correctness (checking for all errors) and clarity (not cluttering the basic flow of code with many error checks).

Exceptions provide a clean way to check for errors without cluttering code. Exceptions also provide a mechanism to signal errors directly rather than using flags or side effects such as fields that must be checked. Exceptions make the error conditions that a method can signal an explicit part of the method's contract. The list of exceptions can be seen by the programmer, checked by the compiler, and preserved by extended classes that override the method.

An exception is *thrown* when an unexpected error condition is encountered. The exception is then *caught* by an encompassing clause up the method invocation stack. If the exception is not caught, a default exception handler takes effect, usually printing useful information about where the exception was thrown (such as a call stack).

## 7.1    Creating Exception Types

Exceptions in Java are objects. All exception types—that is, any class designed for throwable objects—must extend the Java language class `Throwable` or one of its subclasses. The `Throwable` class contains a string that can be used to describe the exception. By convention, new exception types extend `Exception` rather than `Throwable`.

Java exceptions are primarily *checked exceptions,* meaning that the compiler checks that your methods only throw exceptions they have declared themselves to throw. Standard runtime exceptions and errors extend the classes `RuntimeException` and `Error`, thereby creating *unchecked exceptions*. All exceptions you create should extend `Exception`, making them checked exceptions.

Sometimes it is useful to have more data to describe the exceptional condition than just the string that `Exception` provides. In such cases, `Exception` can be extended to create a class that contains the added data (usually set in the constructor).

For example, suppose a `replaceValue` method is added to the `Attributed` interface discussed in Chapter 4. This method replaces the current value of a named attribute with a new value. If the named attribute doesn't exist, an exception should be thrown, since it is reasonable to assume that one should replace only existing attributes. That exception should contain the name of the attribute, and the new value to which the attribute was to be set. To represent the exception, create the `NoSuchAttributeException` class:

```java
public class NoSuchAttributeException extends Exception {
    public String attrName;
    public Object newValue;

    NoSuchAttributeException(String name, Object value) {
        super("No attribute named \"" + name + "\" found");
        attrName = name;
        newValue = value;
    }
}
```

`NoSuchAttributeException` extends `Exception` to add a constructor that takes the name of the attribute and its intended value; it also adds public fields to store the data. The constructor invokes the superclass' constructor with a string description of what happened. This exception type is useful to code that catches the exception because it holds both a human-usable description of the error and the data that created the error. Adding useful data is one reason to create a new exception type.

Another reason to create a new exception type is that the type of the exception is an important part of the exception data, because exceptions are caught according to their type. For this reason, you would invent NoSuchAttributeException even if you did not want to add data, so that a programmer who cared only about such an exception could catch it exclusive of other exceptions that might be generated either by the Attributed interface's methods, or by other methods used on other objects in the same area of code.

In general, new exception types should be created when programmers will want to handle one kind of error and not another. Programmers can then use the exception type to execute the correct code, rather than examining the contents of the exception to determine whether they really care about the exception, or caught an irrelevant exception by accident.

## 7.2 throw

Exceptions are thrown using the throw statement, which takes an object as its parameter. For example, here is an addition to AttributedImpl from Chapter 4 that implements replaceValue:

```
public void replaceValue(String name, Object newValue)
    throws NoSuchAttributeException
{
    Attr attr = find(name);          // look up the attr
    if (attr == null)                // it isn't found
        throw new NoSuchAttributeException(name, this);
    attr.valueOf(newValue);
}
```

The replaceValue method first looks up the current Attr object for the name. If there isn't one, it throws a new object of type NoSuchAttributeException, providing the constructor with the descriptive data. Exceptions are objects, so they must be created before being thrown. If the attribute does exist, its value is replaced with the new value.

An exception can, of course, also be generated by invoking a method that itself throws an exception.

## 7.3 The throws Clause

The first thing the replaceValue method above does is declare which checked exceptions it throws. Java requires the declaration of checked exceptions that methods throw, because programmers invoking a method need to know the exceptions it can throw just as much as they need to know its normal behavior. The checked exceptions that a method throws are as important as the type of value it returns. Both should be declared.

The checked exceptions a method can throw are declared with a `throws` clause, which takes a comma-separated list of exception types.

You can throw exceptions that are extensions of the type of exception in the `throws` clause, because you can use a class polymorphically anywhere its superclass is expected. A method may throw several different classes of exceptions that are all extensions of a particular exception class, and declare only the superclass in the `throws` clause. By doing so, however, you hide potentially useful information from programmers invoking the method, since they don't know which of the possible extended exception types could be thrown. For documentation purposes, the `throws` clause should be as complete and specific as possible.

The contract defined by the `throws` clause is strictly enforced—you can throw only a type of exception that has been declared in the `throws` clause. Throwing any other type of exception is invalid, whether directly using `throw`, or indirectly by invoking another method. If a method has no `throws` clause, it does not mean that *any* exceptions may be thrown: it means *no* exceptions may be thrown.

All of the standard runtime exceptions (such as `ClassCastException` and `ArithmeticException`) are extensions of the `RuntimeException` class. More serious errors are signaled by exceptions that are extensions of `Error`, and these exceptions can occur at any time in any code. `RuntimeException` and `Error` are the only exceptions you do not need to list in your `throws` clauses—they are ubiquitous, and every method can potentially throw these exceptions. This is why they are unchecked by the compiler. The complete list of standard unchecked exception classes is in Appendix B.

Initializers and static initialization code blocks cannot throw checked exceptions, either directly or by invoking a method that throws such an exception. There is nothing to catch and handle exceptions during object construction. When initializing fields, the solution is to initialize them inside a constructor, which *can* throw exceptions. For static initializers, the solution is to put the initialization inside a static block that catches and handles the exception. Static blocks cannot *throw* exceptions, but they can *catch* them.

Java is strict about enforcing checked exception handling because doing so helps avoid bugs that come from not dealing with errors. Experience has shown that programmers forget to handle errors, or defer handling them until some coding future that never arrives. The `throws` clause states clearly which exceptions are being thrown by methods and makes sure they are dealt with in some way by the invoker.

If you invoke a method that lists a checked exception in its `throws` clause, you have three choices:

◆ Catch the exception and handle it.

◆ Catch the exception and map it into one of your exceptions by throwing an exception of a type declared in your own `throws` clause.

◆ Declare the exception in your `throws` clause and let the exception pass through your method (although you might have a `finally` clause that cleans up first; see below for details).

To do any of these things, you need to catch exceptions thrown by other methods, which is the subject of the next section.

### *Exercise 7.1*

Create an `ObjectNotFoundException` class for the `LinkedList` class we've built in previous exercises. Add a `find` method to look for an object in the list, and either returns the `LinkedList` object that contains the desired object, or throws the exception if the object isn't found in the list. Why is this preferable to returning `null` if the object isn't found? What data should `ObjectNotFoundException` contain?  ▲

## 7.4   try, catch, and finally

Exceptions are caught by enclosing code in `try` blocks. The basic syntax for a `try` block is:

```
try
        block
catch (exception_type identifier)
        block
catch (exception_type identifier)
        block

        . . . . .

finally
        block
```

The body of the `try` statement is executed until either an exception is thrown or it finishes successfully. If an exception is thrown, the `catch` clauses are examined in order to find one for an exception of that class or one of the exception's superclasses. If no appropriate `catch` is found, the exception percolates out of the `try` statement into any outer `try` that might handle it. There can be any number of `catch` clauses in a `try`, including none. If no `catch` clause in the method catches the exception, the exception is thrown to the code that invoked this method.

If a `finally` clause is present in a `try`, its code is executed after all other processing in the `try` is complete. This happens no matter how the completion was achieved, whether normally, through an exception, or through a control flow statement like `return` or `break`.

This example code is prepared to handle one of the exceptions `replaceValue` threw:

```
try {
    attributedObj.replaceValue("Age", new Integer(8));
} catch (NoSuchAttributeException e) {
    // shouldn't happen, but recover if it does
    Attr attr = new Attr(e.attrName, e.newValue);
    attributedObj.add(attr);
}
```

The `try` sets up a statement (which must be a block) that does something that is normally expected to succeed. If everything succeeds, the block is finished. If any exception is thrown during execution of the code in the `try` block, either directly via a `throw` or indirectly by a method invoked inside it, execution of the code inside the `try` stops, and the attached `catch` clause is examined to see if it wants to catch the exception that was thrown.

A `catch` clause is somewhat like an embedded method that has one parameter—namely, the exception to be caught. Inside a `catch` clause, you can attempt to recover from the exception, or you can clean up and re-throw the exception so that any code calling yours has a chance to catch it, too. Or a `catch` can do what it needs to, and then fall out the bottom, in which case control flows to the statement after the `try` statement (after executing the `finally` clause, if there is one).

A general `catch` clause—that catches exceptions of type `Exception`, for example—is usually a poor implementation choice, since it will catch *any* exception, not just the specific one we are interested in. Had we used such a clause in our code, it could have ended up handling, for instance, a `ClassCastException` as if it were a missing attribute problem.

Each `catch` clause in a `try` is examined in turn, from first to last, to see if the type of the exception object is assignable to the type declared in the `catch`. When an assignable `catch` clause is found, its block is executed with its identifier set to reference the exception object. No other `catch` clause will be executed. Any number of `catch` clauses can be associated with a particular `try`, as long as each catches a different type of exception.

Because the `catch` clauses are examined in order, a `catch` that picks up one exception type before a `catch` for an extended type of exception is a mistake. The first clause would always catch the exception, and the second clause would never be reached. For this reason, putting a superclass `catch` clause before a `catch` of one of its subclasses is a compile-time error:

```
class SuperException extends Exception { }
class SubException extends SuperException { }

class BadCatch {
    public void goodTry() {
        /* This is an INVALID catch ordering */
        try {
            throw new SubException();
        } catch (SuperException superRef) {
            // Catches both SuperException and SubException
        } catch (SubException subRef) {
            // This would never be reached
        }
    }
}
```

Only one exception is handled by any single encounter with a `try` clause. If a `catch` or `finally` clause throws another exception, the `catch` clauses of the `try` are not reexamined. The `catch` and `finally` clauses are outside the protection of the `try` clause itself. Such exceptions can, of course, be handled by any encompassing `try` block in which the inner `catch` or `finally` clauses were nested.

### 7.4.1   `finally`

The `finally` clause of a `try` statement provides a mechanism for executing a section of code whether or not an exception is thrown. Usually this involves cleaning up internal state or releasing non-object resources, such as open files stored in local variables. Here is a method that closes a file when its work is done, even if an error occurs:

```
public boolean searchFor(String file, String word)
    throws StreamException
{
    Stream input = null;
```

```
try {
    input = new Stream(file);
    while (!input.eof())
        if (input.next() == word)
            return true;
    return false;          // not found
} finally {
    if (input != null)
        input.close();
}
}
```

If the new fails, `input` will never be changed from its initial `null` value. If the new succeeds, `input` will reference the object that represents the open file. When the `finally` clause is executed, the `input` stream is closed only if it has been open. Whether or not the operations on the stream generate an exception, the contents of the `finally` clause ensure that the file is closed, thus conserving the limited resource of simultaneous open files. The `searchFor` method declares that it throws `StreamException` so that any exceptions generated are passed through to the invoking code after cleanup.

A `finally` clause can be used to clean up for `break`, `continue`, and `return` as well, which is why you will sometimes see a `try` clause with no `catch` clauses. When processing any control transfer statement, all `finally` clauses are executed. There is no way to leave a `try` block without executing its `finally` clause.

The example above relies on `finally` in this way to clean up even with a normal `return`. One of the most common reasons `goto` is used in other languages is to ensure that certain things are cleaned up when a block of code is complete, whether or not it was successful. In our example, the `finally` clause ensures that the file is closed on either `return` statement, or if the stream throws an exception.

A `finally` clause is always entered with a reason. That reason may be that the `try` code finished normally, that it executed a control flow statement such as `return`, or that an exception was thrown in code executed in the `try` block. The reason is remembered when the `finally` clause exits by falling out the bottom. However, if the `finally` block creates its own reason to leave by executing a control flow statement (such as `break` or `return`), or by throwing an exception, that reason supersedes the original one, and the original reason is forgotten. For example, consider the following code:

```
try {
    // ... do something ...
    return 1;
```

```
} finally {
    return 2;
}
```

When the `try` block executes its return, the `finally` block is entered with a "reason" of returning the value 1. However, inside the `finally` block the value 2 is returned, so the initial intention is forgotten. In fact, if any of the other code in the `try` block had thrown an exception, the result would still be to return 2. If the `finally` block did not return a value but simply fell out the bottom, the "return the value 1" reason would be remembered and implemented.

## 7.5    When to Use Exceptions

We used the phrase "unexpected error condition" at the beginning of this chapter when describing when to throw exceptions. Exceptions are not meant for simple, expected situations. For example, reaching the end of a stream of input is expected, so the method that returns the next input from the stream has "hit the end" as part of its expected behavior. A return code indicating end-of-input is reasonable, as it is for callers to check the return value, and such a convention is also easier to understand. Compare a typical loop using a return flag,

```
while ((token = stream.next()) != Stream.END)
    process(token);
stream.close();
```

to this loop that relies on an exception to signal the reaching the end of input:

```
try {
    for (;;) {
        process(stream.next());
    }
} catch (StreamEndException e) {
    stream.close();
}
```

In the first case, the flow of control is direct and clear. The code loops until it reaches the end of the stream, and then it closes the stream. In the second case, the code seems to loop forever. Unless you know that end of input is signaled with a `StreamEndException`, you don't know the loop's natural range. Even when you know about `StreamEndException`, this construction still moves the loop termination out of the loop (the `for`) and into the surrounding `try` block, which is confusing.

In some situations no reasonable flag value exists. For example, a class for a stream of `double` values can contain any valid `double`, and there is no possible end-of-stream marker. The most reasonable design is to add an explicit `eof` test method that should be called before any read from the stream:

```
while (!stream.eof())
    process(stream.nextDouble());
stream.close();
```

On the other hand, continuing to read *past* an end-of-file is not expected. It means that the program didn't notice the end and is trying to do something it should never attempt. This is an excellent case for a `ReadPastEndException`. Such behavior is outside the expected use of your stream class, and throwing an exception is the right way to handle it.

Deciding which situations are expected and which are not is a fuzzy area. The point is not to abuse exceptions as a way to report expected situations.

### *Exercise 7.2*

Decide which way you think the following conditions should be communicated to the programmer:

- A program tries to set the capacity of a `PassengerVehicle` object to a negative value.

- A syntax error is found in a configuration file that an object uses to set its initial state.

- A method that searches for a programmer-specified word in a string array cannot find any occurrence of the word.

- A file provided to an "open" method does not exist.

- A file provided to an "open" method exists, but security prevents the user from using it.

- During an attempt to open a network connection to a remote server process, the remote machine cannot be contacted.

- In the middle of a conversation with a remote server process, the network connection stops operating.  ▲

# CHAPTER 8

# Strings

*What's the use of a good quotation if you can't change it?*
—Dr. Who, *The Two Doctors*

**J**AVA strings are standard objects with built-in language support. You have already seen many examples of using quotes to create string objects. You've also seen the + and += operators that concatenate strings to create new strings. The String class, however, has much more functionality to offer. String objects are read-only, so Java also provides a StringBuffer class for mutable strings. This chapter describes the String and StringBuffer classes, including conversion of strings to other types like integers and booleans.

## 8.1  Basic String Operations

The String class provides read-only strings and supports operations on them. Strings can be created implicitly either by using a quoted string (such as "Größe") or by using + or += on two String objects to create a new one.

You can also construct String objects explicitly using the new mechanism. The String class supports the following constructors:

public **String()**
> Constructs a new String with the value "".

public **String(String value)**
> Constructs a new String that is a copy of the specified String object value.

The two basic methods of String objects are length and charAt. The length method returns the number of characters in the string, while charAt returns the char at the specified position. This loop counts the number of each kind of character in a string:

```
for (int i = 0; i < str.length(); i++)
    counts[str.charAt(i)]++;
```

Access to a string position less than zero or greater than length() - 1 throws an IndexOutOfBoundsException, in charAt or any other String method. Such invalid accesses usually occur because of bugs in code.

There are also simple methods to find the first or last occurrence of a particular character or substring in a string. This method returns the number of characters between the first and last occurrences of a particular character in a string:

```
static int countBetween(String str, char ch) {
    int begPos = str.indexOf(ch);
    if (begPos < 0)            // not there
        return -1;
    int endPos = str.lastIndexOf(ch);
    return endPos - begPos - 1;
}
```

This method finds the first and last positions of the character ch in the string str. If the character does not occur twice in the string, the method returns -1. The difference between the two character positions is one more than the number of characters in between (if the two positions were 2 and 3, the number of characters in between is 0).

Several indexing methods overload indexOf for methods that search forward in a string, and lastIndexOf for methods that search backward. Each returns the index of what it found, or -1 if the search was unsuccessful:

| Method | Returns index of... |
| --- | --- |
| indexOf(char ch) | first position of ch |
| indexOf(char ch, int start) | first position of ch $\geq$ start |
| indexOf(String str) | first position of str |
| indexOf(String str, int start) | first position of str $\geq$ start |
| lastIndexOf(char ch) | last position of ch |
| lastIndexOf(char ch, int start) | last position of ch $\leq$ start |
| lastIndexOf(String str) | last position of str |
| lastIndexOf(String str, int start) | last position of str $\leq$ start |

### Exercise 8.1

Write a method that counts the number of occurrences of a given character in a string.  ▲

*Exercise 8.2*

Write a method that counts the number of occurrences of a particular string in another string. ▲

## 8.2   String Comparisons

The String class supports several methods to compare strings and parts of strings. Before we describe the methods, though, we must explain that internationalization and localization issues of full Unicode strings are not addressed with these methods. For example, when comparing two strings to determine which is "greater," characters in strings are compared numerically by their Unicode values, not by their localized notion of order. To a French speaker, c and ç are the same letter with a small diacritical mark the only difference. Sorting a set of strings in French should ignore the difference between them, placing "aça" before "acz." But the Unicode characters are different—c (\u0063) comes before ç (\u00e7) in the Unicode character set, so these strings will actually sort the other way around.

The first compare operation is equals, which returns true if it is passed a reference to a String object with the same contents—that is, the two strings have the same length and exactly the same Unicode characters. If the other object isn't a String, or the contents are different, String.equals returns false.

To compare strings while ignoring case, use the equalsIgnoreCase method. By "ignore case," we mean that Ë and ë are considered the same, but different from E and e. Characters without a case distinction, such as punctuation, compare equal only to themselves. Unicode has many interesting case issues, including a notion of "title case." Case issues in the String class are handled in terms of the case-related methods of the Character class, described in Section 13.5 on page 253.

To sort strings, you need a way to compare them. The compareTo method returns an int that is less than, equal to, or greater than zero when the string on which it is invoked is less than, equal to, or greater than the other. The ordering used is Unicode character ordering.

The compareTo method is useful for creating an internal canonical ordering of strings. A binary search, for example, requires a sorted list of elements, but it is unimportant that the sorted order be local language order. Here is a binary search lookup method for a class that has a sorted array of strings:

```java
private String[] table;

public int position(String key) {
    int lo = 0;
    int hi = table.length - 1;
```

```
        while (lo <= hi) {
            int mid = lo + (hi - lo) / 2;
            int cmp = key.compareTo(table[mid]);
            if (cmp == 0)          // found it!
                return mid;
            else if (cmp < 0)    // search the lower part
                hi = mid - 1;
            else                   // search the upper part
                lo = mid + 1;
        }
        return -1;                 // not found
    }
```

This is the basic binary search algorithm. It first checks the midpoint of the search range to determine if the key is greater than, equal to, or less than the element at that position. If they are the same, the element has been found and the search is over. If the key is less than the element at the position, the lower half of the range is searched; otherwise, the upper half is searched. Eventually the element is found, or the lower end of the range becomes greater than the higher end, in which case the key is not in the list.

In addition to entire strings, regions of strings can also be compared for equality. The method for this is regionMatches, and it has two forms: one that does exact character matching like equals, and one that does case-insensitive matching just like equalsIgnoreCase:

public boolean **regionMatches(int start, String other, int ostart, int len)**
> Returns true if the given region of this String matches the given region of the string other. Checking starts in this string at the position start, and in the other string at position ostart. Only the first len characters are compared.

public boolean **regionMatches(boolean ignoreCase, int start, String other, int ostart, int len)**
> This version of regionMatches behaves exactly like the previous one, but the boolean ignoreCase controls whether case is significant.

For example:

```
class RegionMatch {
    public static void main(String[] args) {
        String str = "Look, look!";
        boolean b1, b2, b3;
```

```
            b1 = str.regionMatches(6, "Look," 0, 4);
            b2 = str.regionMatches(true, 6, "Look", 0, 4);
            b3 = str.regionMatches(true, 6, "Look", 0, 5);

            System.out.println("b1 = " + b1);
            System.out.println("b2 = " + b2);
            System.out.println("b3 = " + b3);
        }
    }
```

Here is its output:

```
    b1 = false
    b2 = true
    b3 = false
```

The first comparison is false because the character at position 6 of the main string is 'l', and the character at position 0 of the other string is 'L'. The second comparison is true because case is not significant. The third comparison yields false because the comparison length is now 5, and the two strings are not the same over five characters, even ignoring case.

You can do simple tests for the beginning and ends of strings using startsWith and endsWith:

public boolean **startsWith(String prefix, int toffset)**
> Returns true if this String starts (at toffset) with the given prefix.

public boolean **startsWith(String prefix)**
> This is a shorthand for startsWith(prefix, 0).

public boolean **endsWith(String suffix)**
> Returns true if this String ends with the given suffix.

In general, strings cannot be compared using == like this:

```
    if (str == "¿Peña?")
        answer(str);
```

This does not compare the contents of the two strings. It compares only one object reference (str) to another (the transient string object representing the constant "¿Peña?"). The references could be to different objects, even if both string objects had the same contents.

However, any two string literals with the same contents will refer to the same `String` object. For example, == probably works correctly in the following code:

```
String str = "¿Peña?";
// ...
if (str == "¿Peña?")
    answer(str);
```

Because `str` is initially set to a string literal, comparing against another string literal is equivalent to comparing the strings for equal contents. But be careful—this trick only works if you are sure that all strings references involved come from string literals. If `str` is changed to refer to a manufactured `String` object, such as the result of a user typing some input, the == operator will return `false`, even if the user types ¿Peña? as their string.

## 8.3    Utility Functions

The `String` class provides two functions that are useful in special applications. One is `hashCode`, which returns a hash based on the contents of the string. Any two strings with the same contents will have the same hash code, although two different strings might also have the same hash. Hash codes are useful for hashtables, such as the `Hashtable` class in `java.util`.

The other utility method is `intern`, which returns a `String` that has the same contents as the one it is invoked on. However, any two strings with the same contents return the same `String` object from `intern`, which enables you to compare string *references* to test equality, instead of the slower test of string *contents*. For example:

```
int putIn(String key) {
    String unique = key.intern();
    int i;
    // see if it's in the table already
    for (i = 0; i < tableSize; i++)
        if (table[i] == unique)
            return i;
    // it's not there--add it in
    table[i] = unique;
    tableSize++;
    return i;
}
```

All the strings stored in the `table` array are the result of an `intern` call. The table is searched for a string that was the result of an `intern` call on another string that had the same contents as the key. If it's found, the search is done. If not, we add the unique representative of the key at the end. Dealing with the results of intern makes comparing object references equivalent to comparing string contents, but much faster.

## 8.4   Making Related Strings

Several String methods return new strings that are like the old one, but with a specified modification. New strings are returned because String objects are read only. Extracting quoted substrings from another string, for example, could be done with a method like this:

```
public static String quotedString(
    String from, char start, char end)
{
    int startPos = from.indexOf(start);
    int endPos = from.lastIndexOf(end);
    if (startPos == -1)     // no start found
        return null;
    else if (endPos == -1)  // no end found
        return from.substring(startPos);
    else                    // both start and end found
        return from.substring(startPos, endPos + 1);
}
```

The quotedString method returns a new String object containing the quoted string inside from that starts with the character start and ends with end. If start is found, but not end, the method returns a new String object containing everything from the start position to the end of the string. quotedString works by using the two overloaded forms of substring. The first form takes only an initial start position, and returns a new string containing everything in the original string from that point on. The second form takes both a start and end position, and returns a new string that contains all the characters in the original string from the start to the endpoint, including the character at the start but not at the end. This "up to but not including the end" behavior is why the method adds one to endPos to include the quotes in the returned string. For example, the string returned by

```
quotedString("Il a dit «Bonjour!»", '«', '»');
```

is

```
«Bonjour!»
```

Here are the rest of the "related string" methods:

public String **replace(char oldChar, char newChar)**
> Returns a new String with all instances of oldChar replaced with the character newChar.

public String **toLowerCase()**
> Returns a new String with each character converted to its lowercase equivalent if it has one.

public String **toUpperCase()**
> Returns a new String with each character converted to its uppercase equivalent if it has one.

public String **trim()**
> Returns a new String with any leading and trailing white space removed.

The concat method returns a new string equivalent to using + on two strings. These two statements are equivalent:

```
newStr = oldStr.concat(" (not)");
newStr = oldStr + " (not)";
```

*Exercise 8.3*

As shown, the quotedString method assumes only one quoted string per input string. Write a version that will pull out all the quoted strings and return an array. ▲

## 8.5   String Conversions

You often need to convert strings to and from something else, such as integers or booleans. Java conversion conventions are such that the type being converted *to* has the method that does the conversion. For example, converting *from* a String *to* an integer requires a static method in class Integer. Here is a table of all the types that Java will convert, and how to convert each to and from a String:

| **Type** | **To** String | **From** String |
| --- | --- | --- |
| boolean | String.valueOf(boolean) | new Boolean(String).booleanValue() |
| int | String.valueOf(int) | Integer.ParseInt(String, int base) |
| long | String.valueOf(long) | Long.ParseLong(String, int base) |
| float | String.valueOf(float) | new Float(String).floatValue() |
| double | String.valueOf(double) | new Double(String).doubleValue() |

For `boolean` and the floating-point values, the technique shown actually creates a `Float` or `Double` object, then asks for its numeric value. There is no floating-point equivalent for `parseInt` that directly parses a value.

There is no method that converts characters of the recognizable Java language forms (\b, \u*ddddd*, etc.) into `char` variables, or vice versa. You can call `String.valueOf` with a single `char`, to obtain a `String` containing that one character.

Neither are there ways to create or decode number strings in the Java language format, with a leading 0 meaning octal, and a leading 0x meaning hexadecimal notation.

Conversion to and from `byte` and `short` are done using `int`, since they fit within the range of an `int` and are always promoted to `int` anyway for evaluation in expressions.

New classes can support string encoding and decoding by having a `toString` method, and a constructor that creates a new object given the string description. Classes with a `toString` method can be used with `valueOf`. The method `valueOf(Object obj)` is defined to return either `"null"` or `obj.toString`. If all classes have a `toString` method, you can convert any object to a `String` by invoking `valueOf`.

## 8.6    Strings and char Arrays

A `String` maps to an array of `char`, and vice versa. You often want to build a string in a `char` array and then create a `String` object from the contents. Assuming that the writable `StringBuffer` class (described later) isn't adequate, several `String` methods and constructors help convert a `String` to an array of `char`, or an array of `char` to a `String`.

For example, to squeeze out all occurrences of a character from a string, a simple algorithm would be

```
public static String squeezeOut(String from, char toss) {
    char[] chars = from.toCharArray();
    int len = chars.length;
    for (int i = 0; i < len; i++) {
        if (chars[i] == toss) {
            --len;
            System.arraycopy(chars, i + 1,
                             chars, i, len - i);
            --i;    // reexamine this spot
        }
}
```

```
        }
        return new String(chars, 0, len);
    }
```

The squeezeOut method first converts its input string from into a character array using the method toCharArray. It then loops searching for toss characters. When an occurrence of toss is found, the length of the returned string is reduced by one, and all the characters in the array are shifted down. i is the decremented so that the new character at position i is examined to see if it should be tossed out. When the method is finished looping over the array, it returns a new String object that contains the squeezed string. The String constructor used takes the source array, the starting position within the array, and the number of characters as arguments.

There is also a String constructor that takes only the character array as a parameter and uses all of it. Both of these constructors make copies of the array, so you can change the array contents after you have created a String from it without affecting the contents of the String.

You can use the two static String.copyValueOf methods instead of the constructors if you prefer. For instance, squeezeOut could have been ended with

```
        return String.copyValueOf(chars, 0, len);
```

There is also a single-argument form of copyValueOf that copies the entire array. For completeness, two static valueOf methods are also equivalent to the two String constructors.

The toCharArray method is simple and sufficient for most needs. When more control is required over copying pieces of a string into a character array, you can use the getChars methods:

**public void getChars(int srcBegin, int srcEnd, char[] dst,
    int dstBegin)**

> Copies characters from this String into the specified array. The characters of the specified substring are copied into the character array, starting at dst[dstBegin]. The specified substring is the part of the string starting at srcBegin, up to but not including srcEnd. Any access outside the bounds of either String or char array throws an IndexOutOfBoundsException.

## 8.7   Strings and byte Arrays

There are methods to convert arrays of 8-bit characters to and from 16-bit Unicode String objects. The methods especially enable creating Unicode strings from ASCII and ISO-Latin-1 characters, which are the first 256 characters of the

Unicode character set. The methods are analogous to their character array counterparts:

public **String(byte[] bytes, int hiByte, int offset, int count)**

This constructor makes a new String whose value is the specified subarray of the array bytes, starting at offset and having count characters. The top 8 bits of each character can be specified in hiByte, which is usually 0, since this constructor is usually used to turn ASCII or ISO-Latin-1 8-bit characters into 16-bit Unicode strings. This throws IndexOutOfBoundsException if the offset and count arguments would make the constructor use elements outside the bounds of the array.

public **String(byte[] bytes, int hibyte)**

This is a shorthand for String(bytes, hibyte, 0, bytes.length).

public void **getBytes(int srcBegin, int srcEnd, byte[] dst,**
  **int dstBegin)**

Copies part of this string into the array dst, starting at dst[dstBegin]. The top 8 bits of each character in the string are lost. The part of the String copied is from position srcBegin up to *but not including* srcEnd. If any access required to execute the method is outside the bounds of the string or array, an IndexOutOfBoundsException is thrown.

Both of the String constructors for building from byte arrays make copies of the data so further modifications to the arrays will not affect the contents of the String.

## 8.8   The StringBuffer Class

If read-only strings were the only kind available, you would have to create a new String object for each intermediate result in a sequence of String manipulations. Consider, for example, how the compiler would evaluate the following expression:

```
public static String guillemete(String quote) {
    return '«' + quote + '»';
}
```

If the compiler were restricted to String expressions, it would have to do the following:

```
quoted = String.valueOf('«').concat(quote)
            .concat(String.valueOf('»'));
```

Each valueOf and concat invocation creates another String object, so this operation would construct four String objects, of which only one would be used afterwards. The others would have taken overhead to create, to set to proper values, and to garbage collect.

The compiler, of course, is more efficient than this. It uses a StringBuffer object to build strings from expressions, creating the final String only when necessary. StringBuffer objects can be modified, so new objects are not needed to hold intermediate results. Using StringBuffer, the previous string expression would be represented as

```
quoted = new StringBuffer().append('«')
            .append(quote).append('»').toString();
```

This creates just one StringBuffer object to hold the construction, appends stuff to it, then uses toString to create a String from the result.

To build and modify a string, you probably want to use the StringBuffer class. The StringBuffer class includes the following constructors:

public **StringBuffer()**
    Constructs a StringBuffer with an initial value of "".

public **StringBuffer(String str)**
    Constructs a StringBuffer with an initial value the same as str.

StringBuffer is similar to String, and it supports methods that have the same names and contracts as some String methods. However, StringBuffer does not extend String or vice versa. They are independent classes—both of them extensions of Object.

### 8.8.1   Modifying the Buffer

There are several ways to modify the buffer of a StringBuffer object, including appending to the end and inserting in the middle. The simplest method is setCharAt, which changes the character at a specific position. Here is a replace method that does what String.replace does, except that it uses a StringBuffer object. The replace method doesn't need to create a new object to hold the results, so successive replace calls can operate on one buffer:

```
public static void
    replace(StringBuffer str, char from, char to)
{
    for (int i = 0; i < str.length(); i++)
        if (str.charAt(i) == from)
            str.setCharAt(i, to);
}
```

The `setLength` method truncates or extends the string in the buffer. If you `setLength` with a length smaller than the length of the current string, the string is truncated to the specified length. If the length is longer than the current string, the string is extended by filling with null characters (\u0000).

There are also `append` and `insert` methods to convert any data type to a `String`, then append the result to the end or insert the result at a specified position. The insert methods shift characters over to make room for inserted characters as needed. Types converted by these `append` and `insert` methods are:

```
Object      String      char[]
boolean     char        int
long        float       double
```

There are also `append` and `insert` methods that take part of a `char` array as an argument. For example, to create a `StringBuffer` that describes the square root of an integer, you could write:

```
String sqrtInt(int i) {
    StringBuffer buf = new StringBuffer();

    buf.append("sqrt(").append(i).append(')');
    buf.append(" = ").append(Math.sqrt(i));
    return buf.toString();
}
```

The `append` and `insert` methods return the `StringBuffer` object itself, enabling us to append to the result of a previous append.

The `insert` methods take two parameters. The first is the index at which to insert characters into the `StringBuffer`. The second is the value to insert, after conversion to a `String` if necessary. Here is a method to put the current date at the beginning of a buffer:

```
public static StringBuffer addDate(StringBuffer buf) {
    String now = new java.util.Date().toString();
    buf.ensureCapacity(buf.length() + now.length() + 2);
    buf.insert(0, now).insert(now.length(), ": ");
    return buf;
}
```

First create a string with the current time using `java.util.Date`, whose default constructor creates an object that represents the time it was created. Ensure that the buffer is big enough to include the new characters we will add, so that the buffer will have to grow at most once, instead of once for each `insert`. Then insert the string that represents "now," followed by a simple separator string.

Return the buffer you were passed so that invoking code can use the same kind of method concatenation that proved useful in StringBuffer's own methods.

The reverse method reverses the order of characters in the StringBuffer. For example, if the contents of the buffer are "good", the contents after invoking reverse are "doog".

### 8.8.2 Getting Data Out

To get a String object from a StringBuffer object, you invoke toString.

There are no StringBuffer methods to remove a part of a buffer—you have to create a character array from the buffer and build a new buffer with the remaining contents. This is the most likely use for the getChars method, which is analogous to String.getChars.

public void **getChars(int srcBegin, int srcEnd, char[] dst,**
  **int dstBegin)**

    Copies the characters of the specified part of the buffer (determined by srcBegin and srcEnd) into the array dst, starting at dst[dstBegin]. Copying starts at the position srcBegin and goes up to, *but does not include*, the position at srcEnd. srcBegin must be a legal index in the buffer, and srcEnd can be no greater than the current string buffer length (which is one beyond the legal last index). If either index is invalid, an IndexOutOfBoundsException is thrown.

Here is a method that uses getChars to remove part of a buffer:

```
public static StringBuffer
    remove(StringBuffer buf, int pos, int cnt)
{
    if (pos < 0 || cnt < 0 || pos + cnt > buf.length())
        throw new IndexOutOfBoundsException();

    int leftover = buf.length() - (pos + cnt);
    if (leftover == 0) {    // a simple truncation
        buf.setLength(pos);
        return buf;
    }

    char[] chrs = new char[leftover];
    buf.getChars(pos + cnt, buf.length(), chrs, 0);
    buf.setLength(pos);
```

```
        buf.append(chrs);
        return buf;
    }
```

First ensure that the array references will stay in bounds. You could handle the actual exception later, but checking now gives you more control. Then calculate how many bytes are left over after the removed portion. If none, truncate and return. Otherwise, retrieve them with `getChars`. Then truncate the buffer and append the leftover characters before returning.

### 8.8.3 Capacity Management

The buffer of a `StringBuffer` object has a capacity, which is the length of the string it can store before it must allocate more space. The buffer grows automatically as characters are added, but it is more efficient to specify the size of the buffer only once.

The initial size of a `StringBuffer` object can be set by using the constructor that takes a single `int`:

public **StringBuffer(int capacity)**
> Construct a `StringBuffer` with the given initial `capacity` and an initial value of "".

public synchronized void **ensureCapacity(int minimum)**
> Ensure that the capacity of the buffer is at least the specified `minimum`.

public int **capacity()**
> Returns the current capacity of the buffer.

You can use these methods to avoid growing the buffer multiple times. Here, for example, is a rewrite of the `sqrtInt` method from page 155 that ensures you allocate new space for the buffer at most once:

```
    String sqrtIntFaster(int i) {
        StringBuffer buf = new StringBuffer(50);
        buf.append("sqrt(").append(i).append(')');
        buf.append(" = ").append(Math.sqrt(i));
        return buf.toString();
    }
```

The only change is to use a constructor that creates a `StringBuffer` object large enough to contain the result string. The value 50 is somewhat larger than required; therefore, the buffer will never have to grow.

## Exercise 8.4

Write a method to convert strings containing decimal numbers into comma-punc-tuated numbers, with a comma every third digit from the right. For example, given the string "1543729", the method should return the string "1,543,729".  ▲

## Exercise 8.5

Modify the method to accept parameters specifying the separator character to use and the number of digits between separator characters.  ▲

# CHAPTER 9

# Threads

*How can you be in two places at once when you're not anywhere at all?*
—Firesign Theater

**W**E are used to writing programs that operate one step at a time, in a sequence. In this picture, the value of a bank balance is fetched, it is increased by the value of the deposit, then it is copied back into the account record:

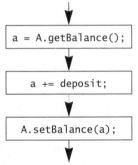

```
a = A.getBalance();
```

```
a += deposit;
```

```
A.setBalance(a);
```

Both real bank tellers and computer programs go through similar sequences. Such a sequence of steps, executed one at a time, is called a *thread*. This *single-threaded* programming model is how programmers are used to working in most programming languages.

In a real bank, more than one thing happens at a time. Multiple tellers are independently updating bank accounts:

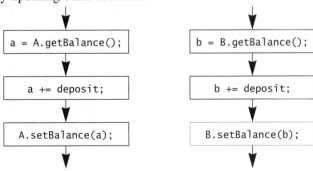

```
a = A.getBalance();
```
```
b = B.getBalance();
```

```
a += deposit;
```
```
b += deposit;
```

```
A.setBalance(a);
```
```
B.setBalance(b);
```

Inside a computer, the analogue to having multiple real-world bank tellers is called *multithreading*. A thread, like a bank teller, can perform a task independent of other threads. And just as two bank tellers can use the same filing cabinets, threads can share access to objects.

This shared access is simultaneously one of the most useful features of multithreading, and one of its greatest pitfalls. A get–modify–set sequence like this has what is known as a *race hazard* exists when two threads can potentially modify the same piece of data in an interleaved way such that the state of the object becomes corrupted. In the bank example, imagine someone walks up to a bank teller to deposit money into an account.

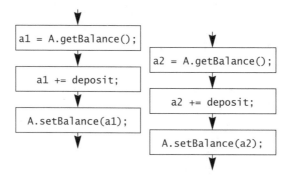

At almost the same time, a second customer asks another teller to handle a deposit into the same account. Each teller goes over to the filing cabinet to get the account information (in the days of bank offices that had paper files!) and gets the same information. Then they go back to their desks, add in the deposit, and go back to the filing cabinet to record their independent results. Done like this, only the last deposit recorded actually affects the balance; the first transaction is effectively lost.

In a real bank this problem was handled by having the tellers put notes into the file saying "I'm working on this one, wait until I'm done." Essentially the same thing is done inside the computer: a *lock* is associated with an object to tell when it is or is not being used.

Many real-world software problems can best be solved by using multiple threads of control. For example, an interactive program that displays data graphically often needs to let users change display parameters in real time. Interactive programs often obtain their best dynamic behavior using threads. Single-threaded systems usually provide an illusion of multiple threads either by using interrupts, or by *polling*. Polling mixes display and user input parts of an application, and in particular, the display code must be written so it will poll often enough to respond to user input in fractions of a second. Display code must either ensure that display operations take minimal time, or must interrupt its own operations to poll. The consequent mixing of two unrelated functional aspects of a program leads to complex and frequently unmaintainable code.

These kinds of problems are more easily solved in a multithreaded system. One thread of control updates the display with current data, and another thread responds to user input. If user input is complex—filling out a form, for example—display code can run independently until it receives new data. In a polling model, either display updates would have to stop for complex input, or complicated hand-shaking would have to occur so that display updates could continue while the user typed data into the form. Such a model of sharing control within a process can be directly supported in a multithreaded system instead of being handcrafted for each new polling case.

## 9.1 Creating Threads

Threads, like strings, are defined by a class in the standard Java libraries. To create a thread of control, you start by creating a Thread object:

```
Thread worker = new Thread();
```

After a Thread object is created, you can configure it, and then run it. Configuring a thread involves setting its initial priority, name, and so on. When the thread is ready to run, you invoke its start method. The start method spawns a new thread of control based on the data in the Thread object, and then returns. Then start invokes the new thread's run method, making the thread active.

When a thread's run method returns, the thread has exited. A thread can be explicitly stopped by invoking the stop method on it, or its execution can be suspended with suspend, or manipulated in many other ways we shall soon describe.

The standard implementation of Thread.run does nothing. You either need to extend Thread to provide a new run method, or create a Runnable object and pass it to the thread's constructor. We first discuss how to create new kinds of threads by extending Thread. We discuss the Runnable technique later (see "Using Runnable" on page 177).

Here is a simple two-threaded program that prints the words "ping" and "PONG" at different rates:

```
class PingPong extends Thread {
    String word;            // what word to print
    int delay;              // how long to pause

    PingPong(String whatToSay, int delayTime) {
        word = whatToSay;
```

```java
            delay = delayTime;
    }

    public void run() {
        try {
            for (;;) {
                System.out.print(word + " ");
                sleep(delay);   // wait until next time
            }
        } catch (InterruptedException e) {
            return;                    // end this thread
        }
    }
    public static void main(String[] args) {
        new PingPong("ping",  33).start(); // 1/30 second
        new PingPong("PONG", 100).start(); // 1/10 second
    }
}
```

We define a type of thread called PingPong. Its run method loops forever, printing its word field and sleeping for delay microseconds. PingPong.run cannot throw exceptions because Thread.run, which it overrides, doesn't throw any. Accordingly, we must catch the InterruptedException that sleep can throw.

Now we can create some actual threads, and PingPong.main does just that. It creates two PingPong objects, each with its own word and delay cycle, and invokes each thread object's start method. Now the threads are off and running. Here is some example output:

```
ping PONG ping ping PONG ping ping ping PONG ping
ping PONG ping ping ping PONG ping ping PONG ping
ping ping PONG ping ping ping PONG ping ping PONG
ping ping ping PONG ping ping ping PONG ping ping
PONG ping ping ping PONG ping ping ping PONG ping
ping ping PONG ping ping PONG ping ping ping PONG ...
```

A thread can have a name, either as a String parameter to the constructor, or as the parameter of a setName call. You can get the current name of a thread by invoking getName. Thread names are strictly for programmer convenience; they are not used by the Java runtime.

You can obtain the Thread object for the current running thread by invoking the static method Thread.currentThread.

## 9.2    Synchronization

Recall the bank teller example from the beginning of this chapter. When two tellers (threads) need to use the same file (object), there is a possibility of interleaved operations that can corrupt the data. In the bank they *synchronize* their access by putting little notes in their filing cabinets. The equivalent when multithreading is putting a *lock* on an object. When an object is locked by some thread, only that thread can access the object.

### 9.2.1    synchronized Methods

To make a class usable in a multithreaded environment, appropriate methods are declared synchronized, where "appropriate" is defined later. If one thread invokes a synchronized method on an object, that object is *locked*. Another thread invoking a synchronized method on that same object will block until the lock is released.

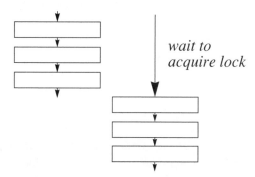

*wait to acquire lock*

Synchronization forces execution of the two threads to be *mutually exclusive* in time. Nesting method invocations are handled in the obvious way: when a synchronized method is invoked on an object that is already locked by that same thread, the method executes, but the lock is not released until the outermost synchronized method returns.

Synchronization makes the interleaved execution example work: if the code sequence is a synchronized method, then when the second thread attempts to access the object while the first thread is using it, the second thread is blocked until the first finishes.

For example, if the Account class were written to live in a multithreaded environment, here is how it would look:

```
class Account {
    private double balance;
```

```
    public Account(double initialDeposit) {
        balance = initialDeposit;
    }
    public synchronized double getBalance() {
        return balance;
    }
    public synchronized void deposit(double amount) {
        balance += amount;
    }
}
```

Now we can explain what is "appropriate" in the context of synchronizing methods.

The constructor does not need to be synchronized because it is executed only when creating an object, which can happen only in one thread for any given new object. The balance field is protected from unsynchronized change by the synchronized accessor methods. This is yet another reason not to have public or protected data, but to use accessor methods: you can control synchronization of their access.

If the value of a field can change, its value should never be read at the same time another thread is writing it. Access to the field needs to be synchronized. If one thread were reading the value while another was setting it, the read might return an invalid partial value. With the synchronized declaration, two or more running threads are assured that they will not interfere with each other. However, there is no guarantee as to the order of operations. If the read starts first, it will finish before the write starts, and vice versa. If you want actions to happen in a guaranteed order, threads must coordinate their activities in some application-specific way.

Class methods can also be synchronized, using a classwide lock for that class. Two threads cannot execute synchronized static methods on the same class at the same time. The per-class lock for a static method has no effect on any objects of that class—you can still invoke synchronized methods on an object while another thread has the class locked in a synchronized static method. Only other synchronized static methods are blocked.

When an extended class overrides a synchronized method, the new method can be synchronized or not. The superclass's method will still be synchronized when it is invoked, so an unsynchronized method in an extended class will not remove the synchronized behavior of the superclass's implementation. If the unsynchronized method uses super.*method*() to invoke the superclass's *method*, the object will become locked at that time, and unlocked when the superclass's *method* returns.

### 9.2.2    synchronized Statements

The `synchronized` statement enables you to execute synchronized code that locks an object without requiring you to invoke a `synchronized` method in that object. The `synchronized` statement has two parts: an object to be locked, and a statement to execute when the lock is obtained. The general form of the `synchronized` statement is

```
synchronized (expr)
    statement
```

The parenthesized expression *expr* must produce an object to lock—usually, an object reference. When the lock is obtained, *statement* is executed as if it were a `synchronized` method on that object. Normally, multiple statements need to be executed while the object is locked, so *statement* is usually a block. Here is a method to replace each element in an array with its absolute value, relying on a `synchronized` statement to control access to the array:

```
/** make all elements in the array nonnegative */
public static void abs(int[] values) {
    synchronized (values) {
        for (int i = 0; i < values.length; i++) {
            if (values[i] < 0)
                values[i] = -values[i];
        }
    }
}
```

The `values` array contains the elements to be modified. We synchronize `values` by naming it as the object of the `synchronized` statement. Now the loop can proceed, assured that the array is not changed during execution by any other code that is similarly synchronized on the `values` array.

There is no requirement that the object of a `synchronized` statement actually be used in the body of the statement. Conceivably, the object's sole function could be to act as a lock object for a larger collection of objects. In such a case the representative object may have little or no direct function, but will be used as the object of all `synchronized` statements that want to manipulate some or all of those other objects.

Another design alternative in such cases is to design the representative class with several `synchronized` methods to operate on the other objects. Not only is this approach a clean encapsulation of the operations, it also eliminates a source of error, namely, programmers forgetting to put accesses inside `synchronized` statements. In some cases, too many operations need to be performed on the objects being protected to encapsulate them all as methods in a class, and you must rely on the synchronized statement to protect multithreaded access.

Sometimes a designer hasn't considered a multithreaded environment when designing a class, and none of its methods are synchronized. To use such a class in a multithreaded environment, you have two choices:

◆ Create an extended class to override the appropriate methods, declare them synchronized, and forward method calls through the super reference.

◆ Use a synchronized statement to access the object in a thread-safe manner.

The extended class is a better general solution—it eliminates the errors of a programmer forgetting to put accesses within a synchronized statement. However, if only one or two places in the code require synchronized access, a synchronized statement may be simpler.

## 9.3   wait and notify

This synchronized locking mechanism suffices for keeping threads from interfering with each other, but you also need a way to communicate from one thread to another. To do this, the wait method is defined to enable waiting until some condition occurs, and notify is defined to tell those waiting that something has occurred.

The wait and notify methods are defined in class Object and are inherited by all classes. They apply to particular objects, just as locks do. When you wait for an event, you're waiting for some other thread to notify you of that event on the same object that you're waiting on.

There is a standard cliché that it is important to use with wait and notify. The thread waiting for a condition should do something like this:

```
synchronized void doWhenCondition() {
    while (!condition)
        wait();
    ... Do what needs doing when the condition is true ...
}
```

A number of things are going on here:

◆ Everything is executed within a synchronized method. This must be so; otherwise, the contents of the object are not stable. For example, if the method is not synchronized, then after the while statement, there is no assurance that the condition is true, because some other thread may have changed the situation which the condition tests.

♦ One of the important aspects of the definition of `wait` is that when it suspends the thread, it *atomically* releases the lock on the object. Saying that the thread suspension and lock release are *atomic* means that they happen together, indivisibly. Otherwise, there would be a race hazard: a `notify` could happen after the lock is released, but before the thread is suspended. The `notify` would have no effect on the thread, effectively getting lost. When a thread is restarted after being notified, the lock is reacquired.

♦ The condition test should *always* be in a loop. Never assume that being woken up means that the condition has been satisfied. In other words, don't change the `while` to an `if`.

On the other side, the `notify` method is invoked by methods that change data that some other thread may be waiting on.

```
synchronized void changeCondition() {
    ... change some value used in a condition test ...
    notify();
}
```

Multiple threads may be waiting on the same object. Using `notify` wakes up the one that has been waiting the longest. If you need to wake up all waiting threads, use `notifyAll`.

This example class implements a queue. The class has methods to insert and remove elements from the queue.

```
class Queue {
        // The first and last elements in the queue
    Element head, tail;

    public synchronized void append(Element p) {
        if (tail == null)
            head = p;
        else
            tail.next = p;
        p.next = null;
        tail = p;
        notify();  // Let waiters know something arrived
    }

    public synchronized Element get() {
        try {
```

```
            while(head == null)
                wait();     // Wait for an element
        } catch (InterruptedException e) {
            return null;
        }

        Element p = head;   // Remember first element
        head = head.next;   // Remove it from the queue
        if (head == null)   // Check for an empty queue
            tail = null;
        return p;
    }
}
```

This implementation of a queue looks very much like a queue used in single-threaded systems. It differs in a few aspects: the methods are synchronized; when an element is appended to the queue, waiters are notified; instead of returning null when the queue is empty, the get method waits for some other thread to insert something. Many threads may be appending elements to the queue (not just one) and many threads may be getting elements from the queue (again, not just one).

## 9.4   Details of wait and notify

There are three forms of wait and two forms of notify. All are methods in the Object class and operate on the current thread:

public final void **wait(long timeout)** throws InterruptedException
> The current thread waits until it is notified, or the specified timeout expires. timeout is in milliseconds. If timeout is zero, the wait will not time out, but will continue until notification.

public final void **wait(long timeout, int nanos)**
> throws InterruptedException
> A finer-grained wait, where the time out interval is the sum of two parameters: a timeout (in milliseconds) and nanos (in nanoseconds, in the range 0–999999).

public final void **wait()** throws InterruptedException
> Equivalent to wait(0).

public final void **notify()**
> Notifies *exactly one* thread waiting for a condition to change. Threads that must wait for a condition to change before proceeding can call some form

of `wait`. You cannot choose which thread will be notified, so use this form of `notify` only when you are sure you know which threads are waiting for what at which times. If you are not sure of any of these factors, you should probably use `notifyAll`.

public final void **notifyAll()**

Notifies *all* of the threads waiting for a condition to change. Waiting threads are generally waiting for another thread to change some condition. The thread effecting a change on which more than one thread is waiting notifies all the waiting threads using this method. Threads that want to wait for a condition to change before proceeding can call some form of `wait`.

These methods are implemented in `Object`. However, they can be invoked only from within `synchronized` code, using the lock for the object on which they are invoked. The invocation can be from the `synchronized` code directly, or indirectly from a method invoked in such code. Any attempt to invoke these methods on objects from outside the `synchronized` code that acquired the lock will throw an `IllegalMonitorStateException`.

## 9.5    Thread Scheduling

Java can run on both single- and multiprocessor machines, with multiple threads or a single thread, so the threading guarantees are general. You can be sure the highest-priority runnable thread will run, and all threads at that priority will get some processor time. Lower-priority threads are guaranteed to run only when higher-priority threads are blocked. Lower-priority threads might, in fact, run anyway, but you cannot rely upon it.

A thread is blocked if it is sleeping or executing any other system or thread function that is blocked. When a thread blocks, Java picks the highest-priority runnable thread (or one of those with the highest priority, if there is more than one thread at that priority), and lets it run.

The Java runtime can suspend even the highest-priority thread to let another thread at the same priority run, which means that all threads with the top priority will eventually run. However, this is a weak guarantee, since "eventually" is not precise. Use priority only to affect scheduling policy for efficiency purposes. Do not rely on thread priority for algorithm correctness.

A thread's priority is initially the same as the priority of the thread that created it. The priority can be changed using `setPriority` with a value between `Thread`'s constants `MIN_PRIORITY` and `MAX_PRIORITY`. The standard priority for the default thread is `NORM_PRIORITY`. The priority of a running thread can be changed at any time. If you assign a thread a priority lower than its current one, the system may let another thread run, because the original thread may no longer be among those with the highest priority. The getPriority method returns the priority of a thread.

Generally, the continuously running part of your application should run in a lower-priority thread than the thread dealing with rarer events such as user input. When a user pushes a "Stop" button, for example, he or she expects the application to stop. If display update and user input are at the same priority, and the display is updating, some time might pass before the user input thread will react to the button. The display thread at a lower priority will still run most of the time because the user interface thread will be blocked waiting for user input. When user input is available, the user interface thread will preempt the display thread to act on the user request. For this reason, a thread that does continual updates often sets its priority to MIN_PRIORITY to avoid hogging all available cycles.

Several static methods of the Thread class control scheduling of the current thread:

public static void **sleep(long millis)** throws InterruptedException
> Puts the currently executing thread to sleep for at least the specified number of milliseconds. "At least" means there is no guarantee the thread will wake up in exactly the specified time. Other thread scheduling can interfere, as can the granularity and accuracy of the system clock, among other factors.

public static void **sleep(long millis, int nanos)**
throws InterruptedException
> Puts the currently executing thread to sleep for at least the specified number of milliseconds and additional nanoseconds. Nanoseconds are in the range 0–999999.

public static void **yield()**
> Yields the currently executing thread so that any other runnable threads can run. The thread scheduler chooses a thread to run from the runnable threads. The thread that is picked could be the one that yielded, since it may be the highest-priority runnable thread.

This program shows how yield works. The application takes a list of words, and creates a thread responsible for printing each word. The first parameter to the application says whether each thread will yield after each println; the second is the number of times each thread should repeat its word. The remaining parameters are the words to be repeated:

```
class Babble extends Thread {
    static boolean doYield;  // yield to other threads?
    static int howOften;     // how many times to print
```

```
    String word;                   // my word

    Babble(String whatToSay) {
        word = whatToSay;
    }

    public void run() {
        for (int i = 0; i < howOften; i++) {
            System.out.println(word);
            if (doYield)
                yield();    // give another thread a chance
        }
    }

    public static void main(String[] args) {
        howOften = Integer.parseInt(args[1]);
        doYield = new Boolean(args[0]).booleanValue();

        // create a thread for each word at max priority
        Thread cur = currentThread();
        cur.setPriority(Thread.MAX_PRIORITY);
        for (int i = 2; i < args.length; i++)
            new Babble(args[i]).start();
    }
}
```

When the threads do not yield, each thread will get large chunks of time, usually enough to finish all the prints without any other thread getting cycles. For example, when run with doYield set to `false` in the following way:

```
Babble false 2 Did DidNot
```

the output is likely to look like this:

```
Did
Did
DidNot
DidNot
```

If each thread yields after each `println`, other printing threads will have a chance to run. When we set doYield to `true` with an invocation like this:

```
Babble true 2 Did DidNot
```

the yields give the other threads a chance to run, and the other threads will yield in turn, producing an output more like this:

```
Did
DidNot
Did
DidNot
```

The output shown above is only approximate. A different thread implementation could give different results, or the same implementation might give different results on different runs of the application. But under all implementations, invoking yield can give other threads a more equitable chance at getting cycles.

## 9.6   Deadlocks

Whenever you have two threads and two objects with locks, you can have a *deadlock*, where each object is waiting for the lock on the other. If object *X* has a synchronized method that invokes a synchronized method on object *Y*, which in turn has a synchronized method invoking a synchronized method on object *X*, both objects will wait for the other to complete in order to get a lock, so neither will run. This situation is also sometimes called a "deadly embrace." Consider this scenario where jareth and cory are objects of some class Friendly:

1. Thread number 1 invokes synchronized method jareth.hug. Thread number 1 now has the lock on jareth.

2. Thread number 2 invokes synchronized method cory.hug. Thread number 2 now has the lock on cory.

3. Now cory.hug invokes synchronized method jareth.hugBack. Thread number 1 is now blocked waiting for the lock on cory to become available (currently held by thread number 2).

4. Finally, jareth.hug invokes synchronized method cory.hugBack. Thread number 2 is now blocked waiting for the lock on jareth to become available (currently held by thread number 1).

We have now achieved deadlock—cory won't proceed until the lock on jareth is released and vice versa, so the two threads are stuck in a permanent purgatory.

You could get lucky, of course, and have one thread complete the entire hug without the other starting up. If steps 3 and 4 happened to occur in the other order, then jareth would complete both hug and hugBack before cory needed the lock on jareth. But a future run of the same application might deadlock just by a different choice of the thread scheduler. Several design changes would fix this problem. The simplest would be to make hug and hugBack not synchronized, but have both methods synchronize on a single object shared by all Friendly objects. This technique would mean that only one hug could happen at a time in all the threads of a single runtime, but it would eliminate the possibility of deadlock. Other, more involved techniques would enable multiple simultaneous hugs without deadlock.

You are responsible for avoiding deadlock. Java neither detects nor prevents deadlocks. Deadlock problems can be frustrating to debug, so you should solve them by avoiding the possibility in your design. The Bibliography has some useful references to give you a background in thread and lock design.

## 9.7 Suspending Threads

Threads can be *suspended* when you want to ensure they will run only when you are ready for them to do so. Consider a user pushing "Cancel" during an expensive operation, for example. You might want to suspend processing to confirm whether the user really wants to cancel the computation. Here is how that code might look:

```
Thread spinner; // the thread doing the processing

public void userHitCancel() {
    spinner.suspend();              // whoa!
    if (askYesNo("Really Cancel?"))
        spinner.stop();             // stop it
    else
        spinner.resume();           // giddyap!
}
```

The userHitCancel method first invokes suspend on the processing thread, to stop the thread running until explicitly resumed. Then the user is asked whether the cancel was intentional. If so, stop ends the thread's life. If not, resume makes it runnable again.

It is harmless to suspend a suspended thread or resume a thread that is not suspended.

## 9.8 Interrupting Threads

Some methods on the Thread class relate to the notion of *interrupting* a thread. They are placeholders for a feature that will soon be added to Java threads. As of this writing these methods are all unimplemented and throw `NoSuchMethodError` if invoked, killing the invoking thread. Possibly by the time you read this, the methods will have been implemented. This section gives a brief overview of the expected functionality.

The "interrupt" concept is useful when you want to give the running thread some control over when it will handle an event. For instance, a display update loop might need to access some database information using a transaction, and would prefer to handle a "stop" request by waiting until the transaction completes normally. The user interface thread might implement "Stop" by interrupting the display thread to give the display thread that control. This will work well as long as the display thread is well-behaved and checks if it has been interrupted at the end of every transaction, stopping if it has been interrupted.

Interrupting a thread will normally not affect what it is doing, but a few methods, such as `sleep` and `wait`, throw `InterruptedException`. If your thread is executing one of these methods when it is interrupted, the method will throw the `InterruptedException`.

The methods that relate to interrupting a thread are `interrupt`, which sends an interrupt to a thread; `isInterrupted`, which tests if a thread has been interrupted; and `interrupted`, a `static` method that tests if the current thread has been interrupted.

## 9.9   Ending Thread Execution

A thread is finished executing when its `run` method returns. This is the normal way to finish up a thread, but you can also force a thread to stop in a couple of ways.

The preferred way is the cleanest, but it requires some work on the programmer's part: rather than doing something violent to a thread, it is usually best to have it stop voluntarily. This is usually done by having a boolean variable that the thread polls. For example:

Thread 1:

```
thread2.stopRequested = true;
```

Thread 2:

```
while (!stopRequested) {
    // do a little work
}
```

The direct way to stop a thread is to call its `stop` method, which throws a `ThreadDeath` object to the target thread. `ThreadDeath` is a subclass of `Error`, not a subclass of `Exception` (see Appendix B for a discussion of why this is so). Programmers should not catch `ThreadDeath` unless they must do some *extraordinary* cleanup operation that a `finally` clause cannot handle. If

ThreadDeath is caught, rethrowing the exception object is critical, so the thread will die. If ThreadDeath is not caught, the top-level error handler simply kills the thread without printing any message.

A thread can also throw ThreadDeath itself to terminate its own execution. This can be useful if a thread is several levels deep below run and there is no easy way to pass up to the run method the fact that the thread should die.

Another form of the stop method can be passed a different exception instead of ThreadDeath. There are usually better ways to send messages to another thread than throwing an exception, but this can be used as a general way to send an exception to a thread. For example, if one thread is performing an extended calculation based on some input values, the user interface might enable the user to change the values while the calculation is in process. You could simply stop the original thread and start a new one. But if some of the old calculation was reusable, you could instead create a new RestartCalculation exception type and use stop to throw the new exception to the thread. The thread could be set up to catch the exception, examine the new user values, preserve what it could from the original calculation, and resume the calculation.

One thread can wait for another thread to finish. This is done using one of the join methods. The simple form waits forever for a particular thread to die:

```
class CalcThread extends Thread {
    private double Result;

    public void run() {
        Result = calculate();
    }

    public double result() {
        return Result;
    }

    public double calculate() {
        // ...
    }
}

class Join {
    public static void main(String[] args) {
        CalcThread calc = new CalcThread();
        calc.start();
        doSomethingElse();
```

```
        try {
            calc.join();
            System.out.println("result is "
                + calc.result());
        } catch (InterruptedException e) {
            System.out.println("No answer: interrupted");
        }
    }

}
```

First a new thread type, CalcThread, is created to calculate a result. We start it, do something else for a while, then join up with the thread. When join returns, CalcThread.run is guaranteed to have finished, and Result will be set. This works whether or not the thread CalcThread finished before doSomethingElse finished. When a thread dies, its object doesn't go away, so you can still access its state.

Two other forms of join take timeout values analogous to sleep. Here are all three forms of join:

public final void **join()** throws InterruptedException
    Waits forever for this Thread to finish.

public final synchronized void **join(long millis)**
    throws InterruptedException
        Waits for this Thread to finish, or the specified number of milliseconds to elapse, whichever is first. A timeout of 0 milliseconds means wait forever.

public final synchronized void **join(long millis, int nanos)**
    throws InterruptedException
        Waits for the Thread to finish, with more precise timing. Again, a total time-out of 0 nanoseconds means wait forever. Nanoseconds are in the range 0–999999.

Invoking a thread's destroy method is drastic. It kills the thread dead with no cleanup. Normal cleanup includes releasing any locks held on objects in the thread, so using destroy could leave other threads blocked forever. Avoid invoking destroy if you possibly can.

## 9.10  Ending Application Execution

Each application starts off with one thread—the one that executes main. If your application creates no other threads, the application will finish when main returns. But if you create other threads, what happens to them when main returns?

There are two kinds of threads: *user* and *daemon*. The presence of a user thread keeps the application running, while a daemon thread is expendable. When the last user thread is finished, any daemon threads are stopped and the application is done. You use the method `setDaemon(true)` to mark a thread as a daemon thread, and use `getDaemon` to test that flag. By default, daemon-ness is inherited from the thread that creates the new thread. This cannot be changed after a thread is started; an `IllegalThreadStateException` is thrown if you try.

If your `main` method spawns a thread, that thread inherits the user-thread status of the original thread. When `main` finishes, the application will continue to run until that other thread finishes, too. There is nothing special about the original thread—it just happened to be the first to get started for a particular run of an application. After that, it is treated just like any other user thread. An application will run until *all* user threads have completed. For all the runtime knows, the original thread was designed to spawn another thread and die, letting that thread do the real work. If you want your application to exit when the original thread dies, you can mark all the threads you create as daemon threads.

## 9.11  Using `Runnable`

The `Runnable` interface abstracts the concept of something that will execute code while it is active. The `Runnable` interface declares a single method:

```
public void run();
```

The `Thread` class implements the `Runnable` interface because a thread is something that executes code when it is active. You have seen that `Thread` can be extended to provide specific computation for a thread, but this is awkward in many cases. First, class extension is single-inheritance—if you extend a class to make it runnable in a thread, extending both the existing class and extending `Thread` is impossible. Also, if you only want to be runnable, inheriting all the overhead of `Thread` is more than you need.

Implementing `Runnable` is easier in many cases. A `Runnable` object can be executed in its own thread by passing it to the `Thread` constructor. If a `Thread` object is constructed with a `Runnable` object, the implementation of `Thread.run` will invoke the runnable object's run method.

Here is a `Runnable` version of the `PingPong` class from page 161. If you compare the versions, you will see that they look almost identical. The major differences are in the supertype (`Runnable` versus `Thread`) and in `main`:

```
class RunPingPong implements Runnable {
    String word;                    // what word to print
    int delay;                      // how long to pause
```

```
RunPingPong(String whatToSay, int delayTime) {
    word = whatToSay;
    delay = delayTime;
}

public void run() {
    try {
        for (;;) {
            System.out.print(word + " ");
            Thread.sleep(delay); // wait until next time
        }
    } catch (InterruptedException e) {
        return;                 // end this thread
    }
}

public static void main(String[] args) {
    Runnable ping = new RunPingPong("ping",  33);
    Runnable pong = new RunPingPong("PONG", 100);
    new Thread(ping).start();
    new Thread(pong).start();
}
}
```

First a new class is defined that implements Runnable. Its implementation of the run method is the same as PingPong's. In main, two RunPingPong objects with different timings are created; a new Thread object is then created for each and started immediately.

Four Thread constructors enable you to specify a Runnable object:

public **Thread(Runnable target)**
> Constructs a new Thread that uses the run method of the specified target.

public **Thread(Runnable target, String name)**
> Constructs a new Thread with the specified name and uses the run method of the specified target.

public **Thread(ThreadGroup group, Runnable target)**
> Constructs a new Thread in the specified ThreadGroup, and uses the run method of the specified target.

public **Thread(ThreadGroup group, Runnable target, String name)**
> Constructs a new Thread in the specified ThreadGroup with the specified name, and uses the run method of the specified target.

## 9.12 `volatile`

The `synchronized` mechanism works nicely, but if you choose not to use it, multiple threads could potentially modify a field at the same time. If you are doing this on purpose (possibly because you have some other way to synchronize access), you should mark that field `volatile`. For example, if you had a value that was continuously displayed by a graphics thread, and which could be changed by non-synchronized methods, the display code might look something like this:

```
currentValue = 5;
for (;;) {
    display.showValue(currentValue);
    Thread.sleep(1000); // wait 1 second
}
```

If there is no way for `showValue` to change the value of `currentValue`, the compiler might assume that it can treat `currentValue` as unchanged inside the loop, and simply use the constant 5 each time it invokes `showValue`.

But if `currentValue` is updated by other threads while the loop is running, the compiler's assumption would be wrong. Declaring the field `currentValue` to be `volatile` prevents the compiler from making such assumptions.

## 9.13 Thread Security and `ThreadGroup`

When programming multiple threads—some of which are created by library calls—it can be useful to place limitations on the threads to protect them from each other.

Threads are split up into *thread groups* for security reasons. A thread group can be contained within another thread group, providing a hierarchy. Threads within a thread group can modify the other threads in the group, including any farther down the hierarchy. A thread cannot modify threads outside of its own group or contained groups.

These restrictions can be used to protect threads from manipulation by other threads. If new threads are placed in a separate thread group inside an existing thread group, the new threads' priorities can be changed, but they can't change either the existing threads' priorities, or those of any other threads outside their group.

Every thread belongs to a thread group. Each `ThreadGroup` object describes the limits on threads in that group. The thread group can be specified in the thread constructor; the default is to place each new thread in the same thread group as the thread that created it. When a thread dies, the thread object is removed from its group.

public **Thread(ThreadGroup group, String name)**
Constructs a new thread in the specified thread group with the specified name (which can be null).

The ThreadGroup object associated with a thread cannot be changed after the thread is created. You can get the group associated with a particular thread by invoking its getThreadGroup method. You can also check if you are allowed to modify a Thread by invoking its checkAccess method, which throws SecurityException if you cannot modify the thread, and just returns (it is a void method) if you can.

Thread groups can be *daemon* groups. A daemon ThreadGroup is automatically destroyed when it becomes empty. Setting a ThreadGroup to be a daemon group does not affect the daemon-ness of any thread or group contained in that group. It only affects what happens when the group becomes empty.

Thread groups can also be used to set an upper limit on the priority of the threads it contains. After invoking setMaxPriority with a maximum priority, any attempt to set a thread priority higher than the thread group's maximum is silently reduced to that maximum. Existing threads are not affected by this invocation. You can ensure that no other thread in the group will ever have a higher priority than a particular thread by setting that thread's priority to MAX_PRIORITY and then setting the group's maximum priority to MAX_PRIORITY-1. The limit also applies to the thread group itself—any attempt to set a new maximum priority for the group that is higher than the current maximum will be silently reduced:

```
static public void maxThread(Thread thr) {
    ThreadGroup grp = thr.getThreadGroup();
    thr.setPriority(Thread.MAX_PRIORITY);
    grp.setMaxPriority(thr.getPriority() - 1);
}
```

This method works by setting the thread's priority to the maximum possible, and then setting the group's maximum allowable priority to less than the thread's priority. The new group maximum is set to one less than the thread's actual priority, not Thread.MAX_PRIORITY-1, because an existing group maximum might limit your ability to set the thread to MAX_PRIORITY. You want the thread's priority to be the highest possible, and the group's maximum priority to be less than the thread's, whatever that may have turned out to be.

ThreadGroup supports the following constructors and methods:

public **ThreadGroup(String name)**
> Creates a new ThreadGroup. Its parent will be the ThreadGroup of the current thread. Like Thread names, the name of a group is not used by the runtime system. A NullPointerException is thrown if the name is null. This is inconsistent with Thread, where the name is optional.

public **ThreadGroup(ThreadGroup parent, String name)**
> Creates a new ThreadGroup with a specified name in the ThreadGroup parent. As with the other constructor, a name must be provided.

public final String **getName()**
> Returns the name of this ThreadGroup.

public final ThreadGroup **getParent()**
> Returns the parent ThreadGroup, or null if it has none.

public final void **setDaemon(boolean daemon)**
> Sets the daemon status of this group.

public final boolean **isDaemon()**
> Returns the daemon flag of the ThreadGroup.

public final synchronized void **setMaxPriority(int maxPri)**
> Sets the maximum priority of the group.

public final int **getMaxPriority()**
> Gets the current maximum priority of the group.

public final boolean **parentOf(ThreadGroup g)**
> Checks if this ThreadGroup is a parent of the group g, or is the group g. This might be better thought of as "part of," since a group is part of itself.

public final void **checkAccess()**
> Throws SecurityException if the current thread is not allowed to modify this group. Otherwise, this method simply returns.

public final synchronized void **destroy()**
> Destroys a ThreadGroup. A thread group that has any threads cannot be destroyed, or this method throws IllegalThreadStateException. This means you cannot use destroy to kill all threads in the group—that must be done manually using the enumeration methods described later. If the group contains other groups, they must also be empty of threads.

You can examine the contents of a thread group using two parallel sets of methods, one for getting the threads contained in the group, and the other for getting the thread groups contained in the group. You will see an example of how these methods are used in the safeExit method on page 267.

```
public synchronized int activeCount()
```
Returns an estimate of the number of active threads in this group, including threads contained in all subgroups. This is an estimate because, by the time you get the number, it may no longer be correct. Threads may have died, or new ones may have been created, during or after the call to `activeCount`.

```
public int enumerate(Thread[] threadsInGroup, boolean recurse)
```
Fills the `threadsInGroup` array with a reference to every active thread in the group, up to the size of the array. If `recurse` is `false`, only threads directly in the group are included; if it is `true`, all threads in the hierarchy will be included. `ThreadGroup.enumerate` gives you control over whether you recurse or not, but `ThreadGroup.activeCount` does not. This means you can get a reasonable estimate of the size of an array needed to hold the results of a recursive enumeration, but you will overestimate the size needed for a non-recursive `enumerate`.

```
public int enumerate(Thread[] threadsInGroup)
```
Equivalent to enumerate(threadsInGroup, true).

```
public synchronized int activeGroupCount()
```
Like `activeCount`, but counts groups, instead of threads, in all subgroups. "Active" means "existing." There is no concept of an inactive group; the term "active" is used for consistency with `activeCount`.

```
public int enumerate(ThreadGroup[] groupsInGroup,
    boolean recurse)
```
Like the `enumerate` methods for threads, but fills an array of `ThreadGroup` references, not `Thread` references.

```
public int enumerate(ThreadGroup[] groupsInGroup)
```
Equivalent to enumerate(groupsInGroup, true).

You can also use a `ThreadGroup` to manage threads in the group. The following methods operate recursively on all threads in this group and all subgroups:

```
public final synchronized void stop()
```
Stops all the threads in this `ThreadGroup` and all subgroups.

```
public final synchronized void suspend()
```
Suspends all the threads in this `ThreadGroup` and all subgroups.

```
public final synchronized void resume()
```
Resumes all the threads in this `ThreadGroup` and all subgroups.

These methods are the only way to directly use a `ThreadGroup` to set parameters on threads.

There are also two static methods in the `Thread` class to act on the current thread's group. They are shorthand for invoking `getCurrentThread`, invoking `getThreadGroup` on that thread, and then invoking the method on that group.

`public static int` **`activeCount()`**
> Returns the number of active threads in the current thread's `ThreadGroup`.

`public static int` **`enumerate(Thread[] tarray)`**
> Returns the value of `enumerate(tarray)` on the current thread's `ThreadGroup`.

The `ThreadGroup` class also supports a method that is invoked when a thread dies because of an uncaught exception:

`public void` **`uncaughtException(Thread thr, Throwable exc)`**
> Invoked when thread `thr` in this group dies because of an uncaught exception `exc`.

This method is public so you can override it to handle uncaught exceptions in your own idiom. The default implementation invokes the `uncaughtException` method of the group's parent group if there is one, and uses the method `Throwable.printStackTrace` if there is no parent group. If you were writing a graphical environment, you might want to display the stack trace in a window rather than simply printing it to `System.out`, which is where `printStackTrace` puts its output. You could override `uncaughtException` in your group to create the window you need and redirect the stack trace into the window.

## 9.14 Debugging Threads

A few `Thread` methods are designed to help you debug a multithreaded application. These print-style debugging aids can be used to print the state of an application. Here are methods you can invoke on a `Thread` object to help with debugging:

`public String` **`toString()`**
> Returns a string representation of the thread, including its name, its priority, and the name of its thread group.

`public int` **`countStackFrames()`**
> Returns the number of stack frames in this thread.

`public static void` **`dumpStack()`**
> Print a stack trace for the current thread on `System.out`.

There are also debugging aids to track the state of a thread group. The following methods can be invoked on `ThreadGroup` objects to print their state:

`public String` **`toString()`**

Returns a string representation of the `ThreadGroup`, including its name and priority.

`public synchronized void` **`list()`**

Lists this `ThreadGroup` recursively to `System.out`.

CHAPTER **10**

# Packages

*A library is an arsenal of liberty.*
—Unknown

**P**ACKAGES have members that are related classes, interfaces, and subpackages. Packages are useful for several reasons:

- Packages create a grouping for related interfaces and classes.
- Interfaces and classes in a package can use popular public names (like `get` and `put`) that make sense in one context but might conflict with the same name in another package.
- Packages can have types and members that are available only within the package. Such identifiers are available to the package code, but inaccessible to outside code.

Let us look at a package for our attribute classes that were illustrated in previous chapters. We name the package `attr`. Each source file whose classes and interfaces belong in the `attr` package states its residence with a `package` declaration:

```
package attr;
```

to declare that all classes and interfaces defined in this source file are part of the `attr` package. A `package` declaration should appear first in your source file, before any class or interface declarations, and only one package declaration can appear in a source file. The package name is implicitly prefixed to each type name contained within the package.

Code defined outside the package that needs types declared within the package can proceed in one of two ways. One way is to precede each type name with the package name. This option is reasonable if you use only a few items from a package.

The other way to access types from a package is to *import* part or all of the package. A programmer who wants to use the `attr` package could put the following line near the top of a source file (after any `package` declaration, but before anything else):

```
import attr.*;
```

and then access the types simply by name, such as `Attributed`. A package imports itself implicitly, so everything defined in a package is available to all types in the package.

The `package` and `import` mechanisms give programmers control over potentially conflicting names. If a package for another purpose (linguistics, maybe) has a class called `Attributed` for language attributes, a programmer wanting to use both packages in the same source file has several options:

◆ Refer to all types by their fully qualified names, such as `attr.Attributed` and `lingua.Attributed`.

◆ Import `attr.Attributed` or `attr.*`, use the simple name `Attributed` for `attr.Attributed`, and use the full name of `lingua.Attributed`.

◆ Do the converse—import `lingua.Attributed` or `lingua.*`, use the simple name `Attributed` for `lingua.Attributed`, and use the full name of `attr.Attributed`.

## 10.1 Package Naming

A package name should be unique for classes and interfaces in the package, so choosing a name that's both meaningful and unique is an important aspect of package design. But with programmers all around the globe developing Java language packages, there is no way to find out who is using what package names. Choosing unique package names is therefore a problem. If you are certain a package will be used only inside your organization, you can choose a name using an internal arbiter to ensure no two projects pick clashing names.

But in the world at large this is insufficient. Java package identifiers are simple names. A good way to ensure unique package names is to use an Internet domain name. If you work at a company named Magic, Inc., the attribute package declaration should be

```
package COM.magic.attr;
```

Notice the components of the domain name are reversed from the normal domain name convention, and that the highest-level domain name (in this case COM) is spelled in capital letters. The capital letters are used to prevent conflicts with package names chosen by those not following the convention, who are unlikely to use all upper-case, but might name a package the same as one of the many high-level domain names.

If you use this convention, your package names will not conflict with anyone else's, except possibly within your organization. If such conflicts arise (likely in a large organization), you can further qualify using a more specific domain. Many large companies have internal subdomains with names like `east`, `europe`, and such. You could further qualify the package name using that subdomain name:

```
package COM.magic.japan.attr;
```

Package names can become quite long with this scheme, but it is relatively safe—no one else using this technique will choose the same package name, and programmers not using the technique are unlikely to pick your names.

Many development environments reflect package names in the file system, often by requiring all code for a single package to be in a particular folder or directory, and the name of the directory to reflect the package name. Consult your development environment's documentation for details.

## 10.2  Package Access

Classes and interfaces within a package have two accesses: package and public. A `public` class or interface is accessible to code outside of that package. Types that are not `public` have package scope: they are available to all other code in the same package, but hidden outside the package, and even from code in nested packages.

Members of a class also specify access. A member not declared `public`, `protected`, or `private` can be used by any code within the package, but is hidden outside the package. In other words, the default access for an identifier is "package," except for members of interfaces, which are public.

Fields or methods not declared `private` in a package are available to all other code in that package. Thus, classes within the same package are "friendly" or "trusted." However, subpackages are not trusted relative to enclosing packages. For example, protected and package identifiers in package `dit` are not available to code in package `dit.dat`, or vice versa.

## 10.3  Package Contents

If a `package` declaration is not provided in a source file, types declared in that source file go into an "unnamed package."

Packages should be designed carefully so they contain only functionally related classes and interfaces. Classes in a package can freely access each other's non-private members. Protecting class members is intended to prevent misuse by classes with access to internal details of other classes. Access restrictions other than `private` do not exist within a package, and unrelated classes could end up working more intimately than expected with other classes.

Packages should also provide logical groupings for programmers looking for useful interfaces and classes. A package of unrelated classes makes the programmer work harder to figure out what is available. Logical grouping of classes enables programmers to reuse your code because they can more easily find what they need.

Keeping packages to related, coherent sets of types means you can use obvious names for types, avoiding name conflicts arising from unrelated types in the same package.

Packages can be nested inside other packages. For example, `java.lang` is a nested package, where `lang` is nested inside the larger `java` package. The `java` package has no contents besides other packages. Nesting allows a hierarchical naming system for related packages.

For example, to create a set of packages for adaptive systems such as neural networks and genetic algorithms, you could create nested packages by naming the packages with dot-separated names:

```
package adaptive.neuralNet;
```

A source file with this declaration lives in the `adaptive.neuralNet` package, which is itself a subpackage of the `adaptive` package. The `adapative` package might contain classes related to general adaptive algorithms, such as generic problem statement classes or benchmarking. Each package deeper in the hierarchy—such as `adaptive.neuralNet` or `adaptive.genetic`—would contain classes specific to the particular kind of adaptive algorithm.

Package nesting is an organizational tool for related packages, but provides no special access between packages. Class code in `adaptive.genetic` cannot access package-private identifiers of the `adaptive` or `adaptive.neuralNet` packages. Package scope applies only to a particular package. Nesting can group related packages and help programmers find classes in a logical hierarchy, but can confer no other benefits.

# CHAPTER 11

# The I/O Package

*From a programmer's point of view,*
*the user is a peripheral that types when you issue a read request.*
—Peter Williams

**J**AVA I/O (input/output) is defined in terms of *streams*. Streams are ordered sequences of data that have a *source* (input streams), or *destination* (output streams). The I/O classes isolate programmers from the specific details of the underlying operating system, while enabling access to system resources through files. After defining some basic interfaces and abstract classes, most stream types (such as those dealing with files) support the methods of these basic streams with few, if any, additions. The best way to understand Java I/O is to understand the basic interfaces and abstract classes. To illustrate the abstractions in action, we use examples from the file-based streams.

The primary exceptions to the basic streams model are data streams that write and read basic Java types like `int` and `String`. These streams support a larger set of methods designed for this particular purpose. They are covered in the second part of this chapter, starting with Section 11.16.

The Java I/O package is named `java.io`, and all code presented in this chapter imports it, even when there is no explicit `import` statement in the example.

As of this writing, there is no standard library to manipulate output formats of numbers or strings, such as minimum or maximum field widths, or desired precision of floating-point output.

## 11.1 Streams

The `java.io` package defines abstract classes for basic input and output streams. These abstract classes are then extended to provide several useful stream types. Stream types are almost always paired: where there is a `FileInputStream`, there is usually a `FileOutputStream`.

In addition, there are classes for handling file names, a read/write stream class named RandomAccessFile, and a tokenizer for breaking an InputStream into tokens.

The IOException class is used by many methods in java.io to signal exceptional conditions. Some extended classes of IOException signal specific problems, but most problems are signaled by an IOException object with a descriptive string. Details are provided in Section 11.20.

Before we discuss specific kinds of input and output streams, it is important to understand the basic InputStream and OutputStream abstract classes. The entire type tree for java.io appears in Figure 11.1 on page 195.

## 11.2  InputStream

The abstract class InputStream declares methods to read input from a particular source. InputStream is the base class of most input streams in java.io, and it supports these methods:

public **InputStream()**
> InputStream supports only a no-arg constructor.

public abstract int **read()** throws IOException
> Reads a single byte of data and returns the byte that was read, in the range 0 to 255, not –128 to 127. The flag value –1 is returned when end of stream is reached. This method blocks until input is available.

public int **read(byte[] buf)** throws IOException
> Reads into an array of bytes. This method blocks until input is available, then fills buf with as many bytes as were read, up to buf.length bytes. It returns the actual number of bytes read, or –1 when the end of the stream is reached.

public int **read(byte[] buf, int off, int len)** throws IOException
> Reads into a subarray of a byte array. This method blocks until input is available, then fills the subarray of buf starting with offset off up to len bytes, or until the end of the buf array is reached.

public long **skip(long count)** throws IOException
> Skips up to count bytes of input, or until the end of the input stream. Returns the actual number of bytes skipped.

public int **available()** throws IOException
> Returns the number of bytes that can be read without blocking.

```
public void close() throws IOException
```
Closes the input stream. This method should be invoked to release any resources (such as file descriptors) associated with the stream. If this method is not invoked, associated resources remain in use, at least until the garbage collector gets around to running a stream's `finalize` method.

The following program counts the total number of characters and the number of white-space characters in a file:

```
import java.io.*;

class CountSpace {
    public static void main(String[] args)
        throws IOException
    {
        InputStream in;
        if (args.length == 0)
            in = System.in;
        else
            in = new FileInputStream(args[0]);

        int ch;
        int total;
        int spaces = 0;
        for (total = 0; (ch = in.read()) != -1; total++) {
            if (Character.isSpace((char)ch))
                spaces++;
        }

        System.out.println(total + " chars, "
            + spaces + " spaces");
    }
}
```

This program either takes a filename from the command line, or reads from its standard input stream, `System.in`. The variable `in` represents the input stream. If a filename is not provided, the standard input stream is used; if one is provided, a `FileInputStream` object is created, which is an extension of `InputStream`.

The `for` loop counts the total number of characters in the file, and the number of spaces, using the `Character` class's `isSpace` method to test which characters are white space. At the end, the results are printed. Here is the output of the program when used on itself:

```
434 chars, 109 spaces
```

You might be tempted to set `total` using `available`, but it won't work when the stream is `System.in`. The `available` method returns the number of bytes that can be read *without blocking*. For a file, the number of bytes available is usually its entire contents. If `System.in` is a stream associated with a keyboard, the answer can be as low as zero: when there is no pending input, the next `read` will block.

## 11.3  OutputStream

The abstract class `OutputStream` is analogous to `InputStream`; it provides an abstraction for streaming bytes out to a destination. Here are its methods:

public **OutputStream()**
    OutputStream supports only a no-arg constructor.

public abstract void **write(int b)** throws IOException
    Writes b as a byte. The byte is passed as an `int` because it is often the result of an arithmetic operation on a byte. Expressions involving bytes are type `int`, so making the parameter an `int` means the result can be passed without a cast to byte. Note, however, that only the lower 8 bits of the integer are transmitted—the upper 24 bits are lost. This method blocks until the byte is written.

public void **write(byte[] buf)** throws IOException
    Writes an array of bytes. This method blocks until the bytes are written.

public void **write(byte[] buf, int offset, int count)**
    throws IOException
    Writes part of an array of bytes, starting at buf[offset], and writing up to count bytes, stopping at the end of the array if that is encountered first.

public void **flush()** throws IOException
    Flushes the stream, so that any bytes held in a buffer are flushed out of the stream.

public void **close()** throws IOException
    Closes the stream. This method must be invoked to release any resources associated with the stream.

Unless stated otherwise, these methods throw `IOException` if they detect an error in the output stream.

Here is an application to copy its input to its output, translating particular characters to other characters along the way. The `Translate` application takes two parameters, a `from` string and a `to` string. Each character in the `from` string is translated into the character in the `to` string at the equivalent position.

```java
import java.io.*;

class Translate {
    public static void main(String[] args) {
        InputStream in = System.in;
        OutputStream out = System.out;

        if (args.length != 2)
            error("must provide from/to arguments");

        String from = args[0], to = args[1];
        int ch, i;

        if (from.length() != to.length())
            error("from and to must be same length");

        try {
            while ((ch = in.read()) != -1) {
                if ((i = from.indexOf(ch)) != -1)
                    out.write(to.charAt(i));
                else
                    out.write(ch);
            }
        } catch (IOException e) {
            error("I/O Exception: " + e);
        }
    }

    public static void error(String err) {
        System.err.print("Translate: " + err);
        System.exit(1); // non-zero means "not good"
    }
}
```

*Exercise 11.1*

Rewrite the `Translate` program shown above as a method that translates the contents of an `InputStream` onto an `OutputStream`, where the mapping and the streams are parameters. For each type of `InputStream` and `OutputStream` you read about in this chapter, write a new `main` method that uses the translation method to operate on a stream of that type. If you have paired input and output streams you can cover both in one `main` method.  ▲

## 11.4  Standard Stream Types

The `java.io` package defines several types of streams, as can be seen in Figure 11.1. The stream types usually have input/output pairs:

- ◆ `Piped` streams are designed as a pair to provide a conduit so that bytes written on a `PipedOutputStream` can be read from a `PipedInputStream`.

- ◆ `ByteArray` streams use a byte array as an input or output stream.

- ◆ `Filter` streams are abstract classes representing byte streams with some filtering operation applied as bytes are read. A `FilterInputStream` object gets input from another `InputStream` object, processes (filters) the bytes in some manner, and returns the filtered result. You build sequences of filtered streams by chaining various filters into one large filter. Output can be filtered similarly with various `FilterOutputStream` classes.

- ◆ `Buffered` streams extend the `Filter` streams to add buffering, so that `read` and `write` need not access the file system for every invocation.

- ◆ `Data` streams are broken into two parts. The `DataInput` and `DataOutput` interfaces define methods to read and write representations of built-in types, where the output of one is recognizable as input to the other. These interfaces are implemented by the `DataInputStream` and `DataOutputStream` classes.

- ◆ `File` streams extend the `Filter` streams to tie the stream of bytes to a file. They add several methods specific to characteristics of files.

The I/O package also has input and output streams that have no output or input counterpart:

- ◆ `SequenceInputStream` converts a sequence of `InputStream` objects into a single `InputStream`, so a list of concatenated input streams can be treated as a single input stream.

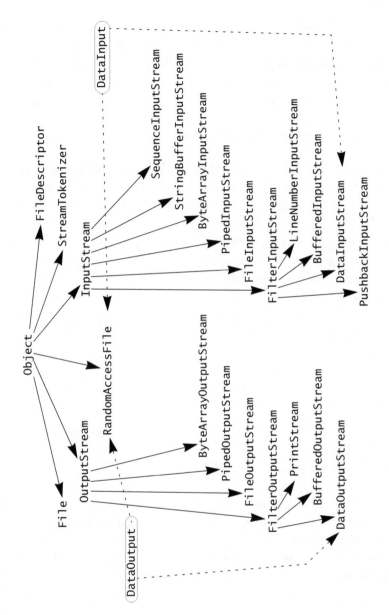

**Figure 11.1** Type Tree for *java.io*

---

- ◆ StringBufferInputStream uses a StringBuffer object as an input stream.
- ◆ LineNumberInputStream extends FilterInputStream to track line numbers of the input stream.

◆ PushbackInputStream extends FilterInputStream to add a one-byte pushback buffer useful for scanning and parsing.

◆ PrintStream extends OutputStream to provide print and println methods for formatting printed data in human-readable form. System.out and System.err are of this type.

In addition to these stream types, a few other useful I/O classes are provided:

◆ File (not to be confused with the File stream classes) provides an abstraction of file pathnames on the local file system, including path component separators, the local suffix separator, and useful methods to manipulate filenames.

◆ RandomAccessFile provides mechanisms to deal with files as randomly accessed streams. It implements the DataInput and DataOutput interfaces, as well as most input and output methods of InputStream and OutputStream.

◆ The StreamTokenizer class breaks an InputStream into tokens. This class breaks its input into recognizable "words," often needed when parsing user input.

These classes can be extended to create new kinds of stream classes for specific applications.

## 11.5  Filter Streams

Filter streams add new constructors to the basic ones in the InputStream and OutputStream classes. These new constructors accept a stream of the appropriate type (input or output) to which to connect. Filter streams enable you to chain streams to produce composite streams of greater power. This program prints the line number where the first instance of a particular character is found in a file:

```
import java.io.*;

class FindChar {
    public static void main(String[] args)
        throws Exception
    {
        if (args.length != 2)
            throw new Exception("need char and file");
```

```
        int match = args[0].charAt(0);
        FileInputStream
            fileIn = new FileInputStream(args[1]);
        LineNumberInputStream
            in = new LineNumberInputStream(fileIn);
        int ch;
        while ((ch = in.read()) != -1) {
            if (ch == match) {
                System.out.println("'" + (char)ch +
                    "' at line " + in.getLineNumber());
                System.exit(0);
            }
        }
        System.out.println(ch + " not found");
        System.exit(1);
    }
}
```

This program creates a FileInputStream named fileIn to read from the named file, then inserts a LineNumberInputStream named in before it. LineNumberInputStream objects get their bytes from the input stream they are attached to, keeping track of line numbers. When we read bytes from in, we are really reading bytes from fileIn, which reads them from the input file. When this program is run on itself looking for the letter 'I', its output is

```
'I' at line 10
```

You can chain any number of FilterInputStream objects. The original source of bytes can be an InputStream object that is not a FilterInputStream. Chaining of streams is the primary feature provided by Filter streams, and since the original source isn't reading bytes from another input stream, it isn't required to be a FilterInputStream.

FilterOutputStream objects can similarly be chained, so that bytes written to one output stream will filter and write bytes to the next output stream. All the streams, from the first to the next-to-last, must be FilterOutputStream objects, but the last may be any kind of OutputStream.

Filter streams enhance the behavior of standard streams. For example, to ensure that the current line number from System.in is always known, you could put this line at the start of the program:

```
LineNumberInputStream
    lnum = new LineNumberInputStream(System.in);
System.in = lnum;
```

All the other code can do the normal operations on `System.in`, but now line numbers will be tracked. To obtain the current line number at any later time, you write:

```
lnum.getLineNumber()
```

A `LineNumberInputStream` attached to another `InputStream` fulfills the same contract as the other stream, if `InputStream` is the only type that it is known as. `System.in` can only be assumed to have the type `InputStream`, so code that uses it can only rely upon it supporting that contract. The `LineNumberInputStream` supports that and more, so it is legitimate to replace it with what is effectively the original object with line number tracking added.

### Exercise 11.2

Extend `FilterInputStream` to create a class of object that will read in and return one line of input at a time with a method that blocks until a full line of input is available.  ▲

### Exercise 11.3

Extend `FilterOutputStream` to create a class of object that converts each word in the output into titlecase.  ▲

### Exercise 11.4

Create a pair of `Filter` stream classes that compress data into some format, with the `CompressInputStream` being able to decompress the bytes that the compressing `CompressOutputStream` class created.  ▲

## 11.6  PrintStream

`PrintStream` is used every time a `print` or `println` method invocation appears in a program. `PrintStream` extends `FilterOutputStream`, so you can filter bytes on their way downstream. It provides `print` and `println` methods for the following types:

```
char     int     float    Object   boolean
char[]   long    double   String
```

In addition, a simple `println` with no parameters ends the current line without printing any other information.

PrintStream supports two constructors. One is the `FilterOutputStream` constructor that takes a downstream object. The other has a boolean second parameter to control autoflushing. If the autoflush boolean is `true`, writing a newline character '\n' invokes flush. Otherwise, newlines are treated like any other character, and flush is not invoked. Autoflush behavior cannot be changed after the stream is constructed.

When autoflush is turned on, any invocation of either write method that writes an array of bytes invokes flush. Newlines inside arrays do not cause auto-flushing, no matter what the state of the autoflush boolean is.

The print(String) and print(char[]) methods are synchronized. All the other print and println methods are written in terms of these two methods, so printing on a PrintStream object is thread-safe.

## 11.7  Buffered Streams

The BufferedInputStream and BufferedOutputStream classes support objects that buffer their data to avoid every read or write going directly to the next stream. These classes are often used in conjunction with File streams—accessing a disk file is relatively inefficient, and buffering helps reduce file accesses.

When a buffered stream is created, its buffer size can be specified explicitly, or it can use a default size. The buffered stream creates a byte array to hold bytes on their way through the stream.

When a read is invoked on an empty BufferedInputStream, it invokes a read on its source stream, fills the buffer with as many bytes as available, and returns the requested data from that buffer.

BufferedOutputStream behaves similarly. When a write fills up the buffer, the destination stream's write is invoked to flush the buffer.

Here is how to create a buffered output stream to write data to a file:

```
OutputStream bufferedFile(String path)
    throws IOException
{
    OutputStream out = new FileOutputStream(path);
    return new BufferedOutputStream(out);
}
```

You create a FileOutputStream with the path, put a BufferedOutputStream in front of it, and return the buffered stream object. This scheme enables you to buffer output destined for the file.

To invoke methods on the FileOutputStream object, you must retain a reference to it, because there is no way to obtain the downstream object from a Filter stream. In such cases, you must ensure that the buffered stream is flushed before operating on downstream objects, because bytes written to the buffered stream may not have yet been written downstream.

## 11.8   ByteArray Streams

To build a string representing printable data, or decode data, arrays of bytes can be treated as the sources of input streams or the destinations of output streams. ByteArray streams provide these capabilities. ByteArray stream methods are synchronized so they are thread-safe.

The ByteArrayInput class uses a byte array as its input source. It has two constructors:

public **ByteArrayInputStream(byte[] buf)**
>    Creates a ByteArrayInputStream from the specified array of bytes. The input array is used directly, not copied. When the end of buf is reached, that is the end of input from the stream.

public **ByteArrayInputStream(byte[] buf, int offset, int length)**
>    Creates a ByteArrayInputStream from the specified array of bytes, using only the subarray of buf from buf[offset] to buf[offset+length-1] or the end of the array, whichever is smaller.

The ByteArrayOutputStream class provides a dynamically growing byte array to hold output. It adds constructors and methods:

public **ByteArrayOutputStream()**
>    Creates a new ByteArrayOutputStream with a default size.

public **ByteArrayOutputStream(int size)**
>    Creates a new ByteArrayOutputStream with the specified initial size.

public synchronized byte[] **toByteArray()**
>    This method returns a copy of the data so the bytes in the array can be modified without changing the bytes of the output.

public int **size()**
>    Returns the current buffer size.

public String **toString(int hiByte)**
>    Creates a new String object from the contents of the byte stream. The top 8 bits of each 16-bit character in the string are set to the lower 8 bits of hiByte. The no-argument form of toString is also overridden to be equivalent to toString(0).

## 11.9   StringBufferInputStream

The StringBufferInputStream reads from a String instead of a byte array. It provides a single constructor that is the string from which to read. Each character in the string is treated as a byte. For example, this program factors numbers read either from the command line or System.in:

```
class Factor {
    public static void main(String[] args) {
        if (args.length == 0) {
            factorNumbers(System.in);
        } else {
            InputStream in;
            for (int i = 0; i < args.length; i++) {
                in = new StringBufferInputStream(args[i]);
                factorNumbers(in);
            }
        }
    }
    // ...
}
```

If the command is invoked without parameters, factorNumbers parses numbers from the standard input stream. When the command line has some parameters on it, a StringBufferInputStream is created for each parameter, and factorNumbers is invoked on each one. factorNumbers treats its input as a stream of bytes containing numbers to be parsed, whether they come from the command line or standard input.

Note that StringBufferInputStream operates on String objects, not StringBuffer objects.

There is no StringBufferOutputStream. A similar effect can be obtained by using the toString method on ByteArrayOutputStream.

## 11.10  File Streams and FileDescriptor

Much input and output in applications reads data from files and writes data to them. Two streams in java.io deal with file I/O—FileInputStream and FileOutputStream. Each type is instantiated with one of three constructors:

◆ A constructor that takes a String that is the name of the file

◆ A constructor that takes a File that refers to the file (see "The File Class" on page 214)

◆ A constructor that takes a FileDescriptor object

A FileDescriptor object represents a system-dependent value that describes an open file. A file descriptor object can be obtained only from a File stream object or RandomAccessFile object, by invoking its getFD method. FileDescriptor objects are used to create a new File or RandomAccessFile stream to the same file as another stream without needing to know the file's pathname. You must be careful to avoid interactions between two streams doing different things with the same file. There is no way to know what happens, for example, when two threads write to the same file using two different FileOutputStream objects at the same time.

The FileOutputStream's flush method guarantees that the buffer is flushed to the underlying file. It is *not* a guarantee that the bytes are committed to disk—the underlying file system may do its own buffering.

## 11.11  Piped Streams

Piped streams are used as input/output pairs; bytes written on the input stream of a pair are those read on the output. Piped streams are thread-safe; in fact, the only safe way to use Piped streams is with two threads—one for reading and one for writing. Writing on one end of the pipe blocks the thread when the pipe fills up. If the writer and reader are the same thread, that thread blocks permanently.

This example creates a new thread to read from the output of some data generator object that writes its output onto an OutputStream object:

```
class Pipe {
    public static void main(String[] args) {
        try {
            PipedOutputStream out = new PipedOutputStream();
            PipedInputStream in = new PipedInputStream(out);

            // DataGenerator will write its results on
            // the output stream we give it
            DataGenerator data = new DataGenerator(out);
            data.setPriority(Thread.MIN_PRIORITY);
            data.start();

            int ch;
            while ((ch = in.read()) != -1)
                System.out.print((char)ch);
            System.out.println();
        } catch (IOException e) {
            System.out.println("Exception: " + e);
        }
    }
}
```

We create the `Piped` streams, making the `PipedInputStream` a parameter to the constructor for the `PipedOutputStream`. The order is unimportant: the output pipe could be a parameter to the input pipe; what is important is that an input/output pair be attached to each other. We create the new `DataGenerator` object, with the `PipedOutputStream` as the output stream for the generated data. Then we loop, reading bytes from the data generator and writing them to the system output stream. At the end, we make sure the last line of output is terminated.

## 11.12  SequenceInputStream

The `SequenceInputStream` class creates a single input stream from reading one or more input streams, reading the first until its end, then reading the next, and so on through the last. It has two constructors: one for the common case of two input streams, where they are provided as the two parameters to the constructor; the other for an arbitrary number of input streams using the `Enumeration` abstraction, described in detail in Chapter 12. An `Enumeration` is an interface that can be implemented to provide an ordered list of any object type. For `SequenceInputStream`, the enumeration should contain only `InputStream` objects. If it contains anything else, a `ClassCastException` is thrown when the `SequenceInputStream` tries to get that object from the list.

For example, the `Factor` application on page 201 invokes `factorNumbers` for each command-line argument. Each number is factored separately, so it didn't matter that the parameters were split into separate invocations. But if your application were summing the values of numbers in its input stream, the function that added values would need all the values at once. The application below uses `SequenceInputStream` to create a single stream from `StringBufferInputStream` objects for each parameter:

```
import java.io.*;
import java.util.Vector;

class Sum {
    public static void main(String[] args) {
        InputStream in; // stream to read numbers from
        if (args.length == 0) {
            in = System.in;
        } else {
            InputStream stringIn;
            Vector inputs = new Vector(args.length);
            for (int i = 0; i < args.length; i++) {
                String arg = args[i] + " ";
```

```
                stringIn = new StringBufferInputStream(arg);
                inputs.addElement(stringIn);
            }
            in = new SequenceInputStream(inputs.elements());
        }

        try {
            double total = sumStream(in);
            System.out.println("The sum is " + total);
        } catch (IOException e) {
            System.out.println(e);
            System.exit(-1);    // we failed
        }
    }
    // ...
}
```

If there are no parameters, we use System.in for input. If there are parameters, we create a Vector large enough to hold as many StringBufferInputStream objects as there are command-line arguments (Vector is described on page 223). Then we create a stream for each, adding a space at the end to separate the strings. We then add the stream to the streams vector. When the loop is finished, we use the vector's elements method to get an Enumeration object for the elements of the vector. We use that Enumeration in the constructor for SequenceInputStream to create a single stream that concatenates all the streams for the parameters into a single InputStream object. We then invoke sumStream to sum the numbers on that stream and print the results. We show the implementation of sumStream as an example in "StreamTokenizer" on page 206.[1]

We could also create a new implementation of Enumeration that caters only to StringInputStream for each argument on demand. See "Enumeration" on page 221 for details.

## 11.13  LineNumberInputStream

The LineNumberInputStream class provides an object to keep track of line numbers while reading input. The getLineNumber method, described on page 201, returns the current line number. Line numbering starts at 1.

---

[1.] This problem could also be solved by building a single string from the parameters and creating one StringBufferInputStream.

The current line number can be set with setLineNumber. This is useful when multiple input streams are treated as one input stream, but line numbers are needed relative to each stream. For example, if you use SequenceInputStream to read a set of files as one stream, you may want line numbers reported relative to the file the bytes came from.

### *Exercise 11.5*

Write a program that reads a specified file and searches for a specified word, printing out all the lines on which that word is found, preceded by the line's number. ▲

## 11.14 PushbackInputStream

A PushbackInputStream provides single-character pushback. Pushback is useful for breaking input into tokens. Lexical scanners, for example, often need to read one character past the end of a token to determine where it ends. Having seen a character that terminates the current token, the scanner must push that character back onto the input stream so it is available as the start of the next token. This example uses PushbackInputStream to find the longest sequence of any single byte in its input:

```
import java.io.*;

class SequenceCount {
    public static void main(String[] args) {
        try {
            PushbackInputStream
                in = new PushbackInputStream(System.in);
            int max = 0;     // long sequence found
            int maxB = -1;   // byte which made that sequence
            int b;           // current byte in input
            do {
                int cnt;
                int b1 = in.read(); // 1st byte in sequence
                for (cnt = 1; (b = in.read()) == b1; cnt++)
                    continue;
                if (cnt > max) {
                    max = cnt; // remember length
                    maxB = b1; // remember which byte value
                }
```

```
                in.unread(b);  // pushback start of next seq
            } while (b != -1); // till we reach end of input
            System.out.println(max + " bytes of " + maxB);
        } catch (IOException e) {
            System.out.println(e);
            System.exit(1);
        }
    }
}
```

When the end of one sequence has been reached, the first byte of the next sequence has been read. We push this byte back using `unread` so that it is read again when we repeat the do loop for the next sequence.

The pushback buffer is a protected `int` field named `pushBack`. A subclass could provide a different way to modify this character. A value of –1 means the pushback buffer is empty. Any other value means that the `Pushback.read` method returns `pushBack` as the first byte of input.

## 11.15  StreamTokenizer

Tokenizing input data is a common application, and the java.io package provides a `StreamTokenizer` class for simple tokenization problems. It currently deals fully only with the lower 8 bits of Unicode, which are the Latin-1 characters, because the internal array that marks character types has only 256 elements. Characters above `\u00ff` are considered alphabetic characters. While this is usually the case (most characters are alphabetics, after all), you cannot, for example, say your quote character is '✍' (`\u270D`). Even with this limitation, many things can be tokenized with such a stream.

A stream is tokenized by creating a `StreamTokenizer` with an `InputStream` object as its source, and then setting parameters for the scan. A scanner loop invokes `nextToken`, which returns the token type of the next token in the stream. Some token types have associated values that are found in fields in the `StreamTokenizer` object.

This class is designed primarily to parse Java-style input; it is not a general tokenizer. However, many configuration files look similar enough to Java that they can be parsed by this tokenizer. When designing a new configuration file or other data, making it look enough like Java to be parsed with `StreamTokenizer` will save work.

When `nextToken` recognizes a token, it returns the token type as its value, and also sets the `ttype` field to the same value. There are four token types:

- ◆ TT_WORD: A word was scanned. The `String` field `sval` contains the word that was found.
- ◆ TT_NUMBER: A number was scanned. The `double` field `nval` contains the value of the number. Only decimal floating-point numbers (with or without a decimal point) are recognized. The tokenizer does not understand `3.4e79` as a floating-point number, nor `0xffff` as a hexadecimal number.
- ◆ TT_EOL: An end-of-line was found.
- ◆ TT_EOF: The end-of-file was reached.

The input stream is composed of "special" and "ordinary" characters. Special characters are those that the tokenizer treats specially, namely, white space, characters that make up numbers, characters that make up words, and so on. Any other character is considered "ordinary." When an ordinary character is the next character in the input, its token type is itself. For example, if the character '¿' is encountered in the input and is not special, the token return type (and the `ttype` field) is the `int` value of the character '¿'.

As one example, let's look at the implementation of `Sum.sumStream`, from the Sum class on page 203:

```
static double sumStream(InputStream in) throws IOException {
    StreamTokenizer nums = new StreamTokenizer(in);
    double result = 0.0;
    while (nums.nextToken() == StreamTokenizer.TT_NUMBER)
        result += nums.nval;
    return result;
}
```

We create a `StreamTokenizer` object from the input stream, then loop reading tokens from the stream. As long as tokens are numbers, we add the numbers to the burgeoning result. When we run out of numbers, we return the final sum.

Here is another example that reads a file, looking for attributes of the form *name=value*, storing them as attributes in `AttributedImpl` objects, described in "Implementing Interfaces" on page 84:

```
public static Attributed readAttrs(String file)
    throws IOException
{
    FileInputStream fileIn = new FileInputStream(file);
    StreamTokenizer in = new StreamTokenizer(fileIn);
    AttributedImpl attrs = new AttributedImpl();
    Attr attr = null;
```

```
            in.commentChar('#');     // '#' is ignore-to-end comment
            in.ordinaryChar('/');    // was original comment char
            while (in.nextToken() != StreamTokenizer.TT_EOF) {
                if (in.ttype == StreamTokenizer.TT_WORD) {
                    if (attr != null) {
                        attr.valueOf(in.sval);
                        attr = null;          // used this one up
                    } else {
                        attr = new Attr(in.sval);
                        attrs.add(attr);
                    }
                } else if (in.ttype == '=') {
                    if (attr == null)
                        throw new IOException("misplaced '='");
                } else {
                    if (attr == null)         // expected a word
                        throw new IOException("bad Attr name");
                    attr.valueOf(new Double(in.nval));
                    attr = null;
                }
            }
        return attrs;
    }
```

The attribute file uses # to mark comments. Ignoring these comments, the stream is searched for a string token followed by an optional = followed by a string or number. Each such attribute is put into an `Attr` object, which is added to a set of attributes in an `AttributedImpl` object. When the file has been parsed, the set of attributes is returned.

Setting the comment character to # sets its character class. The tokenizer recognizes several character classes that are set by the following methods:

public void **wordChars(int low, int hi)**
> Characters in this range are word characters: they can be part of a TT_WORD token. You can invoke this several times with different ranges. A word consists of one or more characters inside any of the legal ranges.

public void **whitespaceChars(int low, int hi)**
> Characters in this range are white space characters. White space is ignored, except to separate tokens such as two consecutive words. As with the wordChars range, you can make several invocations, and the union of the invocations is the set of white space characters.

public void **ordinaryChar(int ch)**

> The character ch is ordinary. An "ordinary" character is returned as itself, not as a token. Refer to the = in the example above for an illustration.

public void **ordinaryChars(int low, int hi)**

> Characters in this range are ordinary.

public void **commentChar(int ch)**

> The character ch starts a single line comment—characters after ch up to the next end-of-line are treated as one run of white space.

public void **quoteChar(int ch)**

> Matching pairs of the character ch delimit String constants. When a String constant is recognized, the character ch is returned as the token, and the field sval contains the body of the string, with surrounding ch characters removed. When reading string constants, some standard Java \ processing is followed (for example, you can have \t in the string), but not all. The string processing in StreamTokenizer is a subset of the Java strings. In particular, you cannot use \uxxxx, \', \", or (unfortunately) \$Q$, where $Q$ is the quote character ch. You can have more than one quote character at a time on a stream, but strings must start and end with the same quote character. In other words, a string that starts with one quote character ends when the next instance of that same quote character is found; if another quote character is found in between, it is simply part of the string.

public void **parseNumbers()**

> Specifies that numbers should be parsed. The stream parses double-precision floating-point numbers and returns a type of TT_NUMBER with the value in nval. There is no way to turn off just this factor—to turn this off requires either invoking ordinaryChars for all the number characters (don't forget the decimal point and minus sign) or invoking resetSyntax.

public void **resetSyntax()**

> Resets the syntax table so that all characters are ordinary. If you do this and then start reading the stream, nextToken always returns the next character in the stream, just like invoking InputStream.read.

There are no methods to query the character class of a given character, or to add new classes of characters. Here are the default settings for a newly created StreamTokenizer object:

```
wordChars('a', 'z');
wordChars('A', 'Z');
wordChars(128 + 32, 255);
whitespaceChars(0, ' ');
```

```
commentChar('/');
quoteChar('"');
quoteChar('\'');
parseNumbers();
```

Other methods control the basic behavior of the tokenizer:

public void **eolIsSignificant(boolean flag)**

> If flag is true, ends of lines are significant, and TT_EOL may be returned by nextToken. If false, ends of lines are treated as white space, and TT_EOL is never returned. The default is false.

public void **slashStarComments(boolean flag)**

> If flag is true, the tokenizer recognizes /*...*/ comments. The default is false.

public void **slashSlashComments(boolean flag)**

> If flag is true, the tokenizer recognizes // to end-of-line comments. The default is false.

public void **lowerCaseMode(boolean flag)**

> If flag is true, all characters in TT_WORD tokens are converted to their lower case equivalent, if they have one (that is, String.toLowerCase is invoked on the word). The default is false.

There are three miscellaneous methods:

public void **pushBack()**

> Pushes the previously returned token back into the stream. The next invocation to nextToken returns the same token again. There is only a one-token pushback; multiple consecutive invocations to pushBack are equivalent to one invocation.

public int **lineno()**

> Returns the current line number. This is usually useful for reporting errors that you detect.

public String **toString()**

> Returns a String representation of the last returned stream token, including its line number.

### Exercise 11.6

Write a program that takes input of the form "name op value", where name is one of three words of your choosing, op is +, -, or =, and value is a number. Apply each operator to the named value. At the end of the program run, print out the three values. For extra credit, use the `Hashtable` class that was used for `AttributedImpl` so that an arbitrary number of named values, not just three, can be used.  ▲

## 11.16  Data Streams

While reading and writing bytes is useful, there is also a frequent need to transmit data of specific types across a stream. The `DataInput` and `DataOutput` interfaces define methods to transmit Java primitive types across a stream. A default implementation of each interface is provided by the classes `DataInputStream` and `DataOutputStream`. We cover the interfaces first, then their implementations.

The interfaces for data input and output streams are almost mirror images. In the table below, the parallel read and write methods for each type are shown:

| Read | Write | Type |
| --- | --- | --- |
| readBoolean | writeBoolean | boolean |
| readChar | writeChar | char |
| readByte | writeByte | byte |
| readShort | writeShort | short |
| readInt | writeInt | int |
| readLong | writeLong | long |
| readFloat | writeFloat | float |
| readDouble | writeDouble | double |
| readUTF | writeUTF | String in UTF format |

UTF is "Unicode Transmission Format"—Unicode characters are transmitted in Unicode-1-1-UTF-8, which is a compact binary form designed to encode 16-bit Unicode characters in 8-bit bytes.

In addition to these paired methods, `DataInput` has several methods of its own:

`public abstract void` **`readFully(byte[] buf)`** `throws IOException`
    Reads bytes into `buf`, blocking until all bytes are read.

`public abstract void` **`readFully(byte[] b, int off, int len)`**
    `throws IOException`
    Reads bytes into `buf` starting at position `offset`, and continuing until either `len` bytes are read, or until the end of `buf` is reached, blocking until all bytes are read.

`public abstract int` **`skipBytes(int n)`** `throws IOException`
    Skips bytes, blocking until all `n` bytes are skipped.

`public abstract String` **`readLine()`** `throws IOException`
> Reads a `String` until a \n, a \r, or a \r\n pair is reached. The end-of-line sequence is not included in the string. A `null` is returned if end-of-input is reached.

`public abstract int` **`readUnsignedByte()`** `throws IOException`
> Reads an unsigned 8-bit byte, and returns the 8-bit byte as an `int`.

`public abstract int` **`readUnsignedShort()`** `throws IOException`
> Reads an unsigned 16-bit short, and returns the 16-bit short as an `int`, giving a number in the range 0–65535 ($2^{16}$–1).

The `DataInput` interface handles end-of-file by throwing an `EOFException` when it occurs. `EOFException` is an extended class of `IOException`.

The `DataOutput` interface supports signatures equivalent to the three forms of `write` in `OutputStream` and additionally provides the following unmirrored methods:

`public abstract void` **`writeBytes(String s)`** `throws IOException`
> Writes a `String` as a sequence of bytes. The upper byte in each character is lost, so unless you are willing to lose data, this method should be used only for strings that contain characters between \u0000 and \u00ff.

`public abstract void` **`writeChars(String s)`** `throws IOException`
> Writes a `String` as a sequence of `char`.

Reading back strings written with these methods must be done using a loop on `readChar`, since there is no `readBytes` or `readChars` method to read back the same number of characters written using a `writeBytes` or `writeChars` invocation. You need to write the length of the string first, or use an end-of-sequence character to mark its end. You can use `readFully` to read back a full array of bytes if you wrote the length first, but that won't work for `writeChars` because you want `char` values, not `byte` values.

### 11.16.1 The Data Stream Classes

For each `Data` interface, there is a corresponding `Data` stream. In addition, the `RandomAccessFile` class implements both the input and output `Data` interfaces (see "RandomAccessFile" on page 213). Each `Data` class is an extension of its `Filter` class, so `Data` streams can be used to filter other streams. This requires constructors for each that take another input or output stream. The filtering can be used, for example, to write data to a file by putting a `DataOutputStream` in front of a `FileOutputStream` object, and then read it back in by putting a `DataInputStream` in front of a `FileInputStream` object.

*Exercise 11.7*

Add a method to the Body class of Chapter 2 that writes the contents of an object to a DataOutputStream, and add a constructor that will read in the state from a DataInputStream.  ▲

## 11.17  RandomAccessFile

The RandomAccessFile class provides a more sophisticated file mechanism than the File streams. It is not an extension of InputStream or OutputStream, because it can do either or both. The mode is specified as a parameter to the various constructors. RandomAccessFile implements both the DataInputStream and DataOutput interfaces, so it can be used to read and write built-in Java data types.

Although RandomAccessFile is not an extension of the input and output stream classes, it supports methods of the same names and signatures as their read and write invocations. Although this means that you don't have to learn a different set of method names and semantics for the same kind of task, you cannot use a RandomAccessFile where either an InputStream or OutputStream object is required. This fact does not prevent you from using a RandomAccessFile where either a DataInput or DataOutput stream is needed.

The three constructors for RandomAccessFile are:

public **RandomAccessFile(String name, String mode)**
    throws IOException
        Creates a RandomAccessFile with the specified filename and mode. The mode can be either "r" or "rw" for "read" or "read/write," respectively. Any other mode throws IOException.

public **RandomAccessFile(File file, String mode)**
    throws IOException
        Creates a RandomAccessFile from a specified File object and mode.

public **RandomAccessFile(FileDescriptor fd)** throws IOException
        Creates a RandomAccessFile with the FileDescriptor object fd (see "File Streams and FileDescriptor" on page 201).

The "random access" referred to in the name of the class is the ability to set the read/write file pointer to any position in the file, and then perform the operation. Methods added by RandomAccessFile to support this functionality are:

public long **getFilePointer()** throws IOException
        Returns the current location of the file pointer (in bytes) from the beginning of the file.

public void **seek(long pos)** throws IOException
> Sets the file pointer to the specified position in number of bytes from the beginning of the file. The next byte written or read will be the posth byte in the file, where the initial byte is the 0th.

public long **length()** throws IOException
> Returns the file length.

*Exercise 11.8*

Write a program that reads in a file with entries separated by lines starting with %%, and creates a table file with the starting position of each such entry. Then write a program that prints out a random entry using that table (see the Math.random method described in "Math" on page 269).  ▲

## 11.18  The File Class

The File class provides several common manipulations that are useful with file-names. It provides methods to separate pathnames into subcomponents, and for querying the file system about the file a pathname refers to.

A File object actually represents a path, not necessarily an underlying file. For example, to find out if a pathname represents an existing file system object, you first create a File object with the pathname, and then invoke exists on that object.

A path is separated into directory and file parts by a char stored in the static field separatorChar, and available as a String in the static field separator. The last occurrence of this character in the path separates the pathname into directory and file components.

File objects are created using one of three constructors:

public **File(String path)**
> Creates a File object to manipulate the specified path. This method throws a NullPointerException if the path parameter is null.

public **File(String dirName, String name)**
> Creates a File object for the file name in the directory named dirName. If dirName is null, only the name component is used. Otherwise this is equivalent to

```
File(dirName + File.separator + name)
```

public **File(File fileDir, String name)**
> Creates a File object given a directory File object fileDir and the file named name. This is equivalent to

```
File(fileDir.getPath(), name)
```

Four "get" methods retrieve information about components of a `File` object's pathname. Here is a code fragment that invokes each of them:

```
File src = new File("ok", "FileMethods");
System.out.println("getName() = " + src.getName());
System.out.println("getPath() = " + src.getPath());
System.out.println("getAbsolutePath() = "
    + src.getAbsolutePath());
System.out.println("getParent() = " + src.getParent());
```

And here is the output:

```
getName() = FileMethods
getPath() = ok/FileMethods
getAbsolutePath() = /vob/java_prog/src/ok/FileMethods
getParent() = ok
```

Several boolean tests return information about the underlying file represented by a `File` object:

- ◆ `exists`: returns `true` if the file exists in the file system.
- ◆ `canRead`: returns `true` if the file exists and can be read.
- ◆ `canWrite`: returns `true` if the file exists and can be written.
- ◆ `isFile`: returns `true` if the file is a normal file (not a directory or any special type).
- ◆ `isDirectory`: returns `true` if the file is a directory.
- ◆ `isAbsolute`: returns `true` if the path is an absolute pathname.

Several other methods are useful in `File`:

public long **lastModified()**
> Returns the last modification time. The return value should be used only to compare modification dates for different files to check if one has been modified more recently than another, or to check if a file has been modified. The time has no other defined meaning.

public long **length()**
> Returns the file length in bytes.

public boolean **mkdir()**
> Creates a directory, returning `true` on success.

public boolean **mkdirs()**
> Creates all directories in this path, returning `true` if all were created. This is a way to ensure a particular directory is created, even if that means creating other directories that don't currently exist above it in the directory hierarchy.

public boolean **renameTo(File new_name)**
>   Renames a file, returning `true` if the rename succeeded.

public boolean **delete()**
>   Deletes the file or directory named in this `File` object, returning `true` if the deletion succeeded.

public String[] **list()**
>   Lists the files in a directory. If used on something that isn't a directory, it returns `null`. Otherwise, it returns an array of filenames. This list includes all files in the directory except the equivalent of "." and ".." (the current and parent directory, respectively).

public String[] **list(FilenameFilter filter)**
>   Uses the specified filter to list files in a directory (see `FilenameFilter` below).

The overridden method `File.equals` deserves mention. Two `File` objects are considered equal if they have the same path, not if they refer to the same underlying file system object. You cannot use `File.equals` to test if two `File` objects denote the same file.

Files are created using `FileOutputStream` objects or `RandomAccessFile` objects, not using `File` objects.

Finally, the character `File.pathSeparatorChar` and the string `File.pathSeparator` represent the character that separates file or directory names in a search path. For example, UNIX separates components in the program search path using a colon, as in `".:/bin:/usr/bin"`. So `pathSeparatorChar` is a colon on UNIX systems.

The path of the file is a protected `String` field named `path`. Classes extending `File` can directly access or modify it as needed.

### Exercise 11.9

Write a method that, given one or more pathnames, will print all the information available about the file it represents (if any).   ▲

## 11.19  FilenameFilter

The `FilenameFilter` interface provides objects that filter unwanted files from a list. It supports a single method:

boolean **accept(File dir, String name)**
>   Returns `true` if the file named `name` in the directory `dir` should be part of the filtered output.

Here is an example that uses a `FilenameFilter` object to list only directories:

```
import java.io.*;

class DirFilter implements FilenameFilter {
    public boolean accept(File dir, String name) {
        return new File(dir, name).isDirectory();
    }

    public static void main(String[] args) {
        File dir = new File(args[0]);
        String[] files = dir.list(new DirFilter());
        System.out.println(files.length + " dir(s):");
        for (int i = 0; i < files.length; i++)
            System.out.println("\t" + files[i]);
    }
}
```

First we create a `File` object to represent a directory specified on the command line. Then we create a `DirFilter` object and pass it to `list`. For each name in the directory, `list` invokes the `accept` method on the filtering object and includes the name in the list if the filtering object returns `true`. For our `accept` method, `true` means that the named file is a directory.

### *Exercise 11.10*

Using `FilenameFilter`, write a program that takes a directory and a suffix as parameters, and prints out all the files that have that suffix. ▲


## 11.20   The `IOException` Classes

Every I/O-specific error detected by classes in `java.io` is signaled by a subclass of `IOException`. Most classes are designed to be general, so most of the exceptions are not detailed specifically. For instance, `InputStream` methods that throw `IOException` cannot detail which particular exceptions might be thrown, because any particular input stream class might throw a subclass of `IOException` for particular error conditions relevant to that stream. And the filter input and output streams only pass through exceptions from their downstream objects, which can also be of any stream type.

Four specific subclasses of IOException are used in the java.io package:

**EOFException** extends IOException
> Thrown by methods in the Data stream interfaces when you reach the end of input, expectedly or unexpectedly.

**FileNotFoundException** extends IOException
> Thrown by the File stream's constructors when you provide a filename that cannot be found.

**InterruptedIOException** extends IOException
> Thrown by any stream when an I/O operation is interrupted by thread interrupts (see "Interrupting Threads" on page 173). In effect, I/O operations translate an unrecoverable InterruptedException into an InterruptedIOException.

**UTFDataFormatException** extends IOException
> Thrown by DataInputStream.readUTF when the string it is reading has malformed UTF syntax.

Besides these specific exceptions, other exceptional conditions in java.io are signaled with an IOException containing a string that describes the specific error encountered, such as using a disconnected Pipe stream object or trying to push back more than one character onto a PushbackInputStream.

# CHAPTER 12

# Standard Utilities

*Computers are useless—they can only give you answers.*
—Pablo Picasso

**T**HE Java environment provides several standard utility interfaces and classes in the `java.util` package. We've already used a few in earlier chapters, such as the `Date` and `Hashtable` classes. Several other useful utilities are available as interfaces and classes:

*COLLECTIONS:*

- *BitSet:* A dynamically sized bit vector
- *Enumeration:* An interface that returns objects that enumerate a set of values, such as elements contained in a particular hashtable.
- *Vector:* A dynamically sized vector of `Object`.
- *Stack:* An extension of `Vector` that adds methods for a basic last-in first-out stack.
- *Dictionary:* An abstract class for algorithms that map keys to values.
- *Hashtable:* An implementation of `Dictionary` that uses hash codes to map keys to values.
- *Properties:* An extension of `Hashtable` that maps string keys to string values.

*DESIGN PATTERNS:*

- *Observer/Observable:* This interface/class pair enables an object to be Observable by having one or more Observer objects that are notified when something interesting happens in the Observable object.

*MISCELLANEOUS:*

- *Date:* Stores dates to one-second granularity.

- *Random:* Objects that generate sequences of pseudorandom numbers.

- *StringTokenizer:* Splits a string into tokens based on delimiters (by default, white space).

## 12.1  BitSet

The BitSet class provides a way to create a bit vector that grows dynamically. In effect, a BitSet is a set of true and false bits with a size of $2^{32}-1$, all bits initially false. The storage size of the set is only large enough to hold the highest bit index set to true or cleared to false—any bits beyond that are assumed to be false.

A BitSet object can be created with an initial size, or by using the no-arg constructor to get the default size.

public void **set(int bit)**
> Sets the bit at position bit to true.

public void **clear(int bit)**
> Clears the bit at position bit to false.

public boolean **get(int bit)**
> Returns the value of the bit at position bit.

public void **and(BitSet other)**
> Logically ANDS this bit set with other, and change the value of this set to the result.

public void **or(BitSet set)**
> Logically ORS this bit set with other, and change the value of this set to the result.

public void **xor(BitSet set)**
> Logically XORS this bit set with other, and change the value of this set to the result.

public int **size()**
> Returns the highest bit position that can be set or cleared without growing the set.

public int **hashCode()**
> Returns a reasonable hash code for this set, based on the values of its bits. Be careful not to change the values of the bits while the BitSet is in the hashtable, or the set will be lost.

```
public boolean equals(Object other)
```
Returns `true` if all the bits in `other` are the same as those in this set.

Here is a class that uses a `BitSet` to mark which characters occur in a string. It can be printed to show which characters were used in the string.

```java
public class WhichChars {
    private BitSet used = new BitSet();

    public WhichChars(String str) {
        for (int i = 0; i < str.length(); i++)
            used.set(str.charAt(i));      // set bit for char
    }

    public String toString() {
        String desc = "[";
        int size = used.size();
        for (int i = 0; i < size; i++) {
            if (used.get(i))
                desc += (char)i;
        }
        return desc + "]";
    }
}
```

## 12.2  Enumeration

Most collection classes use the `Enumeration` interface as a means to iterate through the values in the collection. It is also used by other classes in the Java libraries and in user code to return an enumeration. Each such class usually creates a private enumeration class to implement the `Enumeration` interface and has one or more methods to return an `Enumeration` object. The `Enumeration` interface declares two methods:

```
public abstract boolean hasMoreElements()
```
Returns `true` if the enumeration contains more elements. This may be called more than once between successive calls to `nextElement()`.

```
public abstract Object nextElement()
```
Returns the next element of the enumeration. Invocations of this method enumerate successive elements. Throws `NoSuchElementException` if no more elements exist.

Here is a typical loop using `Enumeration` to step through the elements in a collection object, in this case with the elements of a `Hashtable`:

```
Enumeration e = table.elements();
while (e.hasMoreElements())
    doSomethingWith(e.nextElement());
```

The contract for `Enumeration` does not include a *snapshot* guarantee. In other words, if the contents of the collection are changed while the enumeration is in use, it may affect the values returned by the methods. For instance, if the implementation of `nextElement` uses the contents of the original collection for its list, removing elements from the list as you enumerate through the list is dangerous. A snapshot would return the elements as they were when the `Enumeration` object was created. You can rely on having a snapshot of the contents only if the method that returns the `Enumeration` object explicitly makes a snapshot guarantee.

## 12.3  Implementing an `Enumeration` Interface

When you write your own collections, you may need to implement your own `Enumeration` interface. The `WhichChars` class above is, in effect, a collection for the set of characters in the initial string. Here is a class that implements `Enumeration` to return the characters represented by the `BitSet` in `WhichChars`:

```
class EnumerateWhichChars implements Enumeration {
    private BitSet bits;
    private int pos;      // next pos to test
    private int setSize; // size of bits (optimization)

    EnumerateWhichChars(BitSet whichBits) {
        bits = whichBits;
        setSize = whichBits.size();
        pos = 0;
    }

    public boolean hasMoreElements() {
        while (pos < setSize && !bits.get(pos))
            pos++;
        return (pos < setSize);
    }

    public Object nextElement() {
```

```
            if (hasMoreElements())
                return new Character((char)pos++);
            else
                return null;
        }
    }
```

This class iterates through the bits in the `BitSet`, returning `Character` objects to hold the character values represented by the set bits in the `BitSet` object. The `hasMoreElements` method advances the current position to the next element to be returned. This is carefully written so that `hasMoreElements` may be invoked several times for each invocation of `nextElement`.

Now a method must be added to the `WhichChars` class to return such an enumeration object:

```
public Enumeration characters() {
    return new EnumerateWhichChars(used);
}
```

Notice that `characters` is declared to return an `Enumeration` object, not an `EnumerateWhichChars` object. `EnumerateWhichChars` is not a public class, which means you can hide the enumeration implementation. Unless you need to return an enumeration with new public functionality, you should hide the enumeration object's type to retain the flexibility to change its implementation.

## 12.4 Vector

The `Vector` class provides a resizeable array of `Object`. Items can be added to the beginning, middle, or end of a vector, and any element in the vector can be accessed with an array index. Java arrays are fixed in size, so a `Vector` object is useful when you do not know the maximum number of objects you will need to store when you must create the array, or where the maximum is large and rarely reached.

There are three kinds of methods in `Vector`:

- ◆ Methods to modify the vector
- ◆ Methods to get values out of the vector
- ◆ Methods that manage how the vector grows when it needs more capacity

The no-arg constructor creates a `Vector` object that uses default capacity management. The other constructors are covered along with the capacity management methods.

Many methods change the contents of a vector. All but setElementAt dynamically change the size of the vector, if needed, to accommodate the request.

```
public final synchronized void setElementAt(Object obj,
    int index)
```
Sets the element at index to be the obj. The existing element at index is dropped from the vector. This throws IndexOutOfBoundsException if given an index larger than the current size of the vector. Use setSize to ensure the index is valid before use (see below).

```
public final synchronized void removeElementAt(int index)
```
Deletes the element at index. Elements in the vector after index are moved down, and the size of the vector is reduced by one.

```
public final synchronized void insertElementAt(Object obj,
    int index)
```
Inserts obj as an element at the position index. Elements in the vector from index on are shifted over to make room.

```
public final synchronized void addElement(Object obj)
```
Adds obj as the last element of the vector.

```
public final synchronized boolean removeElement(Object obj)
```
This is equivalent to using indexOf(obj) and, if the object is found, invoking removeElementAt with the index. If the object is not an element, removeElement returns false (indexOf is described below).

```
public final synchronized void removeAllElements()
```
Removes all elements of the vector. The vector becomes empty.

Here is a Polygon class that will store a list of Point objects that are the polygon's vertices:

```
import java.util.Vector;

public class Polygon {
    private Vector vertices = new Vector();

    public void add(Point p) {
        vertices.addElement(p);
    }

    public void remove(Point p) {
        vertices.removeElement(p);
    }
```

```
        public int numVertices() {
            return vertices.size();
        }

        // ... other methods ...
    }
```

There are several ways to examine the contents of a vector. These methods throw `IndexOutOfBoundsException` if given an invalid index. All methods that search the vector for an element use `Object.equals` to compare the object being searched for to the elements of the `Vector`.

`public final synchronized Object` **`elementAt(int index)`**
> Returns the element at `index`.

`public final boolean` **`contains(Object obj)`**
> Returns `true` if `obj` is in the vector.

`public final synchronized int` **`indexOf(Object obj, int index)`**
> Searches for the first occurrence of `obj`, starting with the `index`[th] position, and returns an index to it, or `-1` if it is not found.

`public final int` **`indexOf(Object obj)`**
> Equivalent to `indexOf(obj, 0)`.

`public final synchronized int` **`lastIndexOf(Object obj, int index)`**
> Searches backwards for `obj`, starting from the `index`[th] position, and returns an index to it, or `-1` if it was not found.

`public final int` **`lastIndexOf(Object elem)`**
> Equivalent to `lastIndexOf(obj, size() - 1)`.

`public final synchronized void` **`copyInto(Object[] anArray)`**
> Copies the elements of this vector into the specified array. This method can also be used to get a snapshot of the contents of the vector.

`public final synchronized Enumeration` **`elements()`**
> Returns an `Enumeration` for the current list of elements. Use the methods of `Enumeration` on the returned object to fetch elements sequentially. The enumerator is not a snapshot. Use `copyInto` if a snapshot is needed.

`public final synchronized Object` **`firstElement()`**
> Returns the first element of the vector. Throws `NoSuchElementException` if the vector is empty.

`public final synchronized Object` **`lastElement()`**
> Returns the last element of the vector. Throws `NoSuchElementException` if the vector is empty. The `firstElement` and `lastElement` pair of methods

can be used to loop through the elements in a vector, but there is a risk of someone modifying the vector while the loop is in progress. Use the `copyInto` method if a snapshot is needed.

The size of the vector is the number of elements that are used in the vector. You can change the size by adding or removing elements, or by using `setSize` or `trimToSize`:

`public final int size()`
> Returns the number of elements currently in the vector. Note that this is not the same as the vector's capacity.

`public final boolean isEmpty()`
> Returns `true` if the vector contains no elements.

`public final synchronized void trimToSize()`
> Trims the vector's capacity to the current size. Use this method to minimize the storage of a vector when its size is stable. Subsequent addition to the vector will make it grow again.

`public final synchronized void setSize(int newSize)`
> Sets the size of the vector to `newSize`. If the size shrinks, elements beyond the end are lost; if the size increases, the new elements are set to `null`.

Correctly managing the capacity of a vector significantly affects its efficiency. If the capacity increment is small, and many elements are added, the vector will spend too much time repeatedly creating a larger buffer to hold new objects and copying them into the new buffer. A better way is to create the vector with a capacity at or near the maximum size you will need. If you know how many values you will add, use `ensureCapacity` to grow the vector at most once. The capacity management parameters are set when the `Vector` is constructed; use any of these constructors to create a `Vector` object:

`public Vector(int initialCapacity, int capacityIncrement)`
> Constructs an empty vector with the specified initial storage capacity and capacity increment. A capacity increment of 0 means to double each time the buffer needs to grow; otherwise, `capacityIncrement` elements will be added to the buffer.

`public Vector(int initialCapacity)`
> Equivalent to `Vector(initialCapacity, 0)`.

`public Vector()`
> Constructs an empty vector with a default initial capacity and a capacity increment of 0.

```
public final int capacity()
```
Returns the current capacity of the vector. This is the number of elements the vector can hold without creating new storage to hold elements.

```
public final synchronized void ensureCapacity(int minCapacity)
```
Ensures that the vector has at least the specified capacity, increasing the capacity if necessary.

Here is a method for `Polygon` that includes another polygon's points:

```
public void merge(Polygon other) {
    int otherSize = other.vertices.size();

    vertices.ensureCapacity(vertices.size() + otherSize);
    for (int i = 0; i < otherSize; i++)
        vertices.addElement(other.vertices.elementAt(i));
}
```

This example uses `ensureCapacity` to ensure that the vector will grow at most once, instead of multiple times as new points are added.

The implementation of `Vector.toString` provides a string that fully describes the vector, including the result of invoking `toString` on each of the contained elements.

In addition to these public methods, protected fields are available to classes that subclass the `Vector` class. Be careful what you do with these fields, because, for instance, methods in `Vector` rely on the buffer size being greater than the number of elements in the stack.

```
protected Object elementData[]
```
The buffer where elements are stored.

```
protected int elementCount
```
The number of elements currently used in the buffer.

```
protected int capacityIncrement
```
The number of elements to add to the capacity when `elementData` runs out of space. If it is 0, the size of the buffer is doubled every time it needs to grow.

### *Exercise 12.1*

Write a program that opens a file and reads in its lines one at a time, storing each line into a `Vector` object sorted by `String.compareTo`. The line-reading class you created in Exercise 11.2 on page 198 should prove useful.  ▲

## 12.5  Stack

The Stack class extends Vector to add methods for a simple last-in first-out stack of Object. Use push to push an object onto the stack, and pop to remove the top element from the stack. The peek method returns the top item on the stack without removing it. The empty method returns true if the stack is empty. Trying to pop or peek in an empty Stack object will throw EmptyStackException.

You can use search to find how far away from the top of the stack a particular object is, with 1 being the top of the stack. If the object isn't found, –1 is returned. The search method uses Object.equals to test if an object in the stack is the same as the one it is searching for.

This example uses Stack to keep track of who currently has borrowed something, such as a toy. The original owner is the first entry in the stack, and when someone borrows the toy, the borrower's name is pushed on the stack. If the borrower lends it to someone else, that person's name is pushed on the stack. When the toy is returned, the borrower's name is popped off the stack. The last name is never popped off the stack, since that would mean losing track of who owns the toy.

```java
import java.util.Stack;

public class Borrow {
    private String itemName;
    private Stack hasIt = new Stack();

    public Borrow(String name, String owner) {
        itemName = name;
        hasIt.push(owner);        // owner's name goes first
    }

    public void borrow(String borrower) {
        hasIt.push(borrower);
    }

    public String currentHolder() {
        return (String)hasIt.peek();
    }
    public String returnIt() {
        String ret = (String)hasIt.pop();
        if (hasIt.empty())        // acidentally popped owner
            hasIt.push(ret);      // put it back
```

```
            return ret;
        }
    }
```

*Exercise 12.2*

Add a method that uses search to find out how many borrowers there are for a borrowed item.  ▲

## 12.6 Dictionary

The Dictionary abstract class is essentially an interface. It defines a set of abstract methods to store an *element* indexed by a particular *key*, and retrieve the element using that key. This is the basic interface for Hashtable, but Dictionary is defined as a separate class so that other implementations can use different algorithms to map keys to elements. The Dictionary returns null to indicate events such as being unable to find a particular entry, so neither the key nor its element may be null. If you provide a null key or element argument, you will get a NullPointerException. If you need a special marker element, some value other than null must be used.

The Dictionary methods are:

public abstract Object **put(Object key, Object element)**
>   Puts element into the dictionary under key. Returns the old element stored under key, or null if there wasn't one.

public abstract Object **get(Object key)**
>   Returns the object associated with the specified key in the dictionary, or null if the key is not defined in the dictionary.

public abstract Object **remove(Object key)**
>   Removes the element corresponding to key, returning the element stored for key, or null if key was not in the dictionary.

public abstract int **size()**
>   Returns the number of elements defined in the dictionary.

public abstract boolean **isEmpty()**
>   Returns true if the dictionary contains no elements.

public abstract Enumeration **keys()**
>   Returns an enumeration of the keys in the dictionary.

public abstract Enumeration **elements()**
>   Returns an enumeration of the elements in the dictionary.

The enumerations returned by `keys` and `elements` are not guaranteed to be snapshots, although if you write a class that implements `Dictionary`, you may choose to add a snapshot guarantee to the contract of your implementation of these methods.

## 12.7  Hashtable

The *hashtable* is a common key/element pair storage mechanism. It has the virtues of generality and simplicity, and it is very efficient, given reasonable hash code generation. The `Hashtable` class implements the `Dictionary` interface. It has a capacity and tools to decide when to grow the table. Growing a hashtable involves re-hashing each element in the table to its new position in the larger table, so sizing a hashtable just once is important.

The other efficiency factor of a hashtable is generation of hash codes from the keys. Hash codes should collide as seldom as possible. Their values should be distributed evenly over the range of possible hash codes, which for `Hashtable` is the full range of `int`. If different keys hash frequently to the same code, that part of the hashtable will get very crowded, and performance will suffer.

The hash code is the return value of the `hashCode` method on the object that is the key. By default, every object has a different hash code. Using random objects as keys results in each having a different hash. `String`, `BitSet`, and most other objects that override the `equal` method normally override `hashCode` as well. This is important, because `Hashtable` uses the hash code to find a set of keys that might match, and invokes `equal` on each object until it finds one equal to the key it is looking for. If `equal` and `hashCode` are not compatible for an object, objects of that type will behave erratically when used as `Hashtable` keys.

You saw an example of `Hashtable` in the `AttributedImpl` class in "Implementing Interfaces" on page 84, where a `Hashtable` object was used to store attributes on an object. In that example, keys were the `String` objects that were the attributes' names, and the `Attr` object itself was the attribute value.

In addition to implementing methods from `Dictionary` (`get`, `put`, `remove`, `size`, `isempty`, `keys`, and `elements`), `Hashtable` supports these methods:

`public synchronized boolean` **`containsKey(Object key)`**
> Returns `true` if the hashtable contains an element under `key`.

`public synchronized boolean` **`contains(Object element)`**
> Returns `true` if the specified `element` is in an element of the hashtable. This operation is more expensive than the `containsKey` method because a hashtable is designed to be efficient at looking up keys, not elements.

`public synchronized void` **`clear()`**
> Empties the hashtable.

```
public synchronized Object clone()
```
Creates a clone of the hashtable. The keys and elements themselves are *not* cloned.

A Hashtable object automatically grows when it gets too full. It is "too full" when it exceeds the table's *load factor*, which is the ratio of the number of elements in the table to the table's current capacity. When the table grows, it chooses a new capacity roughly double the current one. A capacity that is a prime number is critical to good performance, so the Hashtable object may change a specified capacity to a nearby prime number. Both the initial capacity and the load factor can be set by Hashtable constructors:

```
public Hashtable()
```
Constructs a new, empty hashtable with a default initial capacity and load factor of 0.75.

```
public Hashtable(int initialCapacity)
```
Constructs a new, empty hashtable with the specified initialCapacity and a default load factor of 0.75.

```
public Hashtable(int initialCapacity, float loadFactor)
```
Constructs a new, empty hashtable with the specified initial capacity and load factor. The loadFactor is a number between 0.0 and 1.0 that defines the threshold for rehashing the hashtable into a bigger one. If the number of entries in the hashtable increases to more than the current capacity times the load factor, the hashtable will resize itself.

The default size is picked by the implementation to be "reasonable," by the implementor's definition. After the Hashtable is constructed, there is no way to change the load factor, or to explicitly set a new capacity.

When the Hashtable object is resized, the work is done by the method rehash. The rehash method is protected so that extended classes can invoke it when they decide, based on their own requirements, that the time has come for the table to grow. There is no way to set the new size—it is always calculated by rehash.

The implementation of Hashtable.toString provides a string that fully describes the contents of the table, including the result of invoking toString on each of the contained keys and elements.

### Exercise 12.3

The WhichChars class shown on page 221 has a problem marking characters near the top of the Unicode range, because the high character values will leave many unused bits in the lower ranges. Use a Hashtable to solve this problem by storing

Character objects for each character seen. Remember to write an enumerator class.  ▲

### Exercise 12.4

Now use a Hashtable to store a BitSet object for each different top byte (high 8 bits) encountered in the input string, with each BitSet storing the low bytes that have been seen with the particular high byte. Remember to write an enumerator class.  ▲

### Exercise 12.5

Write a program that uses a StreamTokenizer object to break an input file into words and counts the number of times each word occurs in the file, printing the result.  ▲

## 12.8  Properties

Another common key/element pair is a *property list*, consisting of string names and associated string elements. This kind of dictionary often has a backing set of default elements for properties not specified in the table. The Properties class extends Hashtable. Standard Hashtable methods are used for almost all manipulation of a property list, but to get properties, use one of the two getProperty methods:

public String **getProperty(String key)**
> Gets the property element for key. If the key is not found in this property list, the default list (if any) is searched. This method returns null if the property is not found.

public String **getProperty(String key, String defaultElement)**
> Gets the property element for key. If the key is not found in this property list, the default list (if any) is searched. If there is no element for key in either this table or its defaults, the string in defaultElement is returned.

The Properties class has two constructors, a no-arg constructor and one that takes another Properties object as a default property list. If a property lookup fails, the default Properties object is queried. The default properties object can have its *own* default property list, and so on. The chain of property lists and default lists can be arbitrarily deep.

public **Properties()**
> Creates an empty property list.

public **Properties(Properties defaults)**
> Creates an empty property list with the specified default `Properties` object for looking up properties that are not specified in this list.

If a property list has been properly populated with only `String` keys and elements, you can save and restore it from files or other I/O streams using the following methods:

private void **save(OutputStream out, String header)**
> Saves the contents of the property list to an `OutputStream`. The header string is written onto the output stream as a single-line comment. Do not use a multiline header string, or the saved property list will not be loadable. Only properties in this list are saved to the file, not those in the default property list.

public synchronized void **load(InputStream in)** throws IOException
> Loads a property list from an `InputStream`. The property list was presumed to have been created previously by a `save` method invocation. This method loads values only into this property list, not values for default properties.

A snapshot `Enumeration` of the keys in a property list is obtained by invoking the `propertyNames` method:

public Enumeration **propertyNames()**
> Enumerates the keys. This method provides a snapshot.

public void **list(PrintStream out)**
> Lists properties on the given `PrintStream`. Useful for debugging.

The default property list cannot be changed after the object is created. To change the default list, you can subclass the `Properties` class and modify the protected field called `defaults` that contains the default properties list.

## 12.9 Observer/Observable

The `Observer/Observable` types provide a protocol where an arbitrary number of `Observer` objects watch for changes and events in any number of `Observable` objects. An `Observable` object subclasses the `Observable` class, which provides methods to maintain a list of `Observer` objects that want to know about changes in the `Observable` object. All objects in the "interested" list must implement the `Observer` interface. When an `Observable` object experiences a noteworthy change, or an event that `Observer` objects care about, the `Observable` object invokes its `notifyObservers` method, which invokes each `Observer` object's update method. The `Observer` interface's update method is:

`public abstract void `**`update(Observable obj, Object arg)`**
  This method is invoked when the `Observable` object `obj` has a change or an event to report. The `arg` parameter is a way to pass an arbitrary object to describe the change or event to the `Observer`.

The `Observer`/`Observable` mechanism is designed to be general. Each `Observable` class is left to define when, and under what circumstances, an `Observer` object's update method will be invoked.

The `Observable` class implements methods to maintain the list of `Observer` objects, methods to maintain an "object changed" flag, and methods to invoke the update method on any `Observer`. These `Observable` methods maintain the list of `Observer` objects:

`public synchronized void `**`addObserver(Observer o)`**
  Adds an `Observer` to the observer list.

`public synchronized void `**`deleteObserver(Observer o)`**
  Deletes an `Observer` from the observer list.

`public synchronized void `**`deleteObservers()`**
  Deletes all `Observer` objects from the observer list.

`public synchronized int `**`countObservers()`**
  Returns the number of observers in the observer list.

The following methods notify `Observer` objects of changes:

`public synchronized void `**`notifyObservers(Object arg)`**
  Notifies all `Observer` objects in the list that something has happened, then clears the "object changed" flag. For each observer in the list, its update method is invoked with this `Observable` object as the first parameter, and `arg` as the second.

`public void `**`notifyObservers()`**
  Equivalent to `notifyObservers(null)`.

This example illustrates how `Observer`/`Observable` might be used to monitor users of a system. First, define a `Users` class that is an `Observable` type:

```
import java.util.*;

public class Users extends Observable {
    private Hashtable loggedIn = new Hashtable();
```

```
    public void login(String name, String password)
        throws BadUserException
{
    // this method throws BadUserException
    if (!passwordValid(name, password))
        throw new BadUserException(name);

    UserState state = new UserState(name);
    loggedIn.put(name, state);
    setChanged();
    notifyObservers(state);
}

    public void logout(UserState state) {
        loggedIn.remove(state.name());
        setChanged();
        notifyObservers(state);
    }

    // ...
}
```

A `Users` object stores a list of users who are logged in and maintains `UserState` objects for each login. When someone logs in or out, all `Observer` objects will be passed that user's `UserState` object. The `notifyObservers` method sends messages only if the state changes, so we must also invoke `setChanged` on `Users`, otherwise `notifyObservers` would do nothing. Besides `setChanged`, there are two other methods that manipulate the "changed" flag: `clearChanged` marks the `Observable` object as unchanged, and `hasChanged` returns the `boolean` flag.

Here is how an `Observer` that maintains a constant display of logged-in users might implement `update` to watch a `Users` object:

```
import java.util.*;

public class Eye implements Observer {
    Users watching;

    public Eye(Users users) {
        watching = users;
        watching.addObserver(this);
    }
```

```
public void update(Observable users, Object whichState)
{
    if (users != watching)
        throw new IllegalArgumentException();

    UserState state = (UserState)whichState;
    if (watching.loggedIn(state))    // user logged in
        addUser(state);              // add to my list
    else
        removeUser(state);           // remove from list
}
}
```

Each Eye object watches a particular Users object. When a user logs in or out, Eye is notified, because it invoked the Users object's addObserver method with itself as the interested object. When update is invoked, it checks the correctness of its parameters, and then modifies its display depending on whether the user in question has logged in or logged out.

The check for what happened with the UserState object is simple here. It could be avoided by passing a wrapper object describing what had happened and to whom, instead of passing the UserState object itself. This is clearer, and makes it easier to add new actions without breaking existing code.

The Observer/Observable mechanism is a looser, more flexible mechanism, analogous to the wait/notify mechanism for threads described on page 166. The thread mechanism ensures that synchronized access protects you from undesired concurrency. The observation mechanism enables any relationship to be built between two participants, whatever the threading model. Both have producers of information (Observable and the invoker of notify) and consumers of that information (Observer and the invoker of wait), but they fill different needs. Use wait/notify when you design a thread-based mechanism, and use Observer/Observable when you need something more general.

*Exercise 12.6*

Provide an implementation of the Attributed interface that uses Observer/Observable to notify observers of changes.   ▲

## 12.10  Date

The Date class provides you with a mechanism for displaying and calculating with dates and times, although the default display is in a style peculiar to the

United States. You can set and examine the date, taking the local time zone into account if needed.

The Date class is intended to reflect UTC (Coordinated Universal Time), but it cannot always do so exactly. Imprecise behavior is inherited from the time mechanisms of the underlying operating system.[1] Subparts of a date are specified in UTC standard units and ranges. A value that is out of range is interpreted correctly—January 32 is equivalent to February 1, for example. Here are the ranges:

| | |
|---|---|
| year | a year after 1900, always specified with all digits |
| month | 0–11 |
| date | day of the month, 1–31 |
| hours | 0–23 |
| min | 0–23 |
| seconds | 0–61 (provides for leap seconds) |

The Date class is simple to use, but has a lot of methods:

public **Date()**

> Creates a Date object that represents the current date/time.

public **Date(int year, int month, int date, int hrs, int min, int sec)**

> Creates a Date object that represents the given date.

public **Date(int year, int month, int date, int hrs, int min)**

> Equivalent to Date(year, month, date, hrs, min, 0), that is, the beginning of the specified minute.

public **Date(int year, int month, int date)**

> Equivalent to Date(year, month, date, 0, 0, 0), that is, midnight on the given date.

public **Date(String s)**

> Creates a date from a string according to the syntax accepted by parse (described below).

---

[1]. Almost all modern systems assume that one day is 24*60*60 seconds. In UTC, about once a year an extra second, called a "leap second," is added to a day to account for the wobble of the earth. Most computer clocks are not accurate enough to reflect this distinction, so neither is the Date class. Some computer standards are defined in GMT, which is the "civil" name for the standard, where UT is the "scientific" name for the same standard. The distinction between UTC and UT is that UT is based on an atomic clock and UTC is based on astronomical observations. For almost all practical purposes this is an invisibly fine hair to split. See the Bibliography for references to further information.

```
public static long UTC(int year, int month, int date, int hrs,
    int min,int sec)
```
Calculates a UTC value from the specified dates.

```
public static long parse(String s)
```
Given a string representing a time, parse it, and return the time value. It accepts many syntaxes, but most importantly, it accepts the IETF standard date syntax, which looks like this: "Sat, 12 Aug 1995 13:30:00 GMT". It understands the continental U.S. time zone abbreviations, but for general use, a time zone offset should be used: "Sat, 12 Aug 1995 13:30:00 GMT+0430" (4 hours, 30 minutes west of the Greenwich meridian). If no time zone is specified, the local time zone is assumed. GMT and UTC are considered equivalent time zone specifiers.

```
public Date(long date)
```
Creates a date. The fields are normalized before the Date object is created. This method accepts the return value of the class methods parse or UTC.

```
public int getYear()
```
Returns the year, always after 1900.

```
public int getMonth()
```
Returns the month in the range 0–11, representing January–December.

```
public int getDate()
```
Returns the day of the month.

```
public int getDay()
```
Returns the day of the week in the range 0–6, representing Sunday–Saturday.

```
public int getHours()
```
Returns the hour in the range 0–23, with midnight equal to 0.

```
public int getMinutes()
```
Returns the minute in the range 0–59.

```
public int getSeconds()
```
Returns the second in the range 0–61.

```
public long getTime()
```
Returns the time in UTC.

```
public int getTimezoneOffset()
```
Returns the time zone offset in minutes for the current locale that is appropriate for this time. This value would be a constant except for daylight savings time, which, where it is observed, shifts the time zone offset depending on the time of year.

```
public void setYear(int year)
```
Sets the year. The year should be at least 1900.

```
public void setMonth(int month)
```
Sets the month.

```
public void setDate(int date)
```
Sets the date.

```
public void setDay(int day)
```
Sets the day of the week.

```
public void setHours(int hours)
```
Sets the hours.

```
public void setMinutes(int minutes)
```
Sets the minutes.

```
public void setSeconds(int seconds)
```
Sets the seconds.

```
public boolean before(Date other)
```
Returns `true` if this date comes before the `other` date.

```
public boolean after(Date other)
```
Returns `true` if this date comes after the `other` date.

```
public boolean equals(Object other)
```
Returns `true` if this date represents the same time in UTC as the `other` date.

```
public int hashCode()
```
Computes a hash code so that `Date` objects can be used as hashtable keys.

```
public String toString()
```
Converts a date to a `String`, such as `"Fri Oct 13 14:33:57 EDT 1995"`.[2]

```
public String toLocaleString()
```
Converts a date to a `String`, using the locale conventions. In other words, the date will be presented in an order common for the locale set by the underlying operating system. For example, people in the United States are used to seeing the month before the date ("June 13"), whereas in much of Europe the normal order is reversed ("13 June").

```
public String toGMTString()
```
Converts a date to a `String`, using the Internet GMT conventions, of the form

```
d mon yyyy hh:mm:ss GMT
```

where d is the day of the month (one or two digits), mon is the first three letters of the month, yyyy is the four-digit year, hh is the hour of the day (0–23),

---

[2.] The format used is the same as the ANSI C convention for its `ctime` function.

mm is the minute of the hour, and ss is the second of the minute. The time ignores local time zone information.


## 12.11  Random

The Random class creates objects that manage independent sequences of pseudo-random numbers. If you don't care what the sequence is and want it as a sequence of double values, the method java.lang.Math.random creates a single Random object the first time it is invoked, and returns pseudorandom numbers from that object. For more control over the sequence (for example, being able to set the seed), create a Random object and get values from it.

public **Random()**
> Creates a new random number generator. Its seed will be initialized to a value based on the current time.

public **Random(long seed)**
> Creates a new random number generator using the specified seed. Two Random objects created with the same initial seed will return the same sequence of pseudorandom numbers.

public synchronized void **setSeed(long seed)**
> Sets the seed of the random number generator to seed. This method can be invoked at any time and resets the sequence to start from the given seed.

public int **nextInt()**
> Returns a pseudorandom uniformly distributed int value between the two values Integer.MIN_VALUE and Integer.MAX_VALUE, inclusive.

public long **nextLong()**
> Returns a pseudorandom uniformly distributed long value between Long.MIN_VALUE and Long.MAX_VALUE, inclusive.

public float **nextFloat()**
> Returns a pseudorandom uniformly distributed float value between Float.MIN_VALUE and Float.MAX_VALUE, inclusive.

public double **nextDouble()**
> Returns a pseudorandom uniformly distributed double value between Double.MIN_VALUE and Double.MAX_VALUE, inclusive.

public synchronized double **nextGaussian()**
> Returns a pseudorandom Gaussian-distributed double value with mean of 0.0 and standard deviation of 1.0.

*Exercise 12.7*

Given a certain number of six-sided dice, you can calculate the theoretical probabilities of each possible total. For example, with two six-sided dice, the probability of a total of seven is one in six. Write a program that matches the theoretical distribution of sums for a particular number of six-sided dice with the actual results over a large number of "rolls" using Random to generate numbers between one and six. Does it matter which of the number-generating methods you use?   ▲

*Exercise 12.8*

Write a program that tests nextGaussian, displaying the results of a large number of runs as a graph (a bar chart of * characters will do).   ▲

## 12.12 StringTokenizer

The StringTokenizer class breaks a string into parts, using delimiters. A sequence of tokens broken out of a string is, in effect, an ordered enumeration of those tokens, so StringTokenizer implements the Enumeration interface (see page 221). You can pass StringTokenizer objects with methods to handle general enumeration, or use Enumeration methods to iterate. StringTokenizer provides more specifically typed methods if you know you are working on a StringTokenizer object. The StringTokenizer enumeration is not a snapshot, but it doesn't matter, because String objects are read-only. For example, to break a string into tokens separated by spaces and commas, a loop like this could be used:

```
String str = "Gone, and forgotten";
StringTokenizer tokens = new StringTokenizer(str, " ,");
while (tokens.hasMoreTokens())
    System.out.println(tokens.nextToken());
```

By including comma in the list of separators in the StringTokenizer constructor, the tokenizer consumes commas along with spaces, leaving only the words of the string to be returned one at a time. The output of this example is:

```
Gone
and
forgotten
```

The StringTokenizer class has several methods to control what is considered a word, whether it should understand numbers or strings specially, and so on:

```
public StringTokenizer(String str, String delim,
    boolean returnTokens)
```
Constructs a `StringTokenizer` on the string `str`, using the characters in `delim` as the delimiter set. The `returnTokens` boolean determines whether delimiters are returned as tokens or skipped. If they are returned as tokens, each delimiter character is returned separately.

```
public StringTokenizer(String str, String delim)
```
Equivalent to `StringTokenizer(str, delim, false)`, meaning delimiters are skipped, not returned.

```
public StringTokenizer(String str)
```
Equivalent to `StringTokenizer(str, " \t\n\r")`, meaning delimiters are white space characters.

```
public boolean hasMoreTokens()
```
Returns `true` if more tokens exist.

```
public String nextToken()
```
Returns the next token of the string. Throws `NoSuchElementException` if there are no more tokens.

```
public String nextToken(String delim)
```
Switches the delimiter set to the characters in `delim`, and returns the next token. There is no way to set a new delimiter set without getting the next token.

```
public int countTokens()
```
Returns the number of tokens remaining in the string using the current delimiter set. This is the number of times `nextToken` can return before it will generate an exception. When you need the number of tokens, this method is faster than repeatedly invoking `nextToken` because the token strings are merely counted, not constructed and returned.

The two methods `StringTokenizer` inherits from the `Enumeration` interface—`hasMoreElements` and `nextElement`—are equivalent to `hasMoreTokens` and `nextToken`, respectively.

If you need a more powerful mechanism to break a string or any other input into tokens, refer to "StreamTokenizer" on page 206, which describes a class with greater power over how input is understood. To use `StreamTokenizer` on a string, create a `StringBufferInputStream` object for the string. For many cases, however, a simple `StringTokenizer` object is sufficient.

### Exercise 12.9

Write a method that will take a string, break it up using white space as the delimiter, and return a new string with the first letter of each word converted to titlecase as covered in Section 13.5 on page 253.  ▲

# CHAPTER 13

# Programming with Types

*I'm gonna wrap myself in paper,*
*I'm gonna dab myself with glue—*
*Stick some stamps on top of my head!*
*I'm gonna mail myself to you.*
—Woody Guthrie, *The Mail Song*

J AVA language types are represented by classes. There are classes, also known as "wrappers," for almost all primitive types (`int`, `boolean`, and such), and a `Class` class to represent types of classes and interfaces. These classes provide three advantages:

- ◆ Useful static methods for a particular type have a logical and consistent home. For example, the methods to convert a string to a `float` are static methods of the `Float` type class.

- ◆ Descriptive methods and fields also have a logical home. `MIN_VALUE` and `MAX_VALUE` constants are available in the classes for each numeric primitive type; methods that describe the supertypes of a class are available from its `Class` object.

- ◆ For primitive types, wrapper objects can be created to hold their values. Then those objects can be used in any context where an `Object` reference is required. For this reason, classes for primitive types are called *wrapper classes*.

The type hierarchy for these classes looks like this:

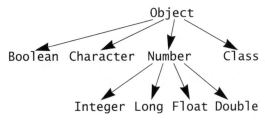

Classes for short and byte are not provided because they are used primarily for storage efficiency. All arithmetic for short and byte is done as int expressions. To store a short or byte value in an object, use an Integer object. Unfortunately this also means that there are no MIN_VALUE and MAX_VALUE constants for byte or short.

This chapter describes how to use these type-related classes. The first part of the chapter covers Class objects that represent particular classes and interfaces. The rest of the chapter is devoted to programming with wrapper classes for primitive types.

## 13.1 Class

Each class and interface in the system has a Class object that represents it. This object can be used for basic queries about the class or interface, and to create new objects of a class.

The Class class enables you to navigate the type system in a program. The type system effectively becomes part of the program environment, to provide many advantages in debugging, self-documentation, and general consistency. It also provides a tool to manipulate classes, primarily for creating objects of types specified in strings, and for loading classes using specialized techniques, such as across the network.

There are two ways to get a Class object: ask an object for its class object using its getClass method, or look it up by its fully qualified (all packages included) name using the static method Class.forName.

The simplest Class methods are those that walk the type hierarchy. This class prints the type hierarchy of the type represented by a particular Class object:

```
public class TypeDesc {
    public static void main(String[] args) {
        TypeDesc desc = new TypeDesc();
        for (int i = 0; i < args.length; i++) {
            try {
                desc.printType(Class.forName(args[i]), 0);
            } catch (ClassNotFoundException e) {
                System.err.print(e);    // report the error
            }
        }
    }

    // by default print on standard output
    public java.io.PrintStream out = System.out;
```

```
    // used in printType() for labeling type names
    private static String[]
        basic    = { "class",   "interface" },
        extended = { "extends", "implements" };

    public void printType(Class type, int depth) {
        if (type == null) // Object's supertype is null
            return;

        // print out this type
        for (int i = 0; i < depth; i++)
            out.print("  ");
        String[] labels = (depth == 0 ? basic : extended);
        out.print(labels[type.isInterface() ? 1 : 0] + " ");
        out.println(type.getName());

        // print out an interfaces this class implements
        Class[] interfaces = type.getInterfaces();
        for (int i = 0; i < interfaces.length; i++)
            printType(interfaces[i], depth + 1);

        // recurse on the superclass
        printType(type.getSuperclass(), depth + 1);
    }
}
```

This example loops through the names provided on the command line and invokes printType on each. It must do this inside a try block in case there is no class of the specified name. Here is its output when invoked on the utility class java.util.Hashtable (the fully qualified name is used because it is required by the forName method):

```
class java.util.Hashtable
  implements java.lang.Cloneable
    extends java.lang.Object
  extends java.util.Dictionary
    extends java.lang.Object
```

The next thing in the source is the declaration of the output stream. It is declared public for brevity, but in a real application it would be private and accessible only by an accessor method. The two String arrays are described shortly.

The `printType` method prints its own type description, then invokes itself recursively to print the description of the type's supertypes. The `depth` parameter keeps track of how far up the type hierarchy it has climbed, indenting each description line depending on its depth. The depth is incremented at each recursion level.

When printing the type, the `isInterface` method determines if the type is an interface. We use the result of `isInterface` to pick an appropriate label to print for the type. At the bottom of the type hierarchy, where `depth` is zero, we want to use "class" and "interface"; higher up in the type hierarchy the type either extends or implements the original type, so we use those terms. This is the purpose of the arrays `Basic` and `Extended`. After we get the right prefix, we use `getName` to print the name of the type. The `Class` class implements the `toString` method, but it already adds "class" or "interface" in front. We want to control the prefix, so we have to create our own implementation.

After printing the type description, `printType` invokes itself recursively. First it recurses to print all the interfaces that the original type implements.[1] Then it prints the superclass this type extends (if any). Eventually it reaches the `Class` object for `Object`, which implements no interfaces and whose `getSuperclass` method returns `null`, and the recursion ends.

### Exercise 13.1

Modify `TypeDesc` to skip printing anything for the `Object` class. It is redundant because everything ultimately extends it. Use the reference for the `Class` object for the `Object` type.   ▲

A `Class` object can use the `newInstance` method to create a new instance (object) of the type it represents. This invokes the class's no-arg constructor, or throws `NoSuchMethodError` if the class doesn't have a no-arg constructor. If the class or the no-arg constructor is not accessible (because it isn't `public` or in the same package), an `IllegalAccessException` is thrown. If the class is `abstract`, or an interface, or the creation fails for some other reason, an `InstantiationException` is thrown. Creating a new object in this way is useful when you want to write general code and let the user specify the class. For example, in the generic sorting algorithm tester in "Designing a Class to Be Extended" on page 72, the user could type the name of the class to be tested and

---

[1.]  If the type we are currently printing is an interface, it actually extends, rather than implementing, its supertype interfaces. Handling this detail would increase the complexity of the code more than was justified for this example.

use that as a parameter to the forName lookup call. Assuming the given class name was valid, newInstance could then be invoked to create an object of that type. Here is a main method for the generic SortDouble class:

```
static double[] testData = { 0.3, 1.3e-2, 7.9, 3.17, };

public static void main(String[] args) {
    try {
        for (int arg = 0; arg < args.length; arg++) {
            String name = args[arg];
            Class classFor =  Class.forName(name);
            SortDouble sorter
                = (SortDouble)classFor.newInstance();
            SortMetrics metrics
                = sorter.sort(testData);
            System.out.println(name + ": " + metrics);
            for (int i = 0; i < testData.length; i++)
                System.out.println("\t" + testData[i]);
        }
    } catch (Exception e) {
        System.err.print(e);            // report the error
    }
}
```

This is almost exactly like BubbleSortDouble.main (see page 76), but we have removed all type names. It can be used for any type that is a SortDouble object and that provides a no-arg constructor. Now we don't have to write a new main for each type of sorting algorithm—this generic main works for all. All we have to do is execute

```
java SortDouble TestClass ...
```

for any sorting class (such as BubbleSortDouble), and it will be loaded and run.

## 13.2  Loading Classes

The Java runtime system loads classes when they are needed. Details of loading classes vary between Java implementations, but most use a "class path" mechanism to search the compiled bytecodes for a class referenced by your code, but not yet loaded into the runtime. This default mechanism works well in many cases, but much of the power of Java is the ability to load classes from places that make sense to your application. To write an application that loads classes in ways different from the default mechanism, you must provide a `ClassLoader` object that can get the bytecodes for class implementations and load them into the runtime.

For example, you might set up a game such that players could write classes to play the game using whatever strategy the player chooses. To make this work, you would provide a `Player` abstract class that players would extend to implement their strategy. When players were ready to try their strategy, they would send the compiled class's bytecodes to your system. The bytecodes would need to be loaded into the game, evaluated, and the score returned to the player. The design would look something like this:

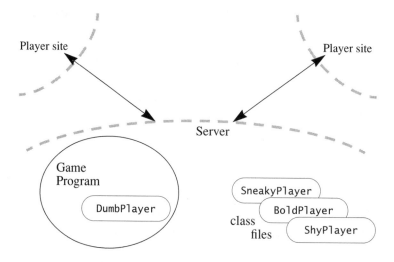

At the server, the game program loads each waiting `Player` class, creates an object of the new type, and runs its strategy against the game algorithm. When the results are known, they will be reported back to the player who submitted the strategy.

The communication mechanism isn't specified here, but it could be as simple as electronic mail, with players mailing in their classes and receiving the results by return mail.

The interesting part is how the game program loads the compiled class files into its runtime. This is the province of a *class loader*. A class loader is defined by extending the abstract `ClassLoader` class and implementing its `loadClass` method:

```
protected abstract Class loadClass(String name,
    boolean resolve) throws ClassNotFoundException
```
> Loads the class of the given name. If `resolve` is `true`, the method must invoke the `resolveClass` method to ensure that all classes referred to by the class are also loaded.

In our example, we would provide a `PlayerLoader` class to read the byte-codes from the player classes and install them as a usable class. The basic loop would look like this:

```
public class Game {
    static public void main(String[] args) {
        String name;      // the class name
        while ((name = getNextPlayer()) != null) {
            try {
                PlayerLoader loader = new PlayerLoader();
                Class
                    classOf = loader.loadClass(name, true);
                Player
                    player = (Player)classOf.newInstance();
                Game game = new Game();
                player.play(game);
                game.reportScore(name);
            } catch (Exception e) {
                reportException(name, e);
            }
        }
    }
}
```

Each new game needs a new `PlayerLoader` object so the new `Player` class will not get mixed up with loaded classes from previous runs. That new loader loads the class, returning the `Class` object that represents it. That `Class` object is used to create a new object of the `Player` class. Then we create a new `game` to play, and play it. When the game is finished the score is reported.

The `PlayerLoader` class extends `ClassLoader` to implement `loadClass`:

```
class PlayerLoader extends ClassLoader {
    private Hashtable Classes = new Hashtable();

    public Class loadClass(String name, boolean resolve)
        throws ClassNotFoundException
    {
        try {
            Class newClass = (Class)Classes.get(name);
            if (newClass == null) { // not yet defined
                try {                   // check if system class
                    newClass = findSystemClass(name);
                    if (newClass != null)
```

```
                           return newClass;
                    } catch (ClassNotFoundException e) {
                        ;                              // keep on looking
                    }

                    // class not found -- need to load it
                    byte[] buf = bytesForClass(name);
                    newClass = defineClass(buf, 0, buf.length);
                    Classes.put(name, newClass);
                }
                if (resolve)
                    resolveClass(newClass);
                return newClass;
            } catch (IOException e) {
                throw new ClassNotFoundException(e.toString());
            }
        }

        // ... bytesForClass() and any other methods ...
    }
```

Any implementation of `loadClass` should load a class only if it hasn't already been loaded, so it keeps a hashtable of already-loaded classes. If a class is already in the table, the associated `Class` object is returned. Otherwise, `loadClass` first checks if it can find the class on the local system by invoking the `ClassLoader` method `findSystemClass`, which looks not only for system classes (those in the `java` packages), but through the class search path as well. If the class is found this way, the `Class` object for it is returned after any necessary loading is done.

If both these simple mechanisms fail, we must read the bytes for the class, which is the purpose of `bytesForClass`:

```
protected byte[] bytesForClass(String name)
    throws IOException, ClassNotFoundException
{
    FileInputStream in = streamFor(name);
    int length = in.available(); // get byte count
    if (length == 0)
        throw new ClassNotFoundException(name);
    byte[] buf = new byte[length];
    in.read(buf);                  // read the bytes
    return buf;
}
```

This method uses `streamFor` (not shown) to get a `FileInputStream` to the class's bytecodes. We then create a buffer for the bytes, read them all in, and return the buffer.

When `loadClass` gets the bytes back, it invokes the `ClassLoader` method `defineClass`, which takes a `byte` array, a start position, and a number of bytes. The bytes in that part of the array are the bytecodes for the class. In our case we use the entire array for the class's bytecodes. When we are finished defining the class, we add the class to the `Classes` hashtable so that we won't load it a second time.

When the class has been successfully loaded, `loadClass` returns the new `Class` object.

There is no way to unload a class when it is no longer needed. You simply stop using it by allowing its class loader object to be garbage-collected.

You can obtain the class loader for a given `Class` object by invoking its `getClassLoader` method. Class loading is discussed in the next section. If the class has no class loader, the method returns `null`.

The class loader only assists in the first stage of making a class available. There are three steps in all:

1. Loading: Getting the bytecodes that implement the class.

2. Linking: Locating the supertypes of the class and loading them if needed.

3. Initialization: Setting the `static` fields of the class to their initial values and executing their initializers, as well as executing any `static` blocks.

### Exercise 13.2

Flesh out `Game` and `Player` to implement a simple game, such as tic-tac-toe. Score some `Player` implementations over several runs each.   ▲

## 13.3  Wrapper Classes: An Overview

Most primitive language types have classes to represent that type. These *wrapper classes* have two primary functions. The first is to provide a home for methods and variables related to the type (such as string conversions and value range constants). Here, for example, is how you might check whether you could use a faster `float` calculation on a particular value, or whether the value requires a larger range than a `float` provides:

```
if (value >= Float.MIN_VALUE && value <= Float.MAX_VALUE)
    return fasterFloatCalc((float)value);
else
    return slowerDoubleCalc(value);
```

The second purpose is to create objects to hold values of a particular primitive type for generically written classes that only know how to handle `Object` references. `Hashtable` objects, for example, store only `Object` references, not primitive types. To use an `int` as a key or value in a `Hashtable` object, you must create an `Integer` object to hold the value:

```
Integer keyObj = new Integer(key);
map.put(keyObj, value);
```

The rest of this chapter covers methods and constants available to each particular wrapper class. Some things are common to all the wrapper classes, so we cover them here before we cover each specific type class.

Each type class has the following constructors and methods:

◆ A constructor that takes the primitive type and creates an object of the type class (for example, there is a `Character(char)` constructor)

◆ A constructor that decodes a single `String` parameter to get the object's initial value

◆ A `toString` method that produces a string version of the type object's value

◆ A *type*`Value` method that produces the primitive type value, such as the `Character.charValue`, `Boolean.booleanValue`

◆ An `equals` method to compare objects of the same type class for equality

◆ A `hashCode` method to return a value-based hash code for use in hashtables

All the wrapper classes have these methods, so they are not listed in each type class's descriptions below. The system property fetch-and-decode methods described in "System Properties" on page 261 are also not discussed here.

The term "radix," used in several places in the wrapper classes, is another word for "numeric base." For example, decoding a `long` "in radix 8" means the same as decoding it "in base 8."

## 13.4 Boolean

The `Boolean` class represents the `boolean` type as a class. Both the `valueOf` method and the constructor that decodes a string understand `"true"`, with any mixture of upper- and lower-case characters, to be `true`; any other string is interpreted as `false`.

## 13.5 Character

The Character class represents the char type as a class. Beyond MIN_VALUE and MAX_VALUE constants, it provides two constants MIN_RADIX and MAX_RADIX, which are the minimum and maximum radices understood by the methods (described below) that translate between a single character digit and its integer value or vice versa. The radix must be in the range 2–36; digits for values above 9 are the letters A through Z or their lowercase equivalents.

public static int **digit(char ch, int radix)**
> Returns the numeric value of the digit ch using the specified radix. If the character is not a valid digit, returns –1.

public static char **forDigit(int digit, int radix)**
> Returns the character value for the specified digit in the specified radix. If the digit is not valid in the radix, the character \u0000 is returned.

The Character class also supports methods to handle the various attributes of characters, including case. There are three cases in Unicode: upper, lower, and title. Upper- and lowercase are familiar to most people. Titlecase is used to distinguish characters that are made up of multiple components and are written differently when used in titles, where the first letter in a word is traditionally capitalized. For instance, in the string "ljepotica",[2] the first letter is the lowercase letter lj (\u01C9, a letter in the "Extended Latin" character set that is used in writing Croatian digraphs). If the word appeared in a book title, and you wanted the first letter of each word to be in uppercase, the correct process would be to use toTitleCase on the first letter of each word, giving you "Ljepotica" (using Lj, which is \u01C8). If you incorrectly use toUpperCase, you would get the erroneous string "LJepotica" (using LJ, which is \u01C7).

All case issues are handled as defined in Unicode. For example, in Georgian, uppercase letters are considered archaic, and translation into uppercase is usually avoided. Therefore, toUpperCase will not change lowercase Georgian letters to their uppercase equivalents, although toLowerCase will translate uppercase Georgian letters to lowercase. Because of details like this, you cannot assume that all characters that are equivalent ignoring case will be the same if you call either toLowerCase or toUpperCase. However, the expression

```
Character.toUpperCase(Character.toLowerCase(ch));
```

---

[2.] The word "ljepotica" is a Croatian diminutive of "beauty," often used as a term of endearment and admiration.

leaves you with a character that you can compare with another similarly constructed character to test for equality ignoring case distinctions. If the two resulting characters are the same, then the original characters were the same except for
possible differences in case.

```
public static boolean isDefined(char ch)
```
> Returns true if ch is a defined Unicode character.

```
public static boolean isLowerCase(char ch)
```
> Returns true if ch is a lowercase letter.

```
public static boolean isUpperCase(char ch)
```
> Returns true if ch is an uppercase letter.

```
public static boolean isTitleCase(char ch)
```
> Returns true if ch is a titlecase letter.

```
public static boolean isDigit(char ch)
```
> Returns true if ch is a digit (see Table 4 on page 300).

```
public static boolean isLetter(char ch)
```
> Returns true if ch is a letter (see note on page 301).

```
public static boolean isLetterOrDigit(char ch)
```
> Returns true if ch is a letter or digit (see Table 5 on page 301).

```
public static boolean isJavaLetter(char ch)
```
> Returns true if ch can start a Java identifier—namely, if it is a letter or
> either '_' or '$'.

```
public static boolean isJavaLetterOrDigit(char ch)
```
> Returns true if ch can occur in a Java identifier after the first character.

```
public static boolean isSpace(char ch)
```
> Returns true if ch is a space, that is, one of ' ', '\t', '\n', '\f', or '\r'.

```
public static char toLowerCase(char ch)
```
> Returns the lowercase character equivalent of ch. If there is no lowercase
> equivalent, ch is returned.

```
public static char toUpperCase(char ch)
```
> Returns the uppercase character equivalent of ch. If there is no uppercase
> equivalent, ch is returned.

```
public static char toTitleCase(char ch)
```
> Returns the titlecase character equivalent of ch. If there is no titlecase
> equivalent, then the result of toUpperCase(ch) is returned.

```
public static int digit(char ch, radix)
```
> Returns the numeric value of ch considered as a digit in the given radix. If the radix is not valid, or if ch is not a digit in the radix, -1 is returned. The letters A-Z and a-z are legal for digits representing values 10 and over.

```
public static char forDigit(int digit, radix)
```
> Returns a character that represents the value digit in the given radix. If digit is greater than radix, or radix is out of range, -1 is returned.

## 13.6  Number

The Number class is an abstract class extended by all wrapper classes that represent numeric primitive types: Integer, Long, Float, and Double. Each has constructors that set the wrapper object's value to either a value of the relevant primitive type or a string that represents a value of that type. The string-based constructors throw NumberFormatException if the string is not valid.

The abstract methods of Number return the value of the object converted to any of the other numeric types:

```
public int intValue()
public long longValue()
public float floatValue()
public double doubleValue()
```

Each extended Number class overrides these methods to convert its own type to any of the others under the same rules used for an explicit cast. For example, given a Float object with the value 32.87, the return value of intValue on the object would be 32, just as (int)32.87 would be 32.

In addition, each numeric type class has the following methods and constants:

◆ A static toString(*type*) method that returns a String object when given a value of the primitive type. If the string is in an improper format for the type, the constructor throws NumberFormatException.

◆ A static valueOf(String) method that returns an object of the numeric type when given a parsable string for that type. All these methods throw NumberFormatException if given a string that is not a proper representation of the primitive type.

◆ Static final constants called MIN_VALUE and MAX_VALUE for the minimum and maximum values variables of that type can take.

## 13.7  Integer

The Integer class extends Number to represent the int type as a class. There are no wrapper classes for short or byte, so these values must be stored in Integer objects. Besides the standard Number methods, Integer supports the following methods:

public static int **parseInt(String str, int radix)**
   throws NumberFormatException
> Returns the value of the integer in str using the specified radix. It throws NumberFormatException if the string cannot be parsed as an int in that radix.

public static int **parseInt(String s)** throws NumberFormatException
> Equivalent to parseInt(str, 10).

public static Integer **valueOf(String s, int radix)**
   throws NumberFormatException
> Like parseInt(str, radix), except it returns an Integer object instead of an int.

public static String **toString(int i, int radix)**
> This additional static method returns a String object representing i in the specified radix. The default static toString method assumes a radix of 10.

In addition, the three static methods toHexString, toOctalString, and toBinaryString convert an int argument to a hexadecimal, octal, or binary string, respectively.

## 13.8  Long

The Long class extends Number to represent the long type as a class. Besides the standard Number methods, Long supports the following methods:

public static long **parseLong(String str, int radix)**
   throws NumberFormatException
> Returns the value of the long in str using the specified radix. It throws NumberFormatException if the string cannot be parsed as a long in that radix.

public static long **parseLong(String str)**
   throws NumberFormatException
> Equivalent to parseLong(str, 10).

```
public static Long valueOf(String str, int radix)
   throws NumberFormatException
```
>
> Like parseLong(str, radix), except it returns a Long object instead of a long.

```
public static String toString(long l, int radix)
```
>
> This additional static method returns a String object representing l in the specified radix. The default static toString method assumes a radix of 10.

Analogous to the equivalent methods in Integer, the static methods toHexString, toOctalString, and toBinaryString convert a long argument to a hexadecimal, octal, or binary string, respectively.

## 13.9 Float and Double

The Float and Double classes extend Number to represent the float and double types as classes. With only a few exceptions, the names of the methods and constants are the same for both types. In the list below, the types for the Float type class are shown, but Float and float can be changed to Double and double, respectively, in all of them to get equivalent fields and methods for the Double type class. Besides the standard Number methods, Float and Double support the following methods:

```
public final static float POSITIVE_INFINITY
```
>
> The value for $+\infty$.

```
public final static float NEGATIVE_INFINITY
```
>
> The value for $-\infty$.

```
public final static float NaN
```
>
> Not-a-Number. This constant provides a tool to get a NaN value, not to test one. To test if a number is NaN, use the isNaN method rather than comparing to this constant.

```
public static boolean isNaN(float val)
```
>
> Return true if val is a Not-a-Number (NaN) value.

```
public static boolean isInfinite(float val)
```
>
> Returns true if val is either positive or negative infinity.

```
public boolean isNaN()
```
>
> Returns true if this object's value is a Not-a-Number (NaN) value.

```
public boolean isInfinite()
```
>
> Returns true if this object's value is either positive or negative infinity.

In addition to the preceding methods, `Float` also has a constructor that takes a `double` argument to use as its initial value, after conversion to `float`.

To manipulate the bits inside a floating-point value's representation, `Double` provides methods to get the bit pattern as a `long`, and a way to convert a bit pattern in a `long` into a `double` value. The `Float` class provides equivalent methods to turn a `float` value into an `int` bit pattern or vice versa:

`public static int `**`floatToIntBits(float value)`**
> Returns the bit representation of a `float` value in an `int`.

`public static float `**`intBitsToFloat(int bits)`**
> Returns the `float` corresponding to a given bit representation.

`public static long `**`doubleToLongBits(double value)`**
> Returns the bit representation of a `double` value as a `long`.

`public static double `**`longBitsToDouble(long bits)`**
> Returns the `double` corresponding to a given bit representation.

### *Exercise 13.3*

Write a program that will read a file with entries of the form "type value", where `type` is one of the type class names (`Boolean`, `Character`, etc.) and `value` is a string that the type's constructor can decode. For each such entry, create an object of the type with that value and add it to a `Vector`. Display the final result when done.   ▲

CHAPTER **14**

# System Programming

*GLENDOWER: I can call spirits from the vasty deep.*
*HOTSPUR: Why, so can I, or so can any man;*
*But will they come when you do call for them?*
—William Shakespeare, *King Henry IV, Part 1*

**T**HIS chapter describes how to access general functions of the Java runtime system and the underlying operating system. Such functions include reading properties, using mathematical functions, executing other programs, controlling memory, and using timing functions. Four classes in `java.lang` provide this access:

- The `Runtime` class represents the state of a Java runtime. This object provides access to functionality that is per-runtime, such as controlling the garbage collector and exiting the runtime.

- The `Process` class represents a running process created with a `Runtime.exec` call.

- The `System` class provides static methods to represent the state of the entire system. As a convenience, several methods in `System` operate on the current runtime.

- The `Math` class provides static methods to compute many standard mathematical functions, such as trigonometric functions and logarithms.

## 14.1 Standard I/O Stream

You can do I/O in standard places using the three system streams that are available as static fields of the `System` class, `System.in`, `System.out`, and `System.err`:

```
public static InputStream in
```
Standard input stream for reading character data.

```
public static PrintStream out
```
Standard output stream for printing messages.

```
public static PrintStream err
```
Standard error stream to print error messages. The user often can redirect standard output to a file. But applications also need to print error messages that the user will still see even if standard output is redirected. The `err` stream is specifically devoted to error messages that are not rerouted with the regular output. Both `out` and `err` are `PrintStream` objects, so you print errors on `err` using the same methods as for `out`.

## 14.2  Memory Management

Although Java has no explicit way to dispose of unwanted objects, you can directly invoke the garbage collector using the `Runtime` class's `gc` method. The `Runtime` class also supports a `runFinalization` method to invoke any pending finalizers. `Runtime` has two methods to report on the memory state:

```
public long freeMemory()
```
Returns an estimate of free bytes in system memory.

```
public long totalMemory()
```
Returns the total bytes in system memory.

The `System` class supports static `gc` and `runFinalization` methods that invoke the corresponding method on the current runtime.

The garbage<sup>collector</sup> may be unable to free additional memory when `Runtime.gc` is invoked. There may be no garbage to collect, and not all garbage collectors can find collectable objects on demand. However, before creating a large number of objects—especially in a time-critical application that might be affected by garbage-collection overhead—invoking `gc` may be advisable. Doing so has two benefits: you start with as much free memory as possible, and you reduce the likelihood of the garbage collector running during the task. Here is a method that frees everything it can at the moment:

```
public static void fullGC() {
    Runtime rt = Runtime.getRuntime();
    long isFree = rt.freeMemory();
    long wasFree;
    do {
        wasFree = isFree;
        rt.gc();
        isFree = rt.freeMemory();
```

```
      } while (isFree > wasFree);
      rt.runFinalization();
}
```

This method loops while the amount of freeMemory is being increased by calls to gc. When the amount of free memory doesn't increase, further calls to gc will likely do nothing. Then we invoke runFinalization to force any pending finalization computation to run right away instead of letting the garbage collector delay it until later.

Usually you will not need to call runFinalization, since finalize methods are called asynchronously by the garbage collector. Under some circumstances, such as running out of a resource that a finalize method reclaims, forcing as much finalization as possible is useful. There is no guarantee that any object awaiting finalization is using some of that resource, so runFinalization may be of no help.

## 14.3   System Properties

Several system properties are available. They are stored by the System class in a Properties object (see "Properties" on page 232). These properties define the system environment and are used by classes that need to know their environment. For example, here is a dump of the properties on one system:

```
#System properties
#Tue Feb 27 19:45:22 EST 1996
java.home=/lab/east/tools/java/java
java.version=1.0.1
file.separator=/
line.separator=\n
java.vendor=Sun Microsystems Inc.
user.name=arnold
os.arch=sparc
os.name=Solaris
java.vendor.url=http://www.sun.com/
user.dir=/vob/java_prog/src
java.class.path=.:./classes:/home/arnold/java/lib/
classes.zip:/home/arnold/java/classes
java.class.version=45.3
os.version=2.x
path.separator=:
user.home=/home/arnold
```

All of the properties shown above are defined on all systems, although the values will certainly vary. Some of the properties are used by classes in the standard packages. The `File` class, for instance, uses the `file.separator` property to build up and break down pathnames. These properties are available for your needs as well. This method looks for a personal configuration file in the user's home folder:

```
public static File personalConfig(String fileName) {
    String home = System.getProperty("user.home");
    if (home == null)
        return null;
    else
        return new File(home, fileName);
}
```

Here are all the methods of the `System` class that deal with the system properties:

**public static Properties getProperties()**
Gets the system properties object.

**public static void setProperties(Properties props)**
Sets the system properties to the specified properties object.

**public static String getProperty(String key)**
Returns the value of the system property named in key. This is equivalent to

```
System.getProperties().getProperty(key);
```

**public static String getProperty(String key, String defaultValue)**
Returns the value of the system property named in key. If it has no definition, returns defaultValue. This is equivalent to

```
System.getProperties().getProperty(key, def);
```

Property values are stored as strings, but some of the strings represent other types, such as integers or booleans. Methods are available to read properties and decode them into the primitive types. These decoding methods are static methods of the primitive type's class. Each method has a `String` parameter that names the property to retrieve. Some forms have a second parameter (shown as def below) which is the default value to return if no property is found with that name. Methods without a default value parameter return an object containing zero for the numeric type, or `false` for `boolean`. All these methods decode values in the standard Java formats for constants of the primitive type.

```
public static boolean Boolean.getBoolean(String name)
public static Integer Integer.getInteger(String name)
public static Integer
            Integer.getInteger(String name, Integer def)
```

```
public static Integer
                Integer.getInteger(String name, int def)
public static Long Long.getLong(String nm)
public static Long Long.getLong(String nm, long def)
public static Long Long.getLong(String nm, Long def)
```

The getBoolean method is irregular. It returns an actual boolean value instead of an object of class Boolean. If the property isn't present, getBoolean returns false.

## 14.4 Creating Processes

As we have discussed, a running Java system can have many threads of execution. Most systems that host a Java environment also have the ability to run multiple programs. Java applications can execute new programs using one of two forms of the method System.exec. Each successful call to exec creates a new Process object that represents the running program. We can query its state and invoke methods to control its progress. The two basic forms of exec are:

public Process **exec(String[] cmdarray)** throws IOException
> This runs the command in cmdarray on the current system and returns a Process object (described below) to represent it. The string in cmdarray[0] is the name of the command, and any subsequent strings in the array are passed to the command as arguments.

public Process **exec(String command)** throws IOException
> This is equivalent to the other form of exec with the string command split into an array wherever white space occurs. Using this form of exec, the previous example would have contained this line instead:

```
String cmd = "/bin/ls " + opts + " " + dir;
Process child = Runtime.getRuntime().exec(cmd);
```

The newly created process is called a child process. By analogy, the creating process is a parent process. The exec methods return a Process object for each child process created. This object represents the child process in two major ways. First, it provides methods to access the input, output, and error streams of the child process:

public abstract OutputStream **getOutputStream()**
> Returns an OutputStream connected to the input of the child process. Data written on this stream is read by the child process as its input. The stream is buffered.

```
public abstract InputStream getInputStream()
```
    Returns an `InputStream` connected to the output of the child process. When the child writes data on its output, it can be read from this stream. The stream is buffered.

```
public abstract InputStream getErrorStream()
```
    Returns an `InputStream` connected to the error output stream of the child process. When the child writes data on its error output, it can be read from this stream. The stream is unbuffered to ensure that errors are reported immediately.

Here, for example, is a program that connects the Java streams to the streams of the new process so that whatever the user types will go to the specified program, and whatever the program produces will be seen by the user:

```
public static Process userProg(String cmd)
    throws IOException
{
    Process proc = Runtime.getRuntime().exec(cmd);
    plugTogether(System.in,  proc.getOutputStream());
    plugTogether(System.out, proc.getInputStream());
    plugTogether(System.err, proc.getErrorStream());
    return proc;
}
```

This assumes that a method `plugTogether` exists to connect two streams together by reading the bytes from one stream and writing them onto the other.

### Exercise 14.1

Write `plugTogether`. Hint: use threads. ▲

The second way a `Process` object represents the child process is by providing methods to control the process and find out its termination status:

```
public abstract int waitFor() throws InterruptedException
```
    Waits indefinitely for the process to complete, returning the value it passed to either `System.exit` or its equivalent (zero means success, nonzero means failure). If the process has already completed, the value is simply returned.

```
public abstract int exitValue()
```
    Returns the exit value for the process. If the process has not completed, `exitValue` throws `IllegalStateException`.

```
public abstract void destroy()
```
>   Kills the process. Does nothing if the process has already finished. If a
>   Process object gets garbage-collected, this does *not* mean that the process
>   is destroyed; it will merely be unavailable for manipulation.

For example, the following method returns a String array that contains the
output of ls with the specified options. It throws an LSFailedException if the
command completed unsuccessfully:

```java
// We have imported java.io.* and java.util.*
public String[] ls(String dir, String opts)
    throws LSFailedException
{
    try {
        // start up the command
        String[] cmdArray = { "/bin/ls", opts, dir };
        Process child = Runtime.getRuntime().exec(cmdArray);
        DataInputStream
            in = new DataInputStream(child.getInputStream());

        // read the command's output
        Vector lines = new Vector();
        String line;
        while ((line = in.readLine()) != null)
            lines.addElement(line);
        if (child.waitFor() != 0)   // if the ls failed
            throw new LSFailedException(child.exitValue());
        String[] retval = new String[lines.size()];
        lines.copyInto(retval);
        return retval;
    } catch (LSFailedException e) {
        throw e;
    } catch (Exception e) {
        throw new LSFailedException(e.toString());
    }
}
```

Process is an abstract class. Each implementation of Java must provide one
or more appropriate extended classes of Process that are able to interact with
processes on the underlying system. Such classes might have extended functionality that would be useful for programming on the underlying system. The local
documentation should contain information on this extended functionality.

Two other forms of exec enable you to specify a set of *environment variables*, which are system-dependent values that can be queried as desired by the new process. Environment variables are passed to exec as a String array, where each element of the array specifies the name and value of an environment variable in the form *name=value*. The name cannot contain any spaces, although the value can be anything. The environment variables are passed as the second parameter:

```
public Process exec(String command, String[] env)
    throws IOException
public Process exec(String[] command, String[] env)
    throws IOException
```

Environment variables are interpreted in a system-dependent way by the child process's program. The environment variable mechanism is supported because existing programs on many different kinds of platforms understand them. To communicate between Java programs, use properties, not environment variables.

### Exercise 14.2

Write a program that runs exec on its command-line arguments and prints out the output from the command with each line preceded by its line number.  ▲

### Exercise 14.3

Write a program that runs exec on command-line arguments and prints out the output from the command, killing the command when a particular string appears in the output.  ▲

## 14.5  Runtime

Objects of the Runtime class represent the state of the runtime system and operations that it can perform. A Runtime object that represents the current runtime can be obtained by invoking the static method Runtime.getRuntime.

One thing the runtime can do is get an input or output stream that translates the local character set into Unicode equivalents. Many existing systems work in localized languages using 8-bit or other character sets that predate Unicode. The runtime provides a way to translate characters from a stream that works in local character sets into their Unicode equivalents. The local keyboard, for example, may generate an 8-bit Oriya character code. When you take the System.in stream that reads from that keyboard and get a localized input stream from it, the 8-bit Oriya characters will be translated into their 16-bit Unicode equivalents in the range \u0b00 \u0b7f. A localized output stream would do the reverse translation.

A runtime can be shut down by invoking its `exit` method, passing a status code. This method kills all threads in the runtime, no matter what state they are in. A `ThreadDeath` exception is not thrown to kill them; they are simply stopped with `finally` clauses not executed. A better way is to kill all threads in your group using `ThreadGroup.stop`, which lets the threads clean up any state they may have pending in their `finally` clauses.

The `exit` status code traditionally is zero to indicate successful completion of a task, and nonzero to indicate failure. There are two ways to signal the success of an application with an exit status. One, immediately invoke `exit` and stop the threads. Two, ensure that all threads are shut down cleanly before invoking `exit`. This example kills all threads in the current group, lets them finish, and then calls `exit`:

```
public static void safeExit(int status) {
    // Get the list of all threads
    Thread myThrd = Thread.currentThread();
    ThreadGroup thisGroup = myThrd.getThreadGroup();
    int count = thisGroup.activeCount();
    Thread[] thrds = new Thread[count + 20]; // +20 for slop
    thisGroup.enumerate(thrds);

    // stop all threads
    for (int i = 0; i < thrds.length; i++) {
        if (thrds[i] != null && thrds[i] != myThrd)
            thrds[i].stop();
    }

    // wait for all threads to complete
    for (int i = 0; i < thrds.length; i++) {
        if (thrds[i] != null && thrds[i] != myThrd) {
            try {
                thrds[i].join();
            } catch (InterruptedException e) {
                // just skip this thread
            }
        }
    }

    // now we can exit
    System.exit(status);
}
```

*Exercise 14.4*

Modify `safeExit` to handle threads that might be created after the invocation of `enumerate`. Also make it skip daemon threads, which presumably expect sudden death.  ▲

## 14.6  Miscellaneous

Two methods in `System` don't belong to any particular category:

`public static long currentTimeMillis()`
> Returns the current time in milliseconds GMT since the epoch (00:00:00 UTC, January 1, 1970). The time is returned in a `long`, so it will not overflow until the year 292280995, which should suffice for most purposes. More sophisticated applications may require the `Date` class: see "`Date`" on page 236.

`public static void arraycopy(Object src, int srcPos, Object dst, int dstPos, int count)`
> Copies the contents of the source array, beginning at `src[srcPos]`, to the destination array, starting at `dst[dstPos]`. Exactly `count` elements will be copied. All the array references must be inside the two arrays, or an `IndexOutOfBoundsException` will be thrown. The data types in the source array must be compatible with the type of the destination array, or an `ArrayStoreException` will be thrown. By "compatible," we mean that in arrays of object references, each object in the source array must be assignable to an entry in the destination array. For arrays of built-in types, the types must be the same, not just assignable; `arraycopy` cannot be used to copy an array of `short` to an array of `int`.
>
> The `arraycopy` method works correctly on overlapping arrays, so it can be used to copy one subpart of an array over another. You can, for example, shift everything in an array one slot towards the beginning, as in the method `squeezeOut` on page 151.

Two tracing methods available in `Runtime` also don't fit in any other category—`traceInstructions` and `traceMethodCalls`. Each takes a boolean argument which, if `true`, turns on tracing of instructions or method calls, respectively. Tracing is turned off when the boolean is `false`. Each runtime implementation is free to do what it wants with these calls, including ignoring them if the local runtime has nowhere to put the trace output. They are likely to work in a development environment.

## 14.7  Security

The System class supports two methods for the SecurityManager object. The SecurityManager class defines methods that govern whether sockets can be opened, files accessed, threads created, and so on. For details on how all this works, see *The Java Language Specification*.

public static void **setSecurityManager(SecurityManager s)**
> Set the system security manager object. This value can be set only once, so that whoever starts up system security can rely on it not being changed.

public static SecurityManager **getSecurityManager()**
> Get the system security interface. A description of the security manager would be too arcane for this general text: see your online documentation for details.

## 14.8  Math

The Math class consists of static constants and methods for common mathematical manipulations. All operations are carried out in double.

The two constants Math.E represents the value $e$ (2.7182818284590452354), and Math.PI represents the value $\pi$ (3.14159265358979323846). In the methods, angles are in radians, and all parameters and return values are double, unless stated otherwise:

| Function | Value |
| --- | --- |
| sin(a) | sine($a$) |
| cos(a) | cosine($a$) |
| tan(a) | tangent($a$) |
| asin(v) | arcsine($v$), with $v$ in the range [–1.0, 1.0] |
| acos(v) | arccosine($v$), with $v$ in the range [–1.0, 1.0] |
| atan(v) | arctangent($v$), returned in the range $[-\pi/2,\pi/2]$. |
| atan2(x,y) | arctangent($x/y$), returned in the range $[-\pi,\pi]$. |
| exp(x) | $e^x$ |
| pow(y,x) | $y^x$ |
| log(x) | ln $x$ (natural log of $x$) |
| sqrt(x) | Square root of $x$ |
| ceil(x) | Smallest whole number $\geq x$ |
| floor(x) | Largest whole number $\leq x$ |
| rint(x) | Return truncated integer value of $x$ as a double |

| Function | Value |
|----------|-------|
| round(x) | Returns (int)floor(x + 0.5), for either float or double types. |
| abs(x) | Return absolute value of $x$ for any numeric type |
| max(x,y) | Return larger of $x$ and $y$ for any numeric type |
| min(x,y) | Return smaller of $x$ and $y$ for any numeric type |

The static method Math.IEEERemainder calculates remainder as defined by the IEEE-754 standard. The remainder operator %, as described in Section 5.15.2 on page 112, obeys the rule

```
(x/y)*y + x%y == x
```

This preserves one kind of symmetry, namely that if x%y is z, then changing the sign of either x or y will only change the sign of z, but never its absolute value. For example, 7%2.5 is 2.0, and -7%2.5 is -2.0. The IEEE standard defines remainder for x and y differently, preserving symmetry of spacing along the number line—the result of Math.IEEERemainder(-7, 2.5) is -0.5. The remainder operator makes values symmetric around zero on the number line, while the IEEE remainder mechanism keeps resulting values y units apart. The method is provided because both kinds of remainder are useful.

The static method random generates a pseudorandom number $r$ in the range $0.0 \leq r < 1.0$. For more control over pseudorandom numbers, see "Random" on page 240

### Exercise 14.5

Write a calculator that has these functions, as well as (at least) the basic operators +, -, *, /, and %. The simplest form is probably a reverse-Polish stack calculator, since operator precedence is not an issue.    ▲

# Native Methods

*They were called "Wonder Workers" by an observer who caught one of them wondering*
*what kind of a wrench to use to hammer a screw into a brick.*
—George Brown, Congressman, San Bernardino, California

SITUATIONS arise where a given application or library cannot be written entirely in Java, and in such cases, the code must be written in some other language more specific to the underlying platform. These special situations tend to fall into three categories:

◆ A large amount of existing code already works. Providing a Java layer for that code is easier than porting it all to Java.

◆ An application must use system-specific features not provided by Java classes.

◆ The Java environment is not fast enough for time-critical applications, and implementation in another language may be more efficient.

To help with these situations, Java supports *native* methods implemented in some local (native) system language, typically C or C++. A method is declared native like this:

```
public native void unlock() throws IOException;
```

The native keyword is just another modifier for the method declaration. A native method is implemented in a native language, so there is no Java code to implement it. However, it is invoked from Java code just like any other method.

A class with a native method cannot be loaded across a network and run in a secure fashion. Specifically, classes with native methods are precluded from use in applets. Even if security is not an issue, native code cannot provide the portability guarantees that compiled Java can. Any Java code that relies on native methods must be ported to each type of platform on which that code is to run.

Native methods may still be worthwhile, especially if you rely on commonly available libraries. But in no case will Java code with native methods be usable as an applet run by remote users, since an applet must run in a portable and secure environment.

Using native methods also sacrifices Java's safety protections, such as array bounds checking and freedom from random pointer bugs. The only restrictions on native methods are those imposed by the language in which they are written.

This chapter describes how to implement a native method in C on a POSIX-compliant system, such as Windows NT and most UNIX implementations. Local details of how to do this vary, and some systems may support other languages besides C and C-linkable languages like C++. These details should be covered in the local documentation. This chapter covers important parts of the C language mapping in use for Sun's Java system in release 1.0.2. Changes and improvements may have been made in the local environment, or a completely different mapping may be in use. Over this we have no control. In particular, the native method binding described here is certain to change in future releases from Sun. Even so, this chapter may help you understand some of the issues involved in a native method binding, no matter what particular binding is in use in your environment.

## A.1   Overview

The following problems must be addressed in any Java to C language mapping:

- ◆ How are names mapped? The complete name of a given Java method is *package.class.method*, but C has neither packages nor classes. The mapping is made even harder because Java identifiers are in Unicode, and C identifiers are in ASCII, so Unicode letters valid in Java identifiers must be mapped to valid identifiers in C.

- ◆ How are different calling paradigms represented? For example, each non-static method in Java has a `this` reference which is, in effect, an implicit parameter to the method. C has neither methods nor implicit parameters.

- ◆ How are types mapped? A native implementation of a method needs to access fields of its `this` object, and possibly methods or fields of objects of other types. How does one represent Java classes in C?

- ◆ How are errors mapped? Java signals errors with exceptions, but C does not have exceptions.

- ◆ How are language safety features mapped? Java checks array bounds and type casts, and supports garbage collection to prevent memory leakage and dangling pointer problems. C and C++ do not have these features, so what happens to such checks? What happens in languages such as Pascal that do have such checks?

♦ How are memory features mapped? How does C code create Java objects?

When dealing with these and other issues, compromises must be made. For example, C and C++ don't have the safety checking features of Java, so the mapping says that C and C++ native methods are unsafe in these ways. Although not ideal for safety, it is a natural mapping into C and C++, where speed is considered more important than safety checks. Providing the checks in C and C++ would require, for instance, accessing all array elements through Java-provided functions that did the checks. This would be both unnatural and slow, and since the reason to use a native method might be speed, the trade-off would be wrong. It would also not work well for existing code that used the normal C and C++ array paradigm.

## A.2 The C and C++ Mapping

The mapping from Java to C is fairly direct. The glue that maps native methods into C calls is a generated header file with the necessary type declarations and function signatures, and generated C stubs to help the Java runtime system invoke them.

We describe only the main points of the mapping here. The source we use as a reference is a LockableFile class in a package called local:[1]

```
package local;

import java.io.*;

class LockableFile extends File {
    LockableFile(String path) {
        super(path);
    }

    // valid parameters to lock()
    public final static int READ = 0,
                            WRITE = 1;

    public native void lock(int type) throws IOException;
    public native void unlock() throws IOException;
```

---

[1] We unfortunately could not use the domain-name convention for packages described on page 187 because it would have made the identifiers too long for the margins of this book.

```
        private int fd = -1;

        static {
            System.load("LockableFile");
        }
    }
```

After this source has been compiled with the Java compiler, you generate the header file by invoking the `javah` utility, naming the class for which you want a header file. A file will be generated with the C declarations and definitions necessary for the mapping. In our example, the command would be

```
javah local.LockableFile
```

This generates a file named after the class according to the name mapping described below. In this case, the header file would be `local_LockableFile.h`. We will show you the contents of the header file and implementation of the native methods throughout the chapter.

The mapping for C++ is the same as the C mapping. In fact, the C++ mapping simply includes the generated header file inside an `extern "C"` declaration:

```
extern "C" {
# include local_LockableFile.h
}
```

The symbols used by the runtime when calling native-method wrappers are created in the C namespace, so rather than C++'s so-called "mangled" namespace, the implementations of native methods must be in C.[2] The primary ramification of using C is that you cannot use C++ overloading for native method implementations. In fact, it is really more proper to say that there is not a C++ mapping for native methods, but because C++ can invoke C functions, you can use the C mapping when writing C++ applications. Clearly, a better C++ mapping is possible and will no doubt be defined in the future.

When you have created the C or C++ code necessary to implement your native methods, you must link the compiled code into your Java application, which requires creating a dynamically linked library and connecting it to your code. The common way to do this is to have a block of `static` code, such as that in the `LocakableFile` class above, that calls one of two static methods from the `System` class that load libraries:

---

[2.] This is not strictly true. With some wrangling the dedicated programmer could work around this limitation, but accepting it is easier both to describe and to do.

`public synchronized void `**`load(String pathname)`**

> Loads a dynamic library, given a complete `pathname`. Local modifications to the path will be made depending on local concerns. This throws `UnsatisfiedLinkError` if the file does not exist, or if symbols required by the library are not found.

`public synchronized void `**`loadLibrary(String libname)`**

> Loads a dynamic library with the specified `libname`. The invocation of `LoadLibrary` should be made in the static initializer of the first class that is loaded (that is, the one with the `main` method being invoked). Linking the same library more than once is ignored. This method throws `UnsatisfiedLinkError` if the library cannot be found.

The `load` method requires a full pathname for the file, but it is the better version to use during development because it reports undefined symbols as undefined symbols. The `loadLibrary` method takes any error, including undefined symbols, and translates it into a "library cannot be found" error. If you have an undefined symbol in your library, this translation hides important information that tells you what is really wrong. If you use the `load` method until the native methods work, then replace it with the `loadLibrary` method, you will get the benefits of more detailed information during development and more portable code afterwards.

These library loading methods of `System` are shortcuts for making the same call on the `Runtime` object that represents the current runtime.

### A.2.1 Names

Method and field names are mapped into C names using their full names including package names, with any `.` replaced by an underscore (`_`). In languages such as C that do not support overloading, you cannot implement more than one native method of the same name in a class, since they would map to the same function name.

Type names are mapped in the same way, except that the type name is preceded by `Class`. The type name for `LockableFile` would be called `Classlocal_LockableFile` in the C source. Each class also needs a handle type, because references are represented internally as handles. The handle name is the same as the class name with `Class` replaced by `H`. So the type of a handle to a `LockableFile` is `Hlocal_LockableFile`.

Characters in names that are in the ASCII character set (characters less than or equal to `\u007f`) are used in C and package names unmodified. All other characters are mapped to `_0dddd` with the *d*'s being the same digits used in their Java character representation. For instance, the character ã, which is `\u00e3`, would appear in an identifier as `_000e3`. A slash (/) in a package name is translated to the underscore character (`_`).

## A.2.2  Methods

Each native method is represented as a function. For example, the `lock` method would be `local_LockableFile_lock`, with the appropriate parameters filled in. The first parameter to the function is a handle to the object on which the method was invoked (the `this` reference). For static methods, the handle is always NULL. There is more discussion on handles below.

Additional glue in the form of stub files is needed to invoke these methods. The stub file is generated by a different invocation of `javah` with the `-stubs` option:

```
javah -stubs local.LockableFile
```

This generates a C source file that must be compiled and loaded into the dynamic library along with your native method implementations. The source file has the same name as the header file, but with the trailing h replaced with a c—in this case, we would have to compile `local_LockableFile.c`.

## A.2.3  Types

The following table shows a typical mapping of Java primitive types to C types when used as method parameters or fields (the mapping for arrays is described below).

| Java Type | C Type |
|-----------|--------|
| boolean | long |
| byte | long |
| short | long |
| int | long |
| long | int64_t |
| float | float |
| double | double |
| char | long |

Each Java class is represented by a C `struct`. All nonstatic fields of the class are members of the `struct`, each with the name it had in Java (except for mapping Unicode characters to _0*dddd* equivalents). This representation means that a class with native methods cannot contain two non-static fields with the same name: the mapping would give a C `struct` with fields of the same name, which is not valid.

This problem shows up in classes that hide fields of any of their superclasses, which is another good reason not to hide field names. However, the problem will apply even to classes with private fields of the same name, since private fields show up in the struct along with all the others. You have no way of knowing whether your class has this problem until it shows up when you write a native method. The problem is worse when the fields being hidden are in superclasses that you cannot change. In such a case, you may be stuck—there is no way to write a native method unless you can modify the field names of the classes.

Each static `final` constant is represented as a `#define` constant preceded by the package and class qualifier. Non-final static fields are not mapped to anything. Here is how the type and constants for `LockableFile` are defined in the header file:

```
typedef struct Classlocal_LockableFile {
    struct Hjava_lang_String *path;
/* Inaccessible static: separator */
/* Inaccessible static: separatorChar */
/* Inaccessible static: pathSeparator */
/* Inaccessible static: pathSeparatorChar */
#define local_LockableFile_READ 0L
#define local_LockableFile_WRITE 1L
    long fd;
} Classlocal_LockableFile;
```

References to objects are represented by a "handle" type, with the `Class` part of the mapped name replaced by H. A reference to the `LockableFile` class would have the name `Hlocal_LockableFile`. Such references are dereferenced by handle methods. The `unhand` macro takes a handle and returns a pointer to the struct the handle represents.

Here are the signatures of the C methods that we will define to implement the native methods of `LockableFile`:

```
extern void local_LockableFile_lock(
                    struct Hlocal_LockableFile *, long);
extern void local_LockableFile_unlock(
                    struct Hlocal_LockableFile *);
```

## A.2.4 Errors

Errors are mapped to exceptions in Java. In C there are no exceptions. To throw an exception from C, use the `SignalError` function to say so, then return. The Java runtime will take the exception signaled by `SignalError` and throw it. There are several examples of how to do this below.

### A.2.5   Language Safety Features

Java's language safety features do not map to C. You are responsible for coding responsibly in C (as you always are) without any automatic help from Java.

### A.2.6   Memory Model

Native methods can create new Java objects using functions described below.

## A.3   An Example

Let us look at how you might implement the native methods of LockableFile. First, you must generate the header and stub file, and compile the stub file. Then you must write the implementations themselves. Here, for example, is an implementation of lock:

```
#include "local_LockableFile.h"
#include <javaString.h>
#include <fcntl.h>
#include <errno.h>

void
local_LockableFile_lock(
    struct Hlocal_LockableFile *this_h,
    long mode)
{
    Classlocal_LockableFile *this = unhand(this_h);
    struct flock lock;

    if (this->fd == -1 && !open_fd(this))
        return;              /* must have been an error */

    if (!setup_lock(&lock, mode))
        return;
    if (fcntl(this->fd, F_SETLKW, &lock) == -1)
        SignalError(EE(),
            "java/io/IOException", strerror(errno));
}
```

First we include the relevant headers. These are the generated header for LockableFile, the general string utility header file <javaString.h>, the system header file <fnctl.h> that defines calls for POSIX locking, and the system header file <errno.h> so we can process the errors we get from system calls.

The first line of the lock implementation translates the handle this_h to a pointer to a Classlocal_LockableFile struct, using the unhand macro to return the object a handle points to. Java null references map to handle pointers that are themselves NULL. To ensure that no errors occur from being passed a null reference, you must check the handle itself before you unhand it, as we demonstrate in later examples.

The second line of local_LockableFile_lock declares a flock structure. The flock structure is used for manipulating POSIX locks. The implementation of open_fd and setup_lock is included in "Internals for LockableFile" on page 280.

Next, we check whether there is a file descriptor. If not, and the function open_fd fails to open the file, it must have generated an error by throwing an exception, so we just return. When there is a file descriptor, the flock structure must be set up using the internal setup_lock function. This can also potentially fail (if mode isn't one of the valid values, for example), and also throw an exception so we can just return. Both open_fd and setup_lock are part of the POSIX-specific code.

We try to get the lock on the file with the F_SETLKW operation of the POSIX fcntl function, which sets the desired lock, waiting if it needs to. If flock returns –1, the lock failed, and we throw an exception by invoking the Java runtime function SignalError:

void **SignalError**(ExecEnv *exenu, char *type, char *constructor)
> Signals that an exception should be thrown when the native method returns. The execution environment exenu should usually be the return value of the function EE, which returns the structure representing the current environment. The type parameter is the full type name of the class of the exception object to be thrown, with each . in the full class name replaced by a /. The final parameter is the exception's descriptive string, or NULL if there is no string.

For our descriptive string, we use the value of the POSIX function strerror, which returns a string that describes the error number. This is about the best we can do to describe exceptions that happen in our native code.

The SignalError function only sets up an exception; it doesn't throw it. C doesn't have exceptions, so it can't throw any. When a function that implements a native method returns, flags are checked to see if an exception was thrown. If one was, the Java runtime throws the exception. This scheme enables the C code to clean up after "throwing" an exception. No cleanup is needed in local_LockableFile, so we return after "throwing" any necessary exception.

The implementation of `unlock` is simpler. We set up the `flock` structure and invoke `fcntl` to set the lock to `F_UNLCK` (unlocked). Again, if it fails we "throw" an exception containing a string explaining the error.

```
void
local_LockableFile_unlock(
    struct Hlocal_LockableFile *this_h)
{
    Classlocal_LockableFile *this = unhand(this_h);
    struct flock lock;

    lock.l_whence = lock.l_start = lock.l_len = 0;
    lock.l_type = F_UNLCK;
    if (fcntl(this->fd, F_SETLKW, &lock) == -1)
        SignalError(EE(),
            "java/io/IOException", strerror(errno));
}
```

Several improvements could be made to this class. There should be a way to test if the file is locked, and by which thread. There should be a nonblocking form of `lock` that would lock if possible, but return otherwise. There should also be specific exceptions for different errors, so that "file doesn't exist" can be distinguished from "permission denied."

### Exercise A.1

If you have access to a non-POSIX system that supports file locking, implement `LockableFile` using its mechanisms.  ▲

### Exercise A.2

If you have access to a POSIX system or have completed Exercise A.1, add the functionality described above as missing from the class.  ▲

### A.3.1  Internals for `LockableFile`

Here, for completeness, are the internal functions used to implement the `LockableFile` class. The static functions `open_fd` and `setup_lock` are used to implement the native methods `lock` and `unlock`:

```
static int
open_fd(Classlocal_LockableFile *this)
{
    char *path = allocCString(this->path);
```

```
        if ((this->fd = open(path, O_RDWR)) == -1)
            SignalError(EE(),
                "java/io/IOException", strerror(errno));
        free(path);          /* we're done with this */
        return (this->fd != -1);
}

static int
setup_lock(
    struct flock *lock,
    long mode)
{
    lock->l_whence = lock->l_start = lock->l_len = 0;
    switch (mode) {
      case local_LockableFile_READ:
        lock->l_type = F_RDLCK;
        break;
      case local_LockableFile_WRITE:
        lock->l_type = F_WRLCK;
        break;
      default:
        SignalError(EE(),
            "java/lang/IllegalArgumentException", NULL);
        return 0;
    }
    return 1;
}
```

## A.4   Strings

Native methods will often need to use Java `String` objects. Several functions defined in the header file `<javaString.h>` help with such tasks. All the functions that convert a Java `String` object to a C string put only the lower eight bits of the Unicode character into the C string. These functions operate upon handle objects passed to the native method, stored in the object's C structure, or created by functions described below.

char ***allocCString**(Hjava_lang_String *str)
> Uses C's `malloc` function to create a buffer big enough to hold the string. You are responsible for calling `free` on the returned pointer when you are done with the space.

char *`javaString2CString`(Hjava_lang_String *str, char buffer[],
  int length)
> Copies up to `length` characters from `str` into `buffer`. You must manage the allocation and deallocation of `buffer`. This function returns `buffer` for convenience.

char *`makeCString`(Hjava_lang_String *str)
> Returns a C string that will be garbage-collected. The garbage collector scans C data as well as Java data to find object references, so the string will not be collected while the native method is using the pointer.

int `javaStringLength`(Hjava_lang_String *str)
> Returns the length of the Java string. This function operates on the handle.

unicode *`javaString2unicode`(Hjava_lang_String *str,
  unicode *buf, int len)
> Copies at most `len` Unicode characters from `str` into the buffer `buf`. The type `unicode` is defined by including `<native.h>`, and it holds a 16-bit character.

You can build new `String` objects by using the function `makeJavaString`:

Hjava_lang_String *`makeJavaString`(char *str, int len)
> Returns a handle to a new `String` object created from the C string `str`, using the first `len` bytes of the string. The length should not include the null byte that by convention terminates C-style strings.

If one of these methods encounters an error, such as running out of memory, it calls `SignalError` with the correct exception and returns `NULL`. In the `NULL` case, you should clean up and return.

Here is how you could write a native method that uses ANSI C's locale-specific `strxfrm` function, which creates an ordering string for the current locale from a standard 8-bit Latin-1 character string. The ordering string can then be used to sort the original string. The current locale defines the sort order—French, Norwegian, or Spanish, for example. You can order two strings in a local language as follows:

1. Call `strxfrm` on the two strings to create ordering strings for each.
2. Compare the ordering strings using `strcmp`, which returns a number less than, equal to, or greater than zero, according to whether the first string is less than, equal to, or greater than the second string.
3. Order the original strings based on the results of `strcmp` for the two ordering strings.

This procedure is useful if your code sorts strings frequently based on their locale-specific ordering. The other option is to use `strcoll` instead of `strcmp`.

strcoll is more expensive than strcmp per call, but doesn't require storing an ordering string for later use. We show the use of strcoll in the next section.

Here is a class that provides some utility methods to handle locale-specific string issues:

```
package local;

public class LocalString {
    /** Return an ordering string for str */
    public native static String xfrm(String str);

    /** Sort the array in the current local */
    public native static String[] sort(String[] input);

    static {
        System.loadLibrary("LocalString");
    }
}
```

The method sort is the one we will discuss in the next section. Here is one way to implement xfrm:

```
HString *
local_LocalString_xfrm(
    struct Hlocal_LocalString *this_h,
    Hjava_lang_String *str_h)
{
    Hjava_lang_String *retval;
    char *str, *xfrm;
    size_t xfrm_len;

    set_locale();
    str = allocCString(str_h);
    if (str == NULL)
        return NULL; /* allocCString() used SignalError() */
    xfrm_len = strxfrm(NULL, str, 0);
    if ((xfrm = (char *)malloc(xfrm_len + 1)) == NULL) {
        SignalError(EE(),
            "java/lang/OutOfMemoryException", NULL);
        return NULL;
    }
    strxfrm(xfrm, str, xfrm_len);
```

```
        retval = makeJavaString(xfrm, xfrm_len);
        free(xfrm);
        free(str);
        return retval;
    }
```

The first thing we must do is set the locale to the local one using the function `set_locale`:

```
    #include <locale.h>

    void
    set_locale()
    {
        static int done_set = 0;

        if (!done_set) {
            setlocale(LC_COLLATE, "");
            done_set++;
        }
    }
```

We use `setlocale` to set the collation algorithm to the one for the locale speci-fied by the user's environment, which is what the "" parameter means. When `set_locale` returns, we allocate a new C string that has the contents of the parameter we were given, and check for errors. Next, we use a form of `strxfrm` that returns the number of characters the ordering string will need. We allocate a buffer for that many characters plus a null byte, and call `strxfrm` to fill the buffer. Now we can use `makeJavaString` to create a new `String` object that contains the ordering string. Before we return that `String`, we must free the memory we allocated. Finally, we return the `String` object containing the ordering string.

Nothing prevents the native C code from modifying the characters in a `Classjava_lang_String` structure for a Java `String` object. However, doing so would violate the guarantee that a `String` object is read-only. Many places in the Java runtime, generated code, and classes rely upon this guarantee. For example, two `String` objects with the same value might share memory to store their contents. Modifying one `String` object would do more than violate a well-understood guarantee—you might also be modifying many other `String` objects.

*Exercise A.3*

Write a native method that prints out the value of a String object. ▲

*Exercise A.4*

Write a native method that returns a system string unavailable in a Java class, such as the name of the current working directory or folder. ▲

*Exercise A.5*

Write a class that uses native methods to provide Java programs access to your system's regular expression library. ▲

## A.5 Arrays

Every array in Java is typed, either as a primitive type such as array of int, or as an array of objects of a class. The type of a Java array is reflected in the C mapping. There are explicit primitive array types, and a general array type for arrays of objects. Each array type has a C structure type that looks like this:

```
typedef struct {
        CType    *body;
} ArrayOfJavaType;
```

Each struct has a field named body that points to the members of the array, where *CType* is the C type to which the Java type is mapped as an array element, and *JavaType* is the name of the Java type. This table shows the C mapping for Java arrays:

| Java Array of . . . | struct name | Type for body | Allocation Type |
|---|---|---|---|
| boolean | ArrayOfInt | long | T_BOOLEAN |
| byte | ArrayOfByte | char | T_BYTE |
| short | ArrayOfShort | short | T_SHORT |
| int | ArrayOfInt | long | T_INT |
| long | ArrayOfLong | int64_t | T_LONG |
| float | ArrayOfFloat | float | T_FLOAT |
| double | ArrayOfDouble | double | T_DOUBLE |
| char | ArrayOfChar | unicode | T_CHAR |
| Object | ArrayOfObject | HObject | T_CLASS |

Elements of an array are accessed by using body[i], up to an index one less than the number of elements in the array. The function obj_length will return the number of elements in a given array.

The basic array creation function is `ArrayAlloc`:

`Handle *ArrayAlloc(int type, int size)`
Create a new array of the given `type`, which should be one of the allocation types in the table above. If `type` is `T_CLASS`, one extra element is created, which points to the class object for the type of objects in that array.

This example is a function that creates an array of a specified type of object:

```
HArrayOfObject *
alloc_class_array(
    char *type,
    int cnt)
{
    HArrayOfObject *retval;

    retval = (HArrayOfObject *)ArrayAlloc(T_CLASS, cnt);
    if (retval == NULL) {
        SignalError(EE(),
            "java/lang/OutOfMemoryException", NULL);
        return NULL;
    }
    unhand(retval)->body[cnt] =
        (HObject *)FindClass(EE(), type, TRUE);
    return retval;
}
```

We first create an array of `T_CLASS`, checking to make sure that it succeeded. We then get the `Class` object for the specified type. The function `FindClass` requires an execution environment, a type name in a C string, and a boolean that says whether to resolve the class name by loading it if it isn't already loaded. The function `EE` returns the current execution environment.

The class object that `FindClass` returns is inserted into the slot past the end of the array, where the runtime looks for the type of an object array to check that each element inserted into the array is of the proper type. To have an array that can hold any object, you can use the class `"java/lang/Object"`.

This implementation of `LocalString.sort` shows how this infrastructure is used. First we see the implementation of `local_LocalString_sort` itself:

```
#include "local_LocalString.h"
#include <stdlib.h>
#include <javaString.h>
```

```
HArrayOfString *
local_LocalString_sort(
    struct Hlocal_LocalString *this_h,
    HArrayOfString *strings_h)
{

    ClassArrayOfString *in_strings;
    HArrayOfString *retval = NULL;
    ClassArrayOfString *retstrs;
    char **strings = NULL;
    int i, str_cnt;

    if (strings_h == NULL) { /* check for null reference */
        SignalError(EE(),
            "java/lang/NullPointerException", "null array");
        return NULL;
    }
    set_locale();

    in_strings = unhand(strings_h);
    str_cnt = obj_length(strings_h);
    strings = (char **)malloc(str_cnt * sizeof *strings);
    if (strings == NULL) {
        SignalError(EE(),
            "java/lang/OutOfMemoryException", NULL);
        return NULL;
    }
    for (i = 0; i < str_cnt; i++) {
        if (in_strings->body[i] == NULL) {
            SignalError(EE(),
                "java/lang/NullPointerException",
                "Null string in array");
            goto cleanup;
        }
        strings[i] = makeCString(in_strings->body[i]);
        if (strings[i] == NULL)
            goto cleanup; /* SignalError() already done */
    }
    qsort(strings, str_cnt, sizeof *strings, cmp);
    retval = (HArrayOfString *)
```

```
          alloc_class_array("java/lang/String", str_cnt);
      retstrs = unhand(retval);
      for (i = 0; i < str_cnt; i++) {
          retstrs->body[i] =
              makeJavaString(strings[i], strlen(strings[i]));
      }

cleanup:
      free(strings);
      return retval;
  }
```

First we check whether we were actually given an array. Then we set the locale, just as in LocalString.xfrm.

Next we create an array of C strings to hold the contents of the String objects to be sorted. To create the C string array, we need to know how many strings there are. We get this number by calling obj_length on the handle to the string array. Then we use malloc to get space for the pointers, and check the malloc's return value.

Checking for errors is important. Native methods that don't check for errors violate the guarantee of safety that Java programmers have. For example, we could omit the check for a null array, but then, instead of getting a NullPointerException, the thread, and possibly the whole program, could die when we used the pointer.

Once we have a place to store the C strings, we loop through the input array storing C string copies of the original strings into our sorting array. Again, we check for null references in the array. In this function we use makeCString primarily to show how it is used. The code is also simpler because the garbage collector removes the returned strings for us in all cases, including errors.

Now strings contains C string versions of the original array. We call the standard C library function qsort to sort the array, using the function given as its final argument, in this case cmp:

```
static int
cmp(const void *str1, const void *str2)
{
    return strcoll(*(char **)str1, *(char **)str2);
}
```

The comparison function cmp casts its pointers back to char ** values (qsort requires void *, relying on the programmer to do the necessary casts). The standard C library function `strcoll` is then used to compare the two C strings in locale-specific fashion. It returns a value less than, equal to, or greater than zero according to whether the first string is less than, equal to, or greater than the second in the current locale's notion of string ordering. The `qsort` function expects its comparison function to return these same values, so the return value of `strcoll` can be used as the return value for `cmp`.

When `qsort` is finished, the strings are sorted according to `strcoll`. All that remains is to create a new array of Java `String` objects and fill it with the results. We use the `alloc_class_array` function shown above to create the array, then loop using `makeJavaString` to create each `String` object. Finally, we free the `strings` array we created with `malloc` and return the result.

### *Exercise A.6*

Modify `LocalStr` so that it works for objects that each have their own locale, instead of assuming that there is only one locale of interest. The methods will no longer be static, and a locale-defining string field will be needed. Remember that the POSIX function `setlocale` sets the locale until the next `setlocale` call. ▲

## A.6 Creating Objects

You can create Java objects in native method implementations by using the function `execute_java_constructor`:

HObject *__execute_java_constructor__(ExecEnv *ee, char *className,
    ClassClass *classObj, char *signature, ...)

> Creates a new object of the given type, specified either by `className` or `classObj`. The other specifier should be `NULL`. The constructor described by the string `signature` is invoked to create the object. Any parameters to the constructor follow the `signature` parameter.

For example, here is how to create a new object of type `Simple` that uses the class's no-arg constructor:

    execute_java_constructor(NULL, "Simple", NULL, "()")

In this case the constructor signature specification is trivial. To use a constructor that takes one or more parameters, their types must be specified in the signature, and their values must come in order after the signature string. Types in the signature strings are similar to those returned by `Class.getName`, which uses single-character abbreviations for primitive types. The single characters for each primitive type are:

```
Z boolean      C char        B byte        S short
I int          J long        F float       D double
```

To avoid conflicts between a class or interface name and these letters, object types are named "L*type*", where *type* is the fully qualified type name of the class or interface with any package-separating dots replaced with a slash, and with a semicolon added at the end. For example, a parameter that is a String object would have the name "Ljava/lang/String;". Arrays are specified by the type of the array preceded by a [ character. An array of long would have the type "[J". If an array has multiple dimensions, more than one bracket precedes the type. A String[][] would have the name "[[Ljava/lang/String;".

If you can't figure out how to specify a type using one of these strings, you can write a Java class that creates an object of the type you need, and invoke getClass().getName() on it to get the translation. Then, if it is a type name, change every . to a /, and put an L at the front and a ; at the end if the L and ; are missing.

Arguments that are objects are passed as handle pointers.

Here is how to create two Attr objects, the first using the one-argument constructor that takes just a name, and the second using the two-argument form that also gives an initial value:

```
oneArgAttr = (struct HAttr *)
    execute_java_constructor(EE(), "Attr", NULL,
        "(Ljava/lang/String;)", attrStr);

twoArgAttr = (struct HAttr *)
    execute_java_constructor(EE(), "Attr", NULL,
        "(Ljava/lang/String;Ljava/lang/Object;)",
        attrStr, attrStr);
```

The semicolon is not a parameter separator, but a type terminator. A constructor that takes two long and two double parameters would be described as "(JJDD)".

## A.7   Invoking Java Methods

Invoking Java methods from native C code is similar to invoking Java constructors. The primary functions are

```
long execute_java_static_method(ExecEnv *, ClassClass *cb,
    char *method_name, char *signature, ...)
```
    Executes a static method of the class described in cb.

```
long execute_java_dynamic_method(ExecEnv *, HObject *obj,
    char *method_name, char *signature, ...)
```
> Executes a non-static (dynamic) method on the given object.

For both of these functions, `method_name` is the name of the method you want to invoke, and `signature` tells which arguments are being provided. For methods, unlike constructors, you must also declare the return type of the method, after the close parenthesis in the signature. The return type is expressed using the same abbreviations as for parameter types, with the addition of V for `void` methods. Examples are shown below. You are responsible for casting the returned `long` to the appropriate return type for the method, or ignoring it for `void` methods.

A class structure for invoking static methods can be obtained using one of the two `FindClass` functions:

```
ClassClass *FindClass(ExecEnv *ee, char *class_name,
    bool_t resolve)
```
> Returns a pointer to the `ClassClass` structure for the named class. As usual, exenv should be the return value of the EE function. The `resolve` boolean is equivalent to the `resolve` boolean used in the `ClassLoader.loadClass` method described in Section 13.2 on page 247.

```
ClassClass *FindClassFromClass(ExecEnv *ee, char *class_name,
    bool_t resolve, ClassClass *from)
```
> Returns a pointer to the class object for the named class, using the `from` class's `ClassLoader` object.

Here is an example that uses `System.out.println()` to report a native method's progress. The `Crunch` class's static native method `grindAway` shown below does some time-consuming number crunching and returns a `double` result:

```
double
Crunch_grindAway(struct HCrunch *this_h)
{
    ClassClass *myClass;
    HObject *out;
    long i;
    double result;
    ExecEnv *ee = EE(); /* used several times */

    myClass = FindClass(ee, "Crunch", TRUE);
    out = (HObject *)execute_java_static_method(ee, myClass,
        "outStream", "()Ljava/io/PrintStream;");
    if (exceptionOccurred(ee))
        return 0.0;
```

```
    for (i = 0; i < NUM_PASSES; i++) {
        execute_java_dynamic_method(ee, out,
            "println", "(I)V", i);
        if (exceptionOccurred(ee))
            return 0.0; /* have to return something
        /* .. crunch away in the i-th pass ... */
    }
    return result;
}
```

The code before the loop retrieves a handle to the `java.io.PrintStream` object in `System.out`. We cannot simply get the value of the static field `System.out` because static fields have no representation in this native method mapping so you must resort to other tactics. Here we create a static method to return the value, and invoke that method from the native code:

```
public static java.io.PrintStream outStream() {
    return System.out;
}
```

First the native code needs a pointer to a `ClassClass` structure for the `Crunch` class, so we call `FindClass`. Now we can call the `execute_java_static_method` function, adding the name of the method we want to invoke, and its signature including its return type. We cast the `long` that is returned to the correct type for the particular method. In this case we only need a generic `HObject` handle, not one for the specific type of `java.io.PrintStream`.

After we invoke the method, we check to see if an exception was raised. This is good practice any time you invoke Java methods or constructors from native code, because otherwise you will continue past an exception and may get into further trouble. When we return in the face of an exception, we return a dummy value, which is ignored.

Once we have the output stream, we start up the multipass computation. Each pass prints out its number using `System.out.println`. The method is invoked using the `execute_java_dynamic_method` function, passing in the object on which the method is being invoked, the method name and its signature, and the parameter. We want the version of `println` that takes an `int` argument, which is a `void` method, so we use the signature string `"(I)V"`, and pass the integer we want to print (`i`) after the signature argument. Again, we check for an exception when the method returns.

For most Java method return types, a simple cast of the returned `long` will be all you need. But the Java types `double` and `long` are 64-bit values, while most existing C compilers have 32-bit `long` types, so the returned `long` is only half of any 64-bit result. Although there are ways to get all 64 bits of such a return value, they are too machine dependent for inclusion in this text, since they rely upon long-word ordering of various types on different machine architectures.

## A.8   A Final Caution

We must caution you once more that the particular binding we describe is subject to change in the future. There are several possible improvements, both in design and in detail. A real C++ binding would have different characteristics, and might influence a different C binding with compatible notions. And designers of future development environments may consider themselves completely unbound to follow any of the particular choices of this binding. We hope that, in any case, this discussion will help you understand some of the issues that confront the designers of a language mapping, and so help you understand the actual native method bindings that you will use.

# Java Runtime Exceptions

*The computer can't tell you the emotional story.*
*It can give you the exact mathematical design but what's missing is the eyebrows.*
—Frank Zappa

**T**HE Java runtime throws two primary kinds of exceptions: runtime exceptions, which are extensions of the RuntimeException class, and errors, which are extensions of the Error class. Both are unchecked exceptions, as defined in Section 7.3 on page 135. Here is the top of the exception type hierarchy:

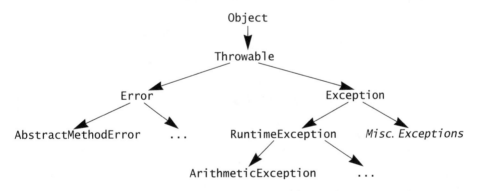

The Error exceptions indicate very serious problems that are usually unrecoverable and should never (well, hardly ever) be caught. Error exception classes are not extensions of RuntimeException, so people who write catch-all catch clauses for Exception or RuntimeException (not always a good idea anyway) won't catch Error exceptions. Of course, the finally clauses of try statements will always be executed as any exception percolates up the call stack, including Error exceptions, so you can always clean up after any exception.

You can extend the RuntimeException and Error classes yourself to create your own unchecked exceptions—that is, exceptions that you can throw *without* declaring them in throws clauses. The only reason you should know this is so that you can be warned against doing it. The throws clause is there to make all the possible behaviors of a method clear to those who invoke it. By making exceptions extensions of RuntimeException or Error, you tell a lie about the exception (that it is thrown by the runtime). You also invalidate the assumptions of programmers using your method that they can understand the method's behavior by reading its throws clause.

Even if you are writing code only for yourself, you should not create unchecked exceptions, because programmers with only a partial understanding of your code would miss an important clue about how it works. And, after all, a few months after you write the code, *you* are one of the people who has to maintain it with only a partial understanding. One way to keep your code clear is to pretend that the RuntimeException and Error classes can't be extended.

All of the Error and RuntimeException classes support at least two constructors: a no-arg constructor, and a constructor that accepts a descriptive String object. Exception classes that directly or indirectly extend RuntimeError or Error are not declared in throws clauses because they are possible at any time, making their declaration redundant.

The CloneNotSupportedException exception extends Exception directly, since any code invoking a clone method that throws it should explicitly handle the exception. This exception is described in "Cloning Objects" on page 67.

This chapter is in two parts—RuntimeException classes and Error classes. Each exception is named along with a description of when it is thrown, what it means, and any additional constructors it provides.

## B.1  RuntimeException Classes

**ArithmeticException** extends RuntimeException
> An exceptional arithmetic condition occurred, such as an integer divided by zero.

**ArrayStoreException** extends RuntimeException
> An attempt was made to store the wrong type of object in an array.

**ClassCastException** extends RuntimeException
> An invalid cast was attempted.

**IllegalArgumentException** extends RuntimeException
> An invalid argument was passed to a method, such as an invocation of String.equals with an Object that was not a String object.

**IllegalMonitorStateException** extends RuntimeException
> The wait/notify mechanism was used outside of synchronized code.

**IllegalThreadStateException** extends IllegalArgumentException
A thread was not in the proper state for the requested operation.

**IndexOutOfBoundsException** extends RuntimeException
The runtime generated this exception when array indices or indices into String objects were beyond the bounds of the object.

**NegativeArraySizeException** extends RuntimeException
Someone tried to create an array with a negative size.

**NullPointerException** extends RuntimeException
A null reference was used to access a field or method. This exception also signals that a method received a null parameter, when null was invalid for that method. In this usage it is like IllegalArgumentException.

**NumberFormatException** extends IllegalArgumentException
A string that was supposed to describe a number did not do so. This is thrown by such methods as Integer.parseInt.

**SecurityException** extends RuntimeException
An attempt to do something was vetoed by the security system, usually the SecurityManager object for this runtime.

## B.2   Error Classes

**AbstractMethodError** extends IncompatibleClassChangeError
An abstract method was invoked. This can happen only in very odd circumstances, so you should never see it.

**ClassFormatError** extends LinkageError
A class or interface that was being loaded was described in an invalid (usually mangled) format.

**IllegalAccessError** extends IncompatibleClassChangeError
An invalid access exception occurred.

**IncompatibleClassChangeError** extends LinkageError
When loading a class or interface, a change was detected that was incompatible with information that used to be known about that class or interface. For example, a nonprivate method was deleted from a class between the time you compiled your code and the time your code was run and tried to use that class.

**InstantiationError** extends IncompatibleClassChangeError
The interpreter tried to instantiate an abstract class or an interface.

**InternalError** extends `VirtualMachineError`
> An internal runtime error occurred. This should "never happen."

**LinkageError** extends `Error`
> `LinkageError` and its subclasses indicate that a class had some dependency on another class that could not then be satisfied.

**NoClassDefFoundError** extends `LinkageError`
> A class could not be found when it was needed.

**NoSuchFieldError** extends `IncompatibleClassChangeError`
> A particular field could not be found in a class or interface.

**NoSuchMethodError** extends `IncompatibleClassChangeError`
> A particular method could not be found in a class or interface.

**OutOfMemoryError** extends `VirtualMachineError`
> You ran out of memory.

**StackOverflowError** extends `VirtualMachineError`
> A stack overflow occurred. This may indicate infinite recursion.

**ThreadDeath** extends `Error`
> A `ThreadDeath` object was thrown in the victim thread when `thread.stop` was called. If `ThreadDeath` is caught, it should be rethrown so that the thread will die. The top-level error handler will not print a message if `ThreadDeath` falls through.

**UnknownError** extends `VirtualMachineError`
> An unknown but serious error occurred.

**UnsatisfiedLinkError** extends `LinkageError`
> An unsatisfied linkage for a native method was encountered. This usually means that the library that implemented a native method had undefined symbols that were not satisfied by any other library.

**VerifyError** extends `LinkageError`
> A verification error occurred, which means that when a class was being loaded it did not pass a verification test. Such tests are designed to ensure that the loaded code does not violate any of the Java safety features.

**VirtualMachineError** extends `Error`
> The virtual machine was broken or ran out of resources.

# Useful Tables

## Table 1  Keywords

Keywords marked with † are unused

| | | | |
|---|---|---|---|
| abstract | double | int | static |
| boolean | else | interface | super |
| break | extends | long | switch |
| byte | final | native | synchronized |
| case | finally | new | this |
| catch | float | null | throw |
| char | for | package | throws |
| class | goto† | private | transient† |
| const† | if | protected | try |
| continue | implements | public | void |
| default | import | return | volatile |
| do | instanceof | short | while |

## Table 2  Special Characters Using \

| Sequence | Meaning |
|---|---|
| \n | newline (\u000A) |
| \t | tab (\u0009) |
| \b | backspace (\u0008) |
| \r | return (\u000D) |
| \f | form feed (\u000C) |
| \\ | backslash itself (\u005C) |
| \' | single quote (\u0027) |
| \" | double quote (\u0022) |
| \ddd | an octal char, with each d being an octal digit (0–7) |
| \udddd | A Unicode char, with each d being a hex digit (0–9, a–f, A–F) |

## Table 3  **Operator Precedence**

| Operator Type | Operator |
|---|---|
| Postfix operators | `[] . (params) expr++ expr--` |
| Unary operators | `++expr --expr +expr -expr ~ !` |
| Creation or cast | `new (type)expr` |
| Multiplicative | `* / %` |
| Additive | `+ -` |
| Shift | `<< >> >>>` |
| Relational | `< > >= <= instanceof` |
| Equality | `== !=` |
| Bitwise AND | `&` |
| Bitwise exclusive OR | `^` |
| Bitwise inclusive OR | `\|` |
| Logical AND | `&&` |
| Logical OR | `\|\|` |
| Conditional | `?:` |
| Assignment | `= += -= *= /= %= >>= <<= >>>= &= ^= \|=` |

## Table 4  **Unicode Digits**

| Unicode | Description |
|---|---|
| `\u0030-\u0039` | ISO-Latin-1 (and ASCII) digits |
| `\u0660-\u0669` | Arabic–Indic digits |
| `\u06f0-\u06f9` | Eastern Arabic–Indic digits |
| `\u0966-\u096f` | Devanagari digits |
| `\u09e6-\u09ef` | Bengali digits |
| `\u0a66-\u0a6f` | Gurmukhi digits |
| `\u0ae6-\u0aef` | Gujarati digits |
| `\u0b66-\u0b6f` | Oriya digits |
| `\u0be7-\u0bef` | Tamil digits (only nine—no zero digit) |
| `\u0c66-\u0c6f` | Telugu digits |
| `\u0ce6-\u0cef` | Kannada digits |
| `\u0d66-\u0d6f` | Malayalam digits |
| `\u0e50-\u0e59` | Thai digits |
| `\u0ed0-\u0ed9` | Lao digits |
| `\uff10-\uff19` | Fullwidth digits |

## Table 5 **Unicode Letters and Digits**

| Unicode | Description |
|---------|-------------|
| \u0041–\u005A | ISO-Latin-1 (and ASCII) uppercase Latin letters ('A'–'Z') |
| \u0061–\u007A | ISO-Latin-1 (and ASCII) lowercase Latin letters ('a'–'z') |
| \u00C0–\u00D6 | ISO-Latin-1 supplementary letters |
| \u00D8–\u00F6 | ISO-Latin-1 supplementary letters |
| \u00F8–\u00FF | ISO-Latin-1 supplementary letters |
| \u0100–\u1FFF | Latin extended-A, Latin extended-B, IPA extensions, spacing modifier letters, combining diacritical marks, basic Greek, Greek symbols and Coptic, Cyrillic, Armenian, Hebrew extended-A, Basic Hebrew, Hebrew extended-B, Basic Arabic, Arabic extended, Devanagari, Bengali, Gurmukhi, Gujarati, Oriya, Tamil, Telugu, Kannada, Malayalam, Thai, Lao, Basic Georgian, Georgian extended, Hanguljamo, Latin extended additional, Greek extended |
| \u3040–\u9FFF | Hiragana, Katakana, Bopomofo, Hangul compatibility Jamo, CJK miscellaneous, enclosed CJK characters and months, CJK compatibility, Hangul, Hangul supplementary-A, Hangul supplementary-B, CJK unified ideographs |
| \uF900–\uFDFF | CJK compatibility ideographs, alphabetic presentation forms, Arabic presentation forms-A |
| \uFE70–\uFEFE | Arabic presentation forms-B |
| \uFF10–\uFF19 | Fullwidth digits |
| \uFF21–\uFF3A | Fullwidth Latin uppercase |
| \uFF41–\uFF5A | Fullwidth Latin lowercase |
| \uFF66–\uFFDC | Halfwidth Katakana and Hangul |

NOTE: A Unicode character is a letter or digit if it is in one of the above ranges and is also a defined Unicode character.

NOTE: A character is a letter if it is in the "Letters and Digits" table and not in the "Digits" table.

**Table 6  Java 1.0 and Java 1.0.2: Differences between Java 1.0 and 1.0.1 that are visible in this book (with the primary affected sections).**

- The MIN_VALUE and MAX_VALUE constants for Character were mistakenly in the Boolean class in Java 1.0. (Section 13.5 on page 253)

- The String and Character class in Java 1.0 dealt only with character class issues (upper- versus lowercase, digits, etc.) in the ISO-Latin-1 subset of Unicode (\u0000 through \u00ff), assuming that all characters outside that range were uncased letters. Also, the Character methods that return data about a character's class beyond upper- and lowercase issues (such as the titlecase methods and isLetter) did not exist. (Section 8.2 on page 145, Section 8.4 on page 149, Section 13.5 on page 253)

- Java 1.0 did not guarantee that String literals with the same value would have the same reference, although they sometimes did. (Section 8.2 on page 145)

- The list of legal letters and digits for identifiers was slightly different in Java 1.0 outside the ISO-Latin-1 range (Table 4 on page 300 and Table 5 on page 301).

- Java 1.0 allowed, and erroneously gave meaning to, the combination of scope keywords private protected.

- Java 1.0 wrapper classes Integer and Long did not have the toHexString, toOctalString, and toBinaryString methods. (Section 13.7 on page 256 and Section 13.8 on page 256).

# Bibliography

*The best book on programming for the layman is* Alice in Wonderland,
*but that's because it's the best book on anything for the layman.*
—Alan J. Perlis

**W**E offer this list of works for further reading on related topics. The list is necessarily duosyncratic—other excellent works exist on most of these topics.

## JAVA TOPICS

- `http://java.sun.com/`, JavaSoft, Sun Microsystems, Inc.
  The latest information on Java and related topics, including Java releases, security issues, and online documentation.

- `http://java.sun.com/Series/`, JavaSoft, Sun Microsystems, Inc.
  The latest information about books in this series, including errata and updates. Of special interest will be those errata and updates for this book.

- *The Unicode Standard: Worldwide Character Encoding*, Version 1.0, Volumes 1 and 2. Addison-Wesley, 1991 and 1992, ISBN 0-201-56788-1 and ISBN 0-201-60845-6.
  Additional data on Unicode 1.1.5 is available at `ftp://unicode.org`.

- *IEEE/ANSI Standard for Binary Floating Point Arithmetic*. Institute of Electrical and Electronics Engineers, 1985, IEEE Std 754-1985.

- `http://tycho.usno.navy.mil`
  U.S. Naval Observatory data on time paradigms used in the Date class.
  See `http://tycho.usno.navy.mil/systime.html`

*OBJECT ORIENTED DESIGN*

◆ *An Introduction to Object-Oriented Programming*, by Timothy Budd. Addison-Wesley, 1991, ISBN 0-201-54709-0
   An introduction to the topic of object-oriented programming, as well as a comparison of C++, Objective C, SmallTalk, and Object Pascal.

◆ *Pitfalls of Object-Oriented Development*, by Bruce F. Webster. M&T Books, 1995, ISBN 1-55851-397-3.
   A collection of traps to avoid for people adopting object technology. Alerts you to problems you're likely to encounter and presents some solutions for them.

◆ *Design Patterns,* by Erich Gamma, Richard Helm, Ralph Johnson, and John Vlissides. Addison-Wesley, 1995, ISBN 0-201-63361-2.

◆ *Object Oriented Analysis and Design, with Applications, 2nd Edition*, by Grady Booch. Benjamin/Cummings, 1994, ISBN 0-8053-5340-2.

◆ *Structured Programming*, by Ole-Johan Dahl, Edsger Wybe Dijkstra, and C. A. R. Hoare. Academic Press, 1972, ISBN 0-12-200550-3.

◆ *Object-Oriented Programming: An Evolutionary Approach, 2nd Edition*, by Brad J. Cox. Addison-Wesley, 1991, ISBN 0-201-54834-8.

*MULTITHREADED PROGRAMMING*

◆ *Programming with Threads*, by Steve Kleiman, Devang Shah, and Bart Smaalders. Prentice Hall, 1996, ISBN 0-13-172389-8.

◆ *The Architecture of Concurrent Programs,* by Per Brinch Hansen. Prentice Hall, 1977, ISBN 0-13-044628-9.

◆ "Monitors: An Operating System Structuring Concept," by C. A. R. Hoare. *Communications of the ACM,* Volume 17, number 10, 1974, pp. 549–557.
   The seminal paper on the concept of monitors as a means to synchronizing multiple concurrent tasks.

*RELATED LANGUAGES*

◆ *The C Programming Language, 2nd Edition*, by Brian W. Kernighan and Dennis M. Ritchie. Prentice Hall, 1988, ISBN 0-13-110362-8 and ISBN 0-13-110370-9 (hardcover).

◆ *The C++ Programming Language, 2nd Edition,* by Bjarne Stroustrup. Addison-Wesley, 1991, ISBN 0-201-53992-6.

◆ *The Evolution of C++*, edited by Jim Waldo. A USENIX Association book from MIT Press, ISBN 0-262-73107-X.

   A history of how we came to be where we are with C++ as told by many of the people who contributed.

◆ "Cedar Language Overview," by J. J. Horning. Xerox internal memo, 1983.

◆ "The Cedar Programming Environment: A Midterm Report and Examination," by Warren Teitelman. Xerox Palo Alto Research Center Report CSL-83-11, June 1984.

◆ *Eiffel: The Language*, by Bertrand Meyer. Prentice Hall, 1992, ISBN 0-13-247925-7.

◆ *Mesa Language Manual,* version 5.0, by James G. Mitchell, William Maybury, and Richard Sweet. Xerox Palo Alto Research Center Report CSL-79-3, April 1979.

◆ *Systems Programming with Modula-3*, edited by Greg Nelson. Prentice Hall, 1991, ISBN-0-13-590464-1.

   Introduces the Modula-3 object-oriented programming language. Chapter 4 is an excellent discussion of thread programming issues. Chapter 8 is an interesting case history of language design.

◆ *Programming in Oberon—Steps Beyond Pascal and Modula*, by Martin Reiser and Niklaus Wirth. Addison-Wesley, 1992, ISBN 0-201-56543-9.

◆ *Objective C: Object-Oriented Programming Techniques,* by Lewis J. Pinson and Richard S. Wiener. Addison-Wesley, 1991, ISBN 0-201-50828-1.

◆ "Self: the Power of Simplicity," by David Ungar and Randall B. Smith. Sun Microsystems Laboratories Technical Report SMLI-TR-94-30, 1994. (Also available in *LISP and Symbolic Computation: An International Journal,* Volume number 4, 3. The Netherlands: Kluwer Academic Publishers, 1991.)

◆ *Data Processing—Programming Languages—SIMULA*. Swedish standard SS 636114, SIS, 1987, ISBN 91-7162-234-9.

◆ *Smalltalk-80: The Language,* by Adele Goldberg and Dave Robinson. Addison-Wesley, 1989, ISBN 0-201-13688-0.

## SOFTWARE ENGINEERING

◆ *The Decline and Fall of the American Programmer*, by Ed Yourdon. Yourdon Press, 1993, ISBN 0-13-203670-3.

   Ed Yourdon writes persuasively about the revolution taking place in programming today. Several chapters discuss issues of object-oriented design and programming. Two chapters of particular interest are "The Lure of the Silver Bullet" and "Programming Methodologies."

♦ *The Mythical Man-Month, Anniversary Edition*, by Frederick P. Brooks, Jr. Addison-Wesley, 1995, ISBN 0-201-83595-9.
  Essays describing how software projects are really managed, and how they should be. Especially read Chapter 16, "No Silver Bullet: Essence and Accidents of Software Engineering." You cannot design good classes without understanding how they will be used and changed over time.

♦ *Peopleware*, by Tom DeMarco and Timothy Lister. Dorset House, 1987, ISBN 0-932633-05-6.

## APPLET-RELATED DESIGN INFORMATION

♦ *Designing Visual Interfaces,* by Kevin Mullet and Darrel Sano. Prentice Hall, 1995, ISBN 0-13-303389-9.
  This book descibes fundamental techniques that can be used to enhance the visual quality of graphical user interfaces.

♦ *About Face,* by Allen Cooper. Prentice Hall, 1995, ISBN 0-13-303389-9.
  Basics of good GUI design in a straightforward presentation.

♦ *Usability Engineering*, by Jakob Nielsen. Academic Press, 1993, ISBN 0-12-518405-0.
  A direct how-to guide on testing your interfaces to make sure they are usable by actual human beings.

♦ *The Visual Display of Quantitative Information,* by Edward R. Tufte. Graphics Press, 1983.
  You shouldn't communicate using graphical media without reading this.

♦ *The Non-Designer's Design Book,* by Robin Williams. Peachpit Press, 1994, ISBN 1-56609-159-4.
  Concentrates on how to use type, space, alignment, and other basic techniques to make your designs visually appealing and user-friendly. Created for paper documents, but the principles apply to HTML documents, displaying data, and user interfaces.

♦ *The Design of Everyday Things,* by Donald A. Norman. Doubleday/Currency, 1988, ISBN 0-385-26774-6
  Discusses usability design for everyday items (doors, typewriters, and so on) with lessons applicable to *any* design, including graphic user interface design.

# Index

*All my life, as down an abyss without a bottom,*
*I have been pouring van-loads of information*
*into the vacancy of oblivion I call my mind.*
—Logan Pearsall Smith

# Colophon

*If I had my life to live again, I'd make the same mistakes, only sooner.*
—Tallulah Bankhead

THIS book is written primarily in eleven point Times, with code text in Lucida Sans Typewriter at 85% of the size of the surrounding text. Some incidental text is in Helvetica.

The text was written in FrameMaker versions 4.0 and 5.0 on several systems: a Sun Sparc-10 and a Sun Sparc-2, both running Solaris 2.4; a Macintosh Quadra 660-AV running system 7.5; a Macintosh Powerbook 170 running system 7.1; and a 486i laptop computer running Windows 3.1.

Non-Latin-1 text on pages 89 and 92 were created on the Powerbook 170 and a Quadra 950 Macintosh running System 7.1 using various fonts, and Adobe Illustrator 5.5 to create encapsulated PostScript drawings of the letters that are included as pictures in the text. The fonts used are Kourier for Cyrillic, ParsZiba for Farsi, Palladam for Tamil, and Ryumin for Kanji.

Code examples were written and compiled on the Sparc systems, then broken into fragments by running a Perl script over the source looking for specially-formatted comments. Source fragments were included in the book by saving the Frame source as MIF documents, running a Perl script on the MIF document to update the source, and re-saving the MIF document as a normal Frame document. The Perl scripts have been posted to the Usenet newsgroup comp.text.frame.

This book itself demonstrates how the Internet provides a powerful tool for collaborations. Ken Arnold worked from Sun Labs in Chelmsford, Massachusetts. James Gosling, Lisa Friendly (Series Editor), and Henry McGilton (Principal Editor) worked from JavaSoft in Palo Alto, California. Bill Joy worked from his eyrie in Sun Central, Aspen, Colorado. Mike Hendrickson of Addison-Wesley worked from headquarters in Reading, Massachusetts. Using email for better than 90% of all communications, we wrote, reviewed, and revised electronically, transmitting copies of the book back and forth between the sites, sometimes daily.